Kozintsev's Shakespeare Films

Kozintsev's Shakespeare Films

Russian Political Protest in *Hamlet* and *King Lear*

Tiffany Ann Conroy Moore

McFarland & Company, Inc., Publishers
Jefferson, North Carolina, and London

LIBRARY OF CONGRESS CATALOGUING-IN-PUBLICATION DATA

Moore, Tiffany Ann Conroy, 1973–
    Kozintsev's Shakespeare films : Russian political protest in Hamlet and King Lear / Tiffany Ann Conroy Moore.
       p.   cm.
    Includes bibliographical references and index.

    ISBN 978-0-7864-7135-5
    softcover : acid free paper ∞

    1. Kozintsev, Grigorii Mikhailovich — Criticism and interpretation. 2. Shakespeare, William, 1564–1616 — Film adaptations — History and criticism. 3. English drama (Tragedy) — Film adaptations. 4. Soviet Union — In motion pictures. I. Title.
PN1998.3.K69M55 2012
791.43'64—dc23   2012039369

BRITISH LIBRARY CATALOGUING DATA ARE AVAILABLE

© 2012 Tiffany Ann Conroy Moore. All rights reserved

No part of this book may be reproduced or transmitted in any form or by any means, electronic or mechanical, including photocopying or recording, or by any information storage and retrieval system, without permission in writing from the publisher.

Front cover image: Grigorii Kozintsev behind the camera at Lenfilm studios, 1969 (© ITAR-TASS/Sovfoto)

Manufactured in the United States of America

McFarland & Company, Inc., Publishers
  Box 611, Jefferson, North Carolina 28640
    www.mcfarlandpub.com

In fond memory of
Kathy Howlett,
not least of all because this project was attempted at her suggestion.

Dedicated to my mother, Marilyn,
for giving me the love of art and literature;
my father, Eugene, for giving me an interest in history and politics;
my sister, Kelly, for the gifts of love and purity of heart.

With special gratitude also for the support and encouragement of
Timothy, my husband.

Table of Contents

Acknowledgments viii

Preface 1

Introduction 3

ONE. Kozintsev's Contexts 1: *Hamlet* in Russia in the 18th and 19th Centuries 25

TWO. Kozintsev's Contexts 2: Soviet *Hamlets* from the Revolution until after Stalin's Death 52

THREE. *Hamlet* in the "Thaw" and Kozintsev's 1964 Film Adaptation 74

FOUR. Kozintsev's Contexts 3: Russian and Soviet *King Lears* from the 18th Century through World War II 106

FIVE. *King Lear* Revisited in the Brezhnev Era: Kozintsev's 1970 Film Adaptation 136

Epilogue 179

Chapter Notes 182

Bibliography 185

Index 193

Acknowledgments

First, I must thank the late Kathy Howlett for all of her help and support. I am so sorry that she departed before I finished this project. Fortunately, Harlow Robinson stepped in to lead the way, and he was endlessly eager, interested and supportive, for which I am truly grateful. I also most thankfully acknowledge Marina Leslie and Ines Hedges, both of whom provided incredibly useful feedback throughout the editing process and have always been forthcoming with advice. While I was at Northeastern University, I received a grant from the Office of the Vice Provost to complete my work, so I must express my appreciation to them generally and to Luis Falcon in particular.

Preface

This study was conceived as a way of putting the Shakespeare films of Soviet director Grigory Kozintsev into their cultural and historical contexts. When I began to study the Soviet-era films of *Hamlet* and *King Lear*, I found a great deal of information was spread out among a number and variety of books, chapters and articles, each with very different goals and perspectives. I determined that putting it all together would be a tremendously useful thing for people who wanted to know more about Kozintsev's Shakespeare, but perhaps were not inclined to attempt to locate and assimilate all this far-flung material. Therefore, what you find here is a narrative that I have composed in order to facilitate the study and enjoyment of Kozintsev's Shakespeare films. Initially, I had thought I might also include Jan Frid's *Twelfth Night* (1955) and Sergei Yutkevich's *Othello* (1955), but, alas, given my linguistic and geographic limitations, I realized that I would not have time or resources to fit these two films into a broader consideration of political protest in Russo-Soviet Shakespeare, despite the fact that their being produced and released just after Stalin's death makes them potentially very good material. Like Kozintsev, Yutkevich also wrote a book on Shakespeare; unlike Kozintsev's, his has still not been translated into English. Since Kozintsev's films have been released on DVD by Ruscico, and one can obtain both of Kozintsev's books in English translations, I determined it was practical to let my focus be on him exclusively. Readers can easily track down copies of the films to view for themselves. If you have any affection for Russian cinema and Shakespeare — which I hope you do, as reader of this book — you will appreciate the aesthetic and dramatic quality therein. Kozintsev's books are somewhat more difficult to find, having been out of print for some time, but they can be located on the internet through purveyors of used books. I highly recommend these books — Kozintsev's passion for his subject, breadth of knowledge and sly brand of humor come through clearly in the translations.

Decisions of scope were very important when I began this project. In order to do justice to the plethora of influences and the multifaceted legacies which intersect and intertwine around and through Kozintsev's films, I have gone back to the very beginnings of Shakespeare's appearance in Russia. Again, in order to limit the scope of what could become another lengthy study in its own right, I determined to focus on *Hamlet* and *King Lear* and to trace their appearances in Russian arts and letters, leaving many other Shakespeare plays out of the narrative, despite their obvious importance. I chose to include Kozintsev's film version of *Don Quixote*, a Spanish Renaissance classic, because he produced it in between his staging of and his filming of *Hamlet*. The themes tackled in this cinematic *Don Quixote*, as well as its situation just after Stalin's death, are germane to a consideration of Kozintsev's Shakespeare productions. Fortunately, this film is also now available on DVD and is easy to order online. Kozintsev's collaborations with Pasternak and Shostakovich have been underplayed in a great deal of the literature about his Shakespeare films. Along with filling in the cultural and political history of the films, I also found it important to share an examination of the relationships Pasternak and Shostakovich had with Shakespeare's works and the ways their perspectives and experiences colored Kozintsev's choices as director and critic.

Over the course of researching and writing this book, I have developed a deep admiration for the tenacity, bravery and idealism of Kozintsev, his collaborators, and his predecessors. As a person living in a place of relative freedom and prosperity, too often mired in cynical irony and detached complacency, I have found the passion, fervor and faith in the power of art as well as the insistence upon the essential dignity of the human person exhibited by Kozintsev and his peers instructive, humbling and inspiring. It is my desire that some of that sense of urgency and vitality can come through in this book.

Introduction

Shakespeare was much admired by Russian and Soviet writers and artists. He was adopted as something of an honorary Russian, influencing Pushkin, among other major literary figures, and was canonized in Russian letters. Soviet academics and leaders, from the mid–19th century onward, were eager to appropriate Shakespeare to the Socialist cause, having been inspired by the statements of Marx and Engels (later also Lenin) on the political importance of some of the plays. Marx and Engels saw in Shakespeare's works evidence of the emerging evils of capitalism and class struggle in the time of the English Renaissance. For example, Laertes was often read by Soviet critics as a champion of the people, a Bolshevik hero; his entrance to avenge his father's murder was depicted on the Soviet stage with the presence of the people rushing in behind him to illustrate his popular revolutionary mandate. He was a leader backed by the worker and peasant storming the palace of Nicholas I. This episode, however, was also represented by other critics, and in performance, in a manner less reflective of the "Party Line." The image of Laertes' return could also be seen as either foolishly rebellious, in the sense of a critique of the rashness of revolutionary zeal, or it could be read as a call-to-arms for Soviet citizens to rise up against their own oppressive regime.

As an example of this so-called "double-voicing," Eisenstein's *Ivan the Terrible, Part 1* (1944) shows a scene in which the people come to laud their new ruler that was certainly intended to be read on two levels. One level indicated the interpretation of events that followed Stalin's wishes for the film, acting as a screen for the other, more resistant level's interpretation to slip by. Stalin instructed Eisenstein personally in the making of his *Ivan* films. Stalin wanted the films to allegorize his own rise to power with that of the 16th century tsar. The final scene in which the people march to the tower in which Ivan hid was, for Stalin, a simile for his own, supposedly popular mandate to take power after Lenin's death. Yet, in the final analysis, the ambivalent characterization of Ivan in the film makes his assumption of power feel more frightening than liberating, and the people seem more misled or coerced than jubilant. Eisenstein's *Ivan* films then, like Kozintsev's Shakespeare films, used an officially-sanctioned story to convey an unofficial, un-sanctioned message. Kozintsev's Shakespearean adaptations and books similarly used old stories of temporally or geographically distant persons and places, much loved and respected by the Party and the people, to analyze the problems of power in the USSR.

Kozintsev's entire career, especially his two books on Shakespeare (*Shakespeare: Time and Conscience* [1966] and *King Lear: The Space of Tragedy* [1973]) deserve careful consideration for the former's illustration of his artistic adaptability in the face of increased Party control over cinema and the latter's illumination of Kozintsev's relationship with Shakespeare and the significance he saw in the plays for the contemporary situation of the Soviet Union. Barbara Leaming's 1988 artistic biography of Kozintsev offers a great deal of information on his artistic career, his relationships with other theater and film practitioners and is helpful for our understanding of how he negotiated the treacherous territory of his political situation. Most of the Shakespeare scholarship within the Russian areas of the USSR took a more conservative approach than did artistic adaptations or translations. However, critical works from beyond the central seat of Soviet power, such as the Polish Jan Kott's *Shakespeare Our Contemporary* (1964), were highly political and extremely influential in Russian-Soviet artistic and intellectual circles. Kozintsev's first book on Shakespeare was titled in Russian *Our Contemporary: William Shakespeare*, in obvious homage to Kott's work. Kott's various presentations and articles point back to Kozintsev's works and Kott attests to his friend's subversive intentions. Kozintsev cites Kott frequently in his books, thereby helping to indirectly illuminate his own political intent in adapting the plays for stage and film.

The lives and works of Kozintsev, Pasternak and Shostakovich (among other artists and critics mentioned in this study) illumine the particular difficulties of living and creating art after the 1917 Revolution. In the course of my discussion, relevant cultural and political events in the USSR provide the necessary context for readers unfamiliar with Soviet history. Each of these artists dealt with overt government censure and threats in ways that are entirely representative of the fate of many of their contemporaries. None of these three men was imprisoned, exiled or killed, but they all had friends or family members who were. Each of these artists shared a tremendous respect for Shakespeare and saw in him a kindred spirit whose works they could adapt in order to express their own perspectives on the chaos and injustice surrounding them. In their Shakespearean adaptations and translations each artist used the material of a distant time and place to speak about their contemporary situation.

Aesopian Discourse and Double-Voicing

In order to correctly and fully comprehend Russian and Soviet works of art, one must understand that many of them are encoded. Many works with subversive messages had to pass the censors of both the pre– and post–Revolutionary eras in order to reach their audiences. Lev Loseff, a Soviet poet and scholar who came to the U.S. in the 1970s, is one of the most often cited critics who writes about Russian and Soviet "doublespeak." Aesopian language is, in his words, "a special literary system, one whose structure allows interaction between author and reader at the same time that it conceals inadmissible content from the censor" (x). The term comes directly from Aesop's fables, which were translated into Russian in 1700. Aesop himself (well, if he existed at all — his very identity might have been a ruse, adding even more layers to his obfuscations) was a slave who used his fables as a way of providing critical commentary against his cultural milieu. The use of the name "Aesopian" then indicated a subversive form of discourse in Russia from as early as the 1860s, when progressives would have had to get their propaganda spread either through non-official channels or with heavy doses of cryptic language (Loseff 2, 4). Political messages had to be cloaked in allegory in order to escape invoking the tsar's wrath. The dominant discourse after the tsarist era was that such hiding was no longer necessary. In an article from 1912, Lenin claimed that the days of Aesopian language had ended: "Accursed days of Aesopian talk, literary bondage, slavish language, ideological serfdom! The proletariat has put an end to this corruption which choked everything alive and fresh in Russia" (quoted in Loseff 7). Yet freedom from the need to cloak one's true feelings about culture and government did not ultimately come about in the Soviet era despite Lenin's assessment. Rather, control over arts and letters only increased, forcing artists and audiences to become even more adept at conducting Aesopian discourse.

In spite of the continuation of the use of double-voicing, the Soviets had to pretend that Lenin was correct and that nobody had to use such subterfuge anymore — in fact, even discussing such a thing became *verboten*. Kozintsev's writings about Shakespeare's difficulties under Elizabeth and James contain only glancing, oblique references to the sort of cloaked messages artists circulated before and after the Bolshevik Revolution. Interestingly, "discussion of anti-censorship tactics is impossible in a state of censorship. Even an investigation into the struggle against censorship and the Aesopian language of past eras automatically acquires, under the conditions of the current censorship, an Aesopian ambiguity" (Loseff 13). Therefore, a seemingly objective, dispassionate account of Elizabethan censorship was in itself a signal to one's audience to begin to look for encoded messages. Kozintsev knew this and was expert at playing the game of only giving away as much information as his audience needed to "get it," while avoiding anything that might pique the interest of the censors.

The Soviet audience was trained and primed to look for and to understand Aesopian discourse: "a sense for reading between the lines becomes unusually keen in the reading public" during the Soviet era (Loseff 17; quoting Jakobson on Pushkin 20). All sorts of texts and performances contained heavy use of irony, allegory and metaphorical language. In texts that seemed removed from the contemporary context, sly references to contemporary life, such as modern slang, snatches of songs, references to places, etc., alerted the reader to the author's desire for his story to be read as an allegory of Soviet life. Kevin Moss writes, "the function of an Aesopian text is to make the reader name, at least to himself, the Soviet realia to which the text does not overtly refer" (Moss 3). Therefore, highly trained audiences carefully analyzed the works of equally skilled fable-producers. Most of these Aesopian works indeed passed the censors, effectively making even the official media into unwitting transmitters of subversive material. All of this created an initiated subculture: as Brian James Baer, another recent scholar, suggests, "the successful decoding of oppositional content (re)produced the individual reader as a member of an alternative 'reading public,' situated within official Soviet Literary culture" (538). As a part of this covert exchange both producers and consumers of Aesopian texts experienced a comforting level of solidarity in their ability to confront reality, however obliquely. "Catharsis," writes Loseff, "is the inner content of an Aesopian literary work, a catharsis which the reader experiences as a victory over repressive authority" (230). Each successful transaction meant a small victory for people who sought the truth amid the chimera of propaganda and repression. It is certainly a bittersweet victory to find subversive messages being unwittingly disseminated by the very same people who would prefer to squash them. Still, one can imagine that the very sanity of millions of Soviet citizens depended upon knowing that someone was out there expressing their true feelings — enabling the shared catharsis so critical to the human experience.

Loseff breaks down the Aesopian scheme into its component parts: "screens" and "markers" (Loseff 51; Moss 3–4, 8; Baer 543). Screens were employed to noisily divert the censor's attentions and markers were things that subtly cued the reader to look for subversive content. Baer notes that markers "cued the 'ideal' reader" to recognize in the artistic work "the realities of contemporary society" (543). There are many examples, among which the use of Shakespeare as material should be included, of "Aesopian works in which temporal and geographical shifts function as screen for the covert text" (Moss 4). Shifting the focus of the audience from the present, for instance, onto the story of a pre–Christian king told by an English man of the Elizabethan age, as in *King Lear*, would serve as both a temporal and a geographical screen. Yet because of the audience's Aesopian orientation, it "is not allowed to relegate the action comfortably to a time fixed and closed off from the present" because of its recognition of the markers that point to the present (Moss 7). To continue with the previous example, the king's jester, Lear's Fool, speaks in colloquial, present-day Russian and sings familiar Russian tunes — these anachronisms collapse the gap between past and present. Many of the Shakespeare translations discussed in the chapters of this project are examples of other types of screens. Eleanor Rowe, in her book on *Hamlet* in Russia, cites many critics within and without the USSR who commented upon the "Aesopian" nature of tsarist and Soviet era art. Rowe explains that under an authoritarian or totalitarian regime, which is typically characterized by the use of far-reaching and officially unimpeachable propaganda, artists must get their resistant political messages out "under the radar" of censors and other silencing mechanisms set up by the government. Therefore, layers of meaning are piled onto the core message of a work by way of irony, metaphor, allegory, analogy and symbolism. In addition to such changes of place and time, "translations and quasi-translations are a popular Aesopian screening device" (Moss 5). As an example, Pushkin's "From Pindemonte" was presented as a phony translation containing many slights upon Nicholas I. Boris Pasternak turned to translating Shakespeare as just such a means to make his views clear without arousing suspicion.

Given the threats of censorship, imprisonment and exile always looming over Soviet writers and artists, Kozintsev's Shakespearean adaptations are in many ways works of bravery. It is the fact that they hid behind the guise of adapting Shakespeare, far removed, or so it seemed, from the

Soviet situation, that they were able to enact subversion in relative safety and hoodwink the censors, although this safety was not always achieved by his collaborators and contemporaries. In his books also, Kozintsev examines Shakespeare from the point of view of a theater practitioner and filmmaker, and draws his readers' attention to the political importance of Shakespeare's works in their own time in order to suggest their relevance to the present. Kozintsev's Shakespeare films are quite similar in this way to the *Ivan* films of Eisenstein, which analogized 20th century Stalin with the 16th century ruler, using a story removed from Soviet time and place to criticize the regime. Kozintsev suggests, while writing on *King Lear*, that Shakespeare's own use of stories from history were crafted to speak to his present audience: "In order to bring contemporary processes into full relief, the shadow of another epoch was cast on the principals and on the course of events" (*STC* 61). Kozintsev avoids being too precise about just what sort of processes were being brought into relief and to what ends, so it is for the reader attuned to the often oblique language of artists and scholars in Soviet Russia to hear Kozintsev state within this analogy of past in present his own project of resistance and critique.

Perhaps the most important element of this or any investigation into the political importance of Russo-Soviet literature and art is the understanding that indirect expression of political protest or critique through works of art and criticism was the long-standing norm — this was no invention of the Soviet era. Even prior to the now well-known repression and censorship of public expression and media in the Soviet era, Russians were not accustomed to voicing explicit, direct and unveiled public critique of the government. Therefore, if researchers look to the official newspapers for editorials, or at public speeches and writings, they will not find a particularly accurate overview of the lives and thoughts of Russia's citizens before 1917. Instead, "Russian political and social realities and problems have traditionally been expressed through the medium of literature and literary criticism" (Rowe vii-viii). In essence, genre itself became a screen. One could write about literature instead of trying to publish political tracts or editorials for the newspapers. To this formula could certainly be added the arts more broadly. An artist can also circumvent the more obvious genres of political expression by looking to theater, poetry, and so forth. The relevance and ubiquity of the arts in the lives of ordinary citizens in Russian culture is perhaps a fact that needs to be established, given the ways in which Westerners' experiences might differ. Literature, criticism, theater, music and later, of course, film as well, formed the stuff of Russian cultural consciousness across a broad spectrum of the population. This was especially true after 1917 when official efforts were made to spread literacy and media to workers and peasants all over the country. Given such a context, the special languages artistic and critical works employed to communicate meaning must be decoded and then juxtaposed against official history, propaganda and dogma before one can comprehend their political potency. Moreover, there existed and still exists in Russia a constant dialogue and interplay between the worlds of criticism and the arts, which readers might also find unlike the West's more stratified academic disciplines and the ensuing gap between practitioners or artists in one camp and reviewers or academics in another. Kozintsev himself provides an example of this Russian interdisciplinarity in being himself a theatrical director, a filmmaker and a literary scholar.

Arthur Mendel, making reference to *Hamlet* in an article from the early 1970s, offers an apt analogy in discussing the oblique communication of Soviet artists and intellectuals, which can be applied to pre–Soviet tsarist rule as well: "They were speaking out against their own Elsinore in the only speech tyranny permits [...] the Aesopian language of literary criticism, traditional among the Russian intelligentsia, that ostensibly talks about other places and other times than the subject is here and now" (quoted in Rowe viii). Fables and parables such as Aesop's are almost always designed to be readable on multiple separable levels: the surface level of plot and character screens the underlying levels of moral messages and social critiques that contain markers of the story's relevance to contemporary society. These moral messages are not projected into the universal void, but rather aim to illustrate the ills of government or the powerful to their audiences. As we shall explore in my discussion of Kozintsev's *Hamlet* film, Hamlet's staging of the play *The Murder of Gonzago* is a sort of Aesopian device designed to accuse Claudius without actually stating as much.

Translation

As with the Aesopian strategy, Russian artists had long turned to translation as a means to speak out under the radar of censors. This phenomenon was especially pronounced in the Soviet period when writers, critics, theater practitioners and film-makers turned to Shakespeare's words and imagery as mouthpiece for their own sentiments: "translation served as sublimation for their creative impulse" (Friedberg 16). Stymied by political pressure, artists did not simply cower in the shadows, they simply sought a clearer route to expression: "Deprived of the possibility of expressing themselves to the full in original writing, Russian poets — especially between the nineteenth and twentieth Party Congresses, used the language of Goethe, Shakespeare, Oberliani or Hugo to talk to the reader" (Etkind quoted in Baer 537). For various reasons, translation provided refuge to intellectuals and artists, such as Pasternak, who undertook his translations when he could not publish his original works. For Maurice Friedberg, whose 1997 book on the politics of translation is an invaluable resource, sanctuary could be found because "literary translation — as opposed to original Soviet writing — was traditionally viewed as a nonpolitical activity. The tendency for prominent victims of Communist thought control to seek refuge in translation when they were no longer allowed to publish original work — foremost among them Boris Pasternak and Anna Akhmatova — served to strengthen this belief" (7). Kozintsev's problems with, and ultimate parting of ways from, his blacklisted partner Leonid Trauberg, and the banning of their 1945 film *Simple People*, also led to his turning to Shakespeare criticism and adaptation. Many of the Soviet literary critics discussed in this project were seeking and finding refuge in Shakespeare, particularly during the Stalin era, using ostensibly objective, impartial historical and literary criticism as a screen for their frustration with the Soviet regime. "Translation [...] became a refuge [...]. The profession thus attracted a disproportionate number of men and, especially, women with politically dubious backgrounds, such as Jews or former inmates of Soviet prisons. Conversely, few professional translators were Communist Party members" (Friedberg 17). One could add actors to the list of "translators" who were former prison inmates. The actor Innokenti Smoktunovski, who played Hamlet in Kozintsev's *Hamlet* film, had been in a prison camp following World War II. Actors are translators and casting choices become significant in an age in which so many people had "politically dubious backgrounds" — using them in a film would have spoken volumes in and of itself. Perhaps the disinterest of the Party in translation was a happy accident, allowing all sorts of material into the public sphere simply because the censors were just plain out of touch.

The effects of translations upon their audiences provided a similar comfort and catharsis to Aesopian discourse. Friedberg states that "during the Soviet period, Russian renditions of foreign writing also helped sustain men and women who were skeptical of official assurances that the social ills and psychological malaise depicted in imported books had no relevance to their own grievances and aspirations" (18). The need for catharsis of fear, grief and trauma, as well as craving for a truthful representation of their experiences, led the audience for translations to find solace, and probably sanity too, in the honesty of translated works. Although they were not the target audience, works that openly critiqued, say, the West would provide vicarious experience of outspokenness. Moreover, like Aesopian discourse (of which translation is a variant), Baer reveals that "translation [...] became a site of resistance to official Soviet culture and values" (537). In this way, translators became almost like spiritual leaders, giving comfort, reassurance and, most importantly, hope, to their audiences. Baer quotes Soviet scholar Vladimir Shlapentokh: "literary translators came to embody resistance, especially during the worst periods of repression. In part through that resistance, the Soviet-era intelligentsia bolstered its 'claim on the spiritual leadership of society'" (539). The underlying ethos was nothing less than a wholesale rejection of the dictates of Socialist realism, Party propaganda and Marxist techniques of historical and literary investigation: "literary translators perpetuated the concepts of timeless 'universal values' and 'world culture' that were in opposition to what they saw as the tendentious, politicized, and class-based official culture of the Soviet Union" (Baer 539). The implication of an interior, spiritual orientation is highly significant. Countless quotations from Kozintsev's books on Shakespeare, especially his later one, perhaps not accidentally published after his death, indicate a deeply spiritual orientation, a sympathy for religious beliefs and an ahistorical, or maybe more accurately, trans-historical, view of the relevance of Shakespeare to the Soviet situation. Baer's observation on this point could very easily apply to Kozintsev, as well as his collaborators Shostakovich and Pasternak: "translators were seen — often in heroic terms — as serving the 'eternal' or universal values of art in preference to the fleeting and shifting political values of the party or state" (551). Kozintsev's depictions of Hamlet and Edgar imply strong parallels to Christ, therefore casting the true hero as one committed to universal metaphysical truths and not the particular historical atheism of the State. For such portrayals of Shakespeare's characters, Kozintsev owed much to Pasternak whose own translations of *Hamlet* and *Lear* played up the religious themes, providing a quiet affirmation and slaking of the Soviet audience's thirst for transcendental truths.

Critical Background

A proper overall reading of the films under consideration must take into account not only their cinematic, aesthetic qualities but their historical, political and cultural contexts as well. There are many fine articles and book chapters dealing with Kozintsev's Shakespeare adaptations. Many of them are more or less formal in approach, not considering the wider, non-aesthetic contexts that might have influenced Kozintsev's works, and avoiding speculation regarding the implications and interpretations likely evoked by these films in their audiences. Similarly, there are many articles presenting compelling formal readings of Kozintsev's Shakespeare films, but few make a case for a politically subversive reading along the lines of what I wish to do here. Critics sometimes write that Kozintsev's *Lear* is "political" without giving any examples of just what particular political issues or events might be suggested by his presentation of the play in film. Or a critic will make reference to Lear himself in the Kozintsev film as a Stalin-figure, but without offering any more precise examples of how Stalin's rulership could be evoked by Lear's actions in the play in the minds of the film's audience. Unfortunately, too many scholars avoid mentioning specific historical contexts or the biographies of Kozintsev's collaborators, the possible relevance (or irrelevance) of previous Shakespearean adaptations, especially in the theater, and the reasons why a Shakespeare play should serve a Soviet artist's needs at all. Since interpretations of the more formal, aesthetic and cinematic facets of the Kozintsev adaptations have been considered sufficiently elsewhere, this project will focus on the films in order to illustrate how they emphasize political themes within the plays that resonated with the contemporary situation of the Soviet audience. Therefore, one will not find much discussion of the influence of the early FEKS years upon Kozintsev's later films, since that is well-documented elsewhere.

Certainly, part of the problem for Western scholars writing in the 1960s, 70s, and well into the 80s and 90s, would have been the dearth of comprehensive or reliable information on the USSR. In addition, Western political pressures, which some American and British academics must have felt keenly given the politically-charged atmosphere at colleges and universities from the 1960s onward, led to promulgations of a Cold War mentality of "us-against-them." Therefore, at times, the more acceptable of possible positions to take in writing about Soviet culture or politics was to dismiss most of it as the result of Communist brainwashing or propaganda. In the past two decades however, critics' readings have become more concerned with the films' historical and political contexts, not only because of the availability of information and the altered political climate, but no doubt also because of the fact that historical, cultural and political literary criticism have become so popular. Therefore, more recent articles and chapters, such as those by Collick, Womack, Sokolyansky and Stribrny, all raise useful issues for a political discussion of the films and further exploration concerning the cultural contexts and importance of Kozintsev's Shakespeare adaptations as well as those of his collaborators and contemporaries.

Still other critics and scholars writing on Kozintsev's Shakespeare, such as Barbara Hodgdon (who sadly has recently passed away), have goals that send their investigations into realms outside the ones taken up here. For instance, a great deal of energy has been, and continues to be (for some reason), spent in defending cinematic adaptations of Shakespeare as valid artistically and as objects of serious academic interest. Therefore, some scholars will argue for and against the aesthetic merits of Shakespeare films and how they do justice to or remain faithful to the play texts, which they inevitably must cut considerably in rendering verbal imagery into a visual medium. At times, these issues become more important than the particular historical, cultural or political contexts in which a film is produced and how this, in turn, enhances our understanding of the plays as adaptable works. In my analysis, the issue of whether or not Kozintsev's adaptations are defensibly "correct," or even good, is not significant. What is important is how he has identified certain issues in the plays, out of a range of possibilities, and has made those speak to the Soviet experience.

A starting point in the shift away from the initial wave of scholarship on Kozintsev and away from an overly simplistic understanding of Soviet Bloc cultural politics was no doubt the appearance of Jan Kott's book *Shakespeare Our Contemporary*, which appeared in English in 1974. Kott's published lecture "On Kozintsev's *Hamlet*" appeared in *The Literary Review* of 1979 and states without hesitation, and with the authority of someone who lived through the Stalin era, that Kozintsev's film is indeed a subversive, politically-motivated interpretation. *Shakespeare Our Contemporary*, first published in Poland around the same time that Kozintsev's *Hamlet* film was released, illustrated to the West the degree to which Shakespeare was being adapted for political purposes, expressly subverting the ideological hegemony of the USSR both inside and outside of Russian regions. Although Kott's orientation and interpretation ultimately differed from Kozintsev's, Kott's cynical reading of political themes in *Hamlet* and other Shakespeare plays illustrates that opinions outside of the official mainstream of Communist Bloc nations were being voiced and heard. Arthur Mendel's 1971 article on *Hamlet* and the Aesopian nature of Soviet art and criticism is yet another work that encouraged Western critics to re-evaluate their reading of Soviet Shakespeare. Mendel's essay was a huge influence on

Rowe's book *Hamlet: A Window on Russia* (released in 1976), which covers Russian artistic adaptations from Pushkin onwards and provides readings attuned to the political contexts of these adaptations. Particularly illuminating is Rowe's observation, following Mendel, and quoted by many of the critics writing on Kozintsev, that one must read this film, and others, in an Aesopian vein. Mendel writes:

> Can there be any doubt [...] that the Soviet critics were practicing what, through *Hamlet*, they preached? They were speaking out against their own Elsinore in the only speech that tyranny permits, the Aesopian language of literary criticism, traditional among the Russian intelligentsia, that ostensibly talks about other times and places when the real subject is the here and now. [...] So when they denounce over and over again the oppressions of Elsinore, the tyrannically ruled and morally corrupt state prison, the "iron ages," "memory wordless, despair soundless, and anger choking in your throat," and when they eulogize this hero because of his conscience, his courage to be and to doubt, his rebellion against all attempts to "equate man with a flute," what other conclusions are we to draw? [746].

Kozintsev, in addition to being a filmmaker and theater director, was an accomplished Shakespearean scholar who published two books on Shakespeare. The first was translated into English in 1966, covering his work and ideas on *Hamlet*, titled *Shakespeare: Time and Conscience* (*STC*). The actual title of this work in Russian is *Our Contemporary: William Shakespeare*, a title designed to evoke a relationship to the Polish Jan Kott's *Shakespeare Our Contemporary* (1964), a highly influential book. Kozintsev was arguably a much better informed Shakespearean than Kott, but the influence of Kott's highly politicized readings of Shakespeare was quite profound in the countries of the Soviet Bloc. Kott's book was widely read in *samizdat* form (i.e., privately-circulated copies of banned or officially edited works designed to avoid official censorship) within the USSR and illustrated quite clearly that not all "Marxists" were interpreting Shakespeare in the same way. Kott's reading contradicts the Marxist view of history as progressive, instead emphasizing the circularity of history, the dimmest view of human nature and evidencing a cynicism quite unlike any mainstream Party-line commentaries. Yet Kozintsev was not a Kottian, however much he admired Kott's work. Kozintsev never succumbed to fatalism, pessimism or nihilism; rather, he was a realist who honestly confronted the problems of his times, but always remained hopeful, believing in human agency and the power of artistic expression to effect positive changes in society.

For Western scholars, reading Soviet critics writing within the USSR also had to undergo a shift away from simply seeing the surface level of meaning. Soviet Party-line Marxist critical interpretations often appear to read Shakespeare only as a sort of proto-Marxist, seeing his characters engaged in class struggle against their oppressors. Thus, in the officially progressive view of history, Shakespeare anticipated the revolutions to come, even if he himself was possessed of limited "consciousness," and was in many respects complicit in the exploitative power structures of his time. Most of the articles in *Shakespeare in the Soviet Union*, a useful anthology of Soviet Shakespeare criticism, which includes a selection from Kozintsev's book on *Lear*, offer a Party-line reading of Shakespeare and his era. Some of the Soviet Shakespeare scholars seem to do this without any under-the-radar qualification, but most seem to offer these readings as a screen for their more oblique, implicit criticisms of the Soviet regime. I will be referring to many of the Soviet critics' works, especially when they seem to speak with two voices. It is likely that Western scholars reading these works decades ago were not attuned to the Aesopian techniques employed therein and therefore most likely did not gain much insight from them until later on.

From the 1980s onwards, it became clear to Western critics that Soviet artists, despite public appearances and statements making them appear as nothing more than Party mouthpieces, were living a sort of double life. Indeed, as they discovered, many works of art in Soviet literature, music, film and theater were actually critical of the regime, just in an indirect or allegorical manner. Taking refuge in stories from the past, Western critics surmised, especially officially-sanctioned ones as most of Shakespeare's works were, artists could critique the Soviet system without overtly doing so, thereby protecting themselves, at least partially, from censure or official reprisals. This subterfuge was not always easy or worthwhile, what with the threat of punishments ranging from job loss and expulsion from unions to sentences in the Gulag, or from internal or external exile to execution. Western critics realized that if they wished to adequately examine Soviet works of art they had to take into account the fact that no one actually living and working within the USSR could publicly and explicitly discuss the many hardships and injustices that formed Soviet reality without exposing him or herself to extreme danger.

The assumption that only those living and working in exile, such as filmmaker Andrei Tarkovsky, or writer Alexander Solzhenitsyn, were critical of the Soviet government was thereby dispelled. Those outside spoke more openly and frankly, to be sure, but those on the inside were talking as well albeit in their own oblique ways, or through privately published and circulated materials. Despite Soviet propaganda and the illusion of absolute control and obedience, works produced abroad, domestically censored, or volatile ones that had been banned altogether were still available within the USSR. Privately-circulated material was common, as was self-publishing, providing an entire subculture of resistance based upon the exchange of banned works or completed versions of officially-edited ones. Once these key elements of Soviet life were understood in the West, rereading of the "clues" left behind by Kozintsev, Pasternak and Shostakovich became possible and yielded new interpretations of their works and uses of Shakespeare.

Boris Pasternak and Dmitri Shostakovich

The artistic careers of Boris Pasternak and Dmitri Shostakovich, both of whom used Shakespearean themes in controversial art that did not always escape the censure of the authorities, are relevant to this book's exploration. The investment of these artists in the freedom of artistic expression is, in its own right, important in putting forth my thesis on the political nature of Kozintsev's films. The fact that Pasternak and Shostakovich used Shakespeare as source and inspiration for works which drew the ire of those committed to the Party propaganda machine makes their inclusion in this project crucial. Very few scholars writing on Kozintsev's films spend sufficient time investigating, for example, Dmitri Shostakovich's Shakespearean adaptation of *Macbeth*, based upon the Leskov story "Lady Macbeth of the Mtsensk District," which brought Stalin's wrath upon Shostakovich during the Terror of the 1930s. Despite the fact that he did not generally enjoy composing for film (which he often did anyway due to pressures from above resulting from Stalin's well-known obsession with cinema), he agreed enthusiastically to work on both of Kozintsev's film adaptations. As Baer observes, there existed in Russian and Soviet arts "an [...] opposition [...] between cultural work done out of love and cultural work done on command" (554). Moreover, for Shostakovich and other musicians, film scoring was, like translation, a means by which to evade close scrutiny by the censors or the censorious eye of Stalin. Shostakovich frequently included musical markers, such as snippets of Soviet or Russian songs, in order to alert audiences to the fact that a screening device was being used in his compositions.

Pasternak's long-standing tension with the Soviet regime, which probably cost him his health in the late 1950s, and his life in 1960, is of interest here too, especially since after he fell out of favor in the 1930s he spent most of his time doing translations, which was a safer endeavor for an artist who was following his own course, not the Party's. Pasternak translated many Shakespeare plays, and his translations reveal a great deal about his own personal beliefs on a range of subjects, including his reactions to the political themes in the plays. For instance, Pasternak's fascination with Orthodox Christianity and Christian symbolism and ritual, which is clearly evidenced in *Doctor Zhivago* (first published outside the USSR in 1957), also permeates his Shakespeare adaptations, especially in his *King Lear* and in the *Hamlet* poem at the end of *Zhivago*. This affection for religion was, of course, totally unacceptable in Soviet Socialist ideology. The abuses suffered by the Orthodox Church, as both a faith-based institution and one synonymous with the tsarist era, made a sympathetic use of Christian themes and images automatically suspect in the eyes of Soviet artists' unions. Such imagery could only be permitted if one intended a condemnation of the Church. Christian imagery also pervades Kozintsev's films, which relied upon Pasternak's translations (although there were many others available in Russian), perhaps in homage to his posthumous collaborator's religious sensibilities. Pasternak saw Hamlet as a Christ-like figure in a distinctly political sense. Pasternak's Hamlet is the Christ who challenges the powers-that-be, and Hamlet's assassination (that is, a politically-motivated murder), is a version of Soviet martyrdom and sainthood.

Shostakovich provided original music for Kozintsev's *Hamlet* and *King Lear* films, as well as their preceding stage productions (Kozintsev's *King Lear* in 1941 and his *Hamlet* in 1954-5). Although it is clear from his own remarks that Shostakovich did not enjoy film scoring in general, it seems that his love for Shakespeare and his long-standing collaborative relationship with Kozintsev, with whom he had worked since the 1920s, made him interested in these projects (Volkov, *Testimony* 83–89). Shostakovich worked with Kozintsev and his partner Leonid Trauberg as early as 1928 for their film *New Babylon* (Volkov 2004, 132) and provided music for six other films with the team of Kozintsev and Trauberg, or Kozintsev alone, between these first collaborations and the post–Stalin Shakespeare films. He provided music for Kozintsev's 1941 Bolshoi Dramatic Theater production of *King Lear*, composing the "Ten Songs of the Fool" as incidental music. He also provided music for the 1954-5 Kozintsev stage production of *Hamlet*, although this music was not recycled for the film version released in 1964. Earlier, in 1932, Shostakovich composed music for an *avant-garde*, farcical, politically cynical version of *Hamlet* by Nikolai Akimov; the play displeased the critics, but the music was well-received (Fay 60). Kozintsev, like Akimov, had started his career in the new experimental and *avant-garde* theater and film world of the 20s and 30s only to have to eschew such "anti-people" or "formalist" forms upon Stalin's institution of cultural controls and the enforcement of Socialist realism.

Shostakovich's opera *Lady Macbeth of Mtsensk District* (adapted from the 1865 Leskov novella), was one of the first major artistic victims of Stalin's Terror campaign in the 1930s. The opera premiered in 1934, initially with great success both in the USSR and abroad. Unfortunately, the artistic repressions of the "anti-formalist" movement caught up with Shostakovich when Stalin's anonymous "Muddle Instead of Music" article lambasting the work appeared in *Pravda* in 1936, ushering in waves of new attacks on art and artists during the first of Stalin's major purges (Volkov 2004, 103–109). This was only the start of Shostakovich's troubles with Stalin and the Soviet cultural authorities. He would be repeatedly vilified and exalted throughout his career, even after the death of the "Great Leader." Yet he continued to write subversive and oppositional music, even while he publicly appeared to be a puppet of the regime. As Gerard McBurney asserts in his 1998 essay on Shostakovich for the collection *Russian Cultural Studies*, Shostakovich's insistence on continuing the inventive compositional tradition of early Soviet music inspired its continuation beyond Stalin's death and survived the most concerted attempts of the cultural police to suppress it. As was the case with many artists, the guise of complicity with the Party's artistic tastes was necessary to stay alive, and by all accounts Shostakovich cared deeply about trying to protect and support his family. It is remarkable that he managed to do so while others who received similarly harsh public censure either were eliminated, exiled, committed suicide or died from diseases related to the stresses and deprivations of Soviet life and Party persecution (as was the case with Pasternak). It seems, by Shostakovich's own accounts, that his survival was partly due to his popularity in the West and Stalin's interest in his work. Other artists popular in the West did not escape the unwelcome attention of the authorities—for instance, Boris Pasternak lost his membership in the Writers Union *after* winning the 1958 Nobel Prize in Literature.

The contradictory nature of the relationship of the musically outspoken Shostakovich and the tyrant leader led Solomon Volkov (and even Shostakovich himself, albeit indirectly), to compare him to the *yurodivy* or holy fool of Russian tradition. In the preface to *Testimony* and in greater length in *Shostakovich and Stalin* (2004), Volkov describes Shostakovich as a *yurodivy*, and Shostakovich himself at various points in *Testimony* (1979) refers to different artists and intellectuals of his time as *yurodivye*. The implication, following Russian examples such as Nikolka in Pushkin's

Boris Godunov, is that this fool is always a little bit insane since his outspokenness entails inviting punishment from the powerful. Boris Pasternak was another "holy fool" of the Soviet era. His works, especially *Doctor Zhivago*, despite earning him the Nobel Prize in 1958, brought him a great deal of trouble with the Soviet government. Like Shostakovich, Pasternak played the difficult game of making art which was subtly subversive, while making official utterances in deference to Party pressures.

Chapter Overviews

Chapter One

My investigation begins with the history of translation, criticism and performance of *Hamlet* in the 18th and 19th centuries in chapter one. Russian translations were immediately controversial and the play was occasionally banned from performance due to its political themes. Most notably, the play was banned during the reigns of Catherine II and Paul I because of the dubiousness of Paul's succession and his mother Catherine's involvement in it. The first chapter also covers the concept of "Hamletism," which was a social movement influenced by an interpretation of Hamlet's character that dominated from the early 19th century into the early 20th. In Hamletism, Hamlet is depicted as lazy, disillusioned and disenfranchised. He is aristocratic and educated, but incapable of directing his energies towards the greater good. Early in the 19th century, Hamlet was Romanticized; his intellectualism and sensitivity were idealized. Later in the 19th century, as the intelligentsia became more radicalized, Hamlet was vilified; he represented all that was holding Russia back from real reform and progress. Some progressives left Hamlet behind altogether, but others reclaimed him, seeing him as more positive and active than negating and passive. Thus, he was recast for the new political climate as a hero. He fought bravely against the corruption of Claudius' regime and was concerned with the fate of his fellow man. It was this Revolutionary Hamlet who survived into the 20th century and this is the characterization favored by Kozintsev.

Chapter Two

The second chapter discusses *Hamlets* of the Soviet era until just after Stalin's death. The play was tacitly banned under Stalin whose own "succession" was not endorsed by Lenin, his predecessor, and who did not appreciate any parallels being drawn between himself and Claudius. Among the few Stalin-era productions were Nikolai Akimov's in 1932, which was satirical and blisteringly political; and a 1938 production by Sergei Radlov, bravely launched during the height of the "Terror" period. After Stalin's death, there was a veritable "*Hamlet*-mania" in the USSR and productions, including one by Kozintsev, sprang up, making pointed comparisons between the "prison" of Denmark and the Soviet Union, and between Claudius and Stalin. Kozintsev's first theatrical *Hamlet*, like that of Nikolai Okhlopkov in 1954, was designed to critique the Stalin era in the wake of Stalin's death in 1953. As such, these productions anticipated the denunciation of Stalin by Khrushchev in 1956.

Chapter Three

Chapter Three considers Kozintsev's film production of *Hamlet*, which was released in the USSR in 1964, a couple of years prior to the publication of its companion study, *Shakespeare: Time and Conscience*. In the intervening years of the "Thaw," some indications of progress for the USSR in terms of artistic freedom and economic development were promising. Yet there were also many setbacks and new forms of repression. By the time of his ousting in 1964, Khrushchev had effectively been thwarted in his plans for reform and most artists continued to suffer under censorship. Kozintsev's *Hamlet* depicts an Elsinore of oppressive and labyrinthine grandeur where spies lurk, monitoring the Court's discourse and activity. Claudius becomes a Renaissance Stalin (and a Khrushchev too, as I suggest); Polonius, one of his opportunistic Party officials; while Rosencrantz and Guildenstern evoke the spies of the Soviet secret police. Hamlet himself comes across as a dissident: hunted, exiled, murdered for his views, yet determined, for his own sake and for the sake of a dead father (emblem of an idealized past regime), to speak the truth through art, specifically theater. This Hamlet becomes a Soviet-artist hero; he suffers the fate of far too many such artists in the era, yet perhaps, by example, inspires others to speak their truths despite fear of personal destruction. A close reading of the film's "Mousetrap" scene and the role of the players illustrates Kozintsev's alignment of Hamlet with Soviet artists and intellectuals. In this scene Hamlet uses a play to depict the crimes of the reigning monarch, suggesting not only fratricide, but that the monarch is a usurper who wields power without the mandate of the people, or even the most basic deference to morality or law. The king, like Stalin viewing *Ivan Part 2*, gets the message, and the brutality and cravenness of his subsequent retaliation mirrors the punishment and harassment meted out to Eisenstein, Pasternak, Shostakovich and many other Soviet artists and intellectuals.

The film suggests the stifling of human expression and limitation of physical movement; the spying and surveillance of the court under Claudius highlight the difficulties faced by persons, especially artists, wishing to speak out against a corrupt regime intent upon keeping power through ideological hegemony and myopia. The play-within-the-play and Hamlet's relationship with the players offer an ideal motif for a cinematic expression of the subversive potential of art. The political implications of the "Mousetrap" (or "Murder of Gonzago") episode urge the audience to read *Hamlet* as a drama about the dangers of creating art that challenges powerful political leaders. The ultimate futility of doing so, when an artist is pitted against a rigid and corrupt system, is suggested by the numerous senseless deaths at the play's close. Kozintsev seized upon an interpretive option that emphasized politics and the relationship of the artist or intellectual to the state.

Hamlet, as Kozintsev writes about at length in *Shakespeare Time and Conscience*, is no longer the "superfluous man" bemoaned by Turgenev and others. He is not the aristocratic parasite of 19th-century "Hamletism," but rather a man of action. No doubt influenced by Pasternak's translation, which casts Hamlet as a Christ-like figure in his will to self-sacrifice and commitment to justice, Kozintsev's Hamlet is the active artist-intellectual, engaged and capable of affecting the social and political world. Even his casting is significant: not only is the actor Innokenti Smoktunovski a strong, masculine actor, but he was imprisoned by Stalin after World War II, which brings a special extra-textual resonance to the work given the post–Stalin-era popularity of *Hamlet* (Stribrny 106).

Chapter Four

The fourth chapter analyzes the uses of *King Lear* from its first appearance through the Second World War. As with *Hamlet*, *King Lear* held the interest of Russian and Soviet translators, critics and artists from the late 18th century. The play served both ends of the political spectrum, being used by some in support of the monarchy, and by others to criticize it. The play held special resonance after the Bolshevik Revolution during the Civil War, the Terror of the 1930s, and World War II. The imagery of the devastation of war, internal and external exile, and the clash of generations and ideologies dramatized in *Lear* was particularly poignant during the time of domestic upheaval from 1917 to 1920. The themes of a despotic, deluded leader whose misdeeds exposed his country to internal and external strife further resonated during the Terror and the Second World War, as the country was traumatized by mass arrests, show trials, imprisonments and assassinations, and then forced to fend off the Germans, losing the lives of millions of people in the process.

Many productions of *Lear* appeared during the war in all regions of the USSR. In addition to its topicality in terms of depicting the horrors of war and foreign invasion, the figure of the egotistical tyrant could not fail to conjure Stalin and Hitler. Kozintsev's staged *Lear* appeared in 1941 in Leningrad during the siege, which was possibly the bleakest of time of the Soviets' engagement in the Second World War. The play's potential as a commentary on war and leadership evokes, among other things, the dissolution of the ill-conceived 1939 Hitler-Stalin pact, which, much like Lear's division of his kingdom, brought destruction and chaos to the people of the Soviet Union.

Chapter Five

Kozintsev's cinematic *King Lear*, produced well into the Brezhnev reign, revisits similar themes, but, as I argue in chapter five, contrary to some other critical assessments, that this film is not merely another portrait of Stalin's horrors, but rather it aims to speak to its own present, critiquing the new leadership of the Soviet Union and its relationship to artists and intellectuals after the promise of the "Thaw" period slipped away. Kozintsev's *Lear* is a dark, dimly prophetic work, which uses the stuff of early medieval legend as metaphor for a country ravaged by years of war and tyranny and, in the Cold War era nuclear arms race, facing even greater destruction as the "promised end" moved from God's hands to humans'. Kozintsev's *Lear* is, in my reading, an overt critique of the Brezhnev-era return to Stalinism. As Moss states of the character of the Burgomaster in an adaptation of *The Adventures of Baron Von Munchausen* presented for Soviet television in the 1970s, "it stands to reason that the ruler of a world which covertly represents the Soviet Union should covertly represent its leader at the time— Brezhnev" (Moss 16, 18). Passages in Kozintsev's book *King Lear: The Space of Tragedy* make it clear that his critique extends to events well after Stalin's death in 1953. Many critics simply assume that Lear is a Stalin figure and leave it at that. Yet there are clearly other objects of Kozintsev's criticism than in his theatrical productions of the 1940s and 1950s. The film's imagery certainly conjures up memories of the violence and devastation of war, from the Russian Civil War of the 1920s, through World War II;

but it also reveals Kozintsev's Cold War fears, post–Cuban Missile Crisis, of a nuclear holocaust. Imagery of the ravaged land and the beleaguered peasantry reminds the viewer of the problems of rural and village life, still beset by the after-effects of war, collectivization, famine, resettlement and depopulation. The image of the Fool draws many historical threads together, for he is at once fool, victimized Russian peasant, Nazi concentration camp or Gulag inmate resurrected at the scene of a nuclear disaster.

Among other directorial choices, emphasis on the figure of the Fool in this production, who is linked to a long tradition of Holy Fools in Russian culture and letters, will be especially important in my reading of *Lear*. Kozintsev extends the role of the Fool, keeping him present until the very end of the film, instead of following Shakespeare's play's somewhat inexplicable disappearance of him after the storm scene. The potency of the Fool character has a similar duality in Early Modern English and Russian culture. The fool, in both traditions, is an entertainer, a jester, a person at the periphery of social and economic norms, a madman (or woman), yet also a visionary, a social critic, a truth-teller, the "conscience of the king." He is unafraid, perhaps because he has so little to lose, to expose the cruelty hypocrisy of the powerful. With the help of Shostakovich's simple, yet haunting music for the Fool's pipe, the pathos of the jester is further highlighted.

Tarkovsky's fool in *Andrei Rublev* (1966) similarly draws the ire of the local clerical hierarchy — serving as Aesopian stand-ins for the Party's watchdogs — during a performance for a group of peasants in a barn. His jesting, singing and dancing are a carnivalesque delight, being both a respite from the serfs' brutal lives, but also a politically subversive act, and one that must be monitored and controlled. The fool's art is not merely entertainment, nor does he act as a mouthpiece of official propaganda. Therefore the audience comes back again, as with *Hamlet*, to the problems of the place and function of art and artists in the Soviet world. Pushkin's fool Nikolka, from the play *Boris Godunov*, has uncommon latitude in criticizing the tsar, uttering things which would leave other people vulnerable to imprisonment or execution for treason or heresy. Critics and artists, among them Shostakovich, saw themselves and their peers as just such *yurodivye*, using art to hold a mirror up to corruption and evil.

Epilogue

The epilogue describes how, after Kozintsev's *Lear*, artists became increasingly bold, as if responding to Edgar's silent delivery of the line, "speak what we feel, not what we ought to say" in the film's final sequence. The audience took up the mandate and the art of double-voicing gave way to more outspoken works published by *samizdat* (self-publishing) and *tamizdat* (publishing abroad) instead of being "screened" in order to get released through official channels. "After almost twenty years [1964–1984] of a flourishing Aesopian literature in the USSR, a similar period has evidently arrived. [...] Writers whose leanings are toward the opposition [...] are not inclined in their work to resort to Aesopian language" (Loseff 229). Similarly, Friedberg contends that "translation [...] contributed over the years to the erosion of Soviet pieties that ultimately led to the collapse of the USSR in 1991," which made the former methods of obfuscation obsolete (Friedberg 18). As a specific theatrical example of this new unobfuscated outspokenness I discuss the famous *Hamlet* production of Moscow's Taganka Theater, which was known for being unusually obvious in its relationship of dissent toward the government and was not particularly concerned with screening its references to contemporary events. Kozintsev's contribution to this movement towards more overt protest, using Shakespeare as a sort of loudspeaker, is a legacy he would have been proud to have seen had he survived past his 68th year. Kozintsev passed away in 1973, just before the publication of his last book, *King Lear: The Space of Tragedy*.

CHAPTER ONE

Kozintsev's Contexts 1: *Hamlet* in Russia in the 18th and 19th Centuries

Kozintsev's stage and film versions of *Hamlet* are politically-charged, based upon a play that was controversial for many Soviets, and distasteful to Stalin to the extent that it was under a tacit ban during his lifetime. Before turning to an investigation of Grigory Kozintsev's stage and film versions of *Hamlet*, this chapter will establish the history of the play in Russian and early Soviet translation, performance and criticism. Emphasized in this survey are those translations, adaptations and performances that have a political orientation or that appear politically-influenced or influential. This background is crucial for understanding Kozintsev's film as an example of an adaptation that is responsive to the history of *Hamlet* and Hamlets in the Russian and European traditions. Kozintsev's career and writings illustrate his extensive knowledge of the history of Elizabethan, European and Russian politics, culture, theater and literature; therefore, a truly thorough reading of his Shakespeare interpretations must consider this background as well in order to enter into the mindset of its subject.

Kozintsev's writing in *Shakespeare: Time and Conscience*, published just after the release of his filmed *Hamlet*, in 1964, illustrates his knowledge of Shakespeare's era, as well as the history of performance, criticism and translation of his plays in Europe and Russia. Nearly all of the translators, critics and performances cited in this chapter were known to Kozintsev and a large number of them are discussed in his books. Kozintsev's interpretations of Shakespeare were informed by his engagement with the plays' own milieu as well as their afterlives. In particular, Kozintsev described and decried the cult of Hamletism that emerged in Russia in the 19th century. Under the influence of Romantic interpretations of *Hamlet*, especially from the German and French, and in sympathy with the Russian figure of the "superfluous man," the image of Hamlet as emblem of the disaffected, apathetic and apolitical intellectuals of the later 19th and early 20th centuries dominated the cultural landscape. Like Anton Chekhov and Alexander Pushkin before him, Kozintsev rejected the "romantic," "decadent" characterization of Hamlet that grew out of French and German thought and helped to create Russian Hamletism. Russia's "superfluous men" of the 19th century were odious to Kozintsev, especially in their connection to Hamlet, whose identification as an idle, disillusioned and ineffectual loafer was far removed from what he saw as Shakespeare's true vision of the character, one that Kozintsev aimed to restore in his own works. Kozintsev saw the Hamletist Hamlet as antithetical to the play's original Shakespearean context. Kozintsev notes that the same sort of interpolated distortion happens with various other literary figures who become "types": they are reduced to certain of their dominant characteristics, simplified and gradually divorced from the works in which they appeared and the historical contexts in which those works circulated. For instance, Kozintsev cites Don Quixote and Tartuffe as similarly fated to become caricatures of themselves (*STC* 107). Kozintsev's restoration of an active, effectual Hamlet followed in the footsteps of Pushkin, Chekhov, and others who resisted Hamletism.

Kozintsev's resistance to the Romantic image of Hamlet also engaged the skirmishes over Shakespeare throughout Russian and early Soviet cultural history: Shakespeare was claimed by both political progressives and conservatives. Kozintsev's remarks on Hamletism speak to the co-optation of Shakespeare more broadly: "It is taken up by various social groups as a weapon, and is sometimes used for ends that contradict one another" (*STC* 107). Even among the progressives, some wished to illustrate Shakespeare's (and Hamlet's) backwardness, his adherence to reactionary, feudal values; while others, in keeping with Marx, Engels, and later, Lenin, saw Shakespeare's plays and characters as anticipating revolution in their resisting the forces of political oppression and emergent capitalism. Kozintsev favored the latter approach and presented a Hamlet actively and heroically opposed to tyranny, oppression and censorship. The Khrushchev "Thaw" period and the dismantling of the Stalin cult are enormously important in understanding Kozintsev's motivations, and these will be treated in my chapters dealing with his theatrical and cinematic adaptations of *Hamlet*. In this chapter, the focus will be on the history of translation, performance and critical interpretation up to Stalin's death, at which time a tremendous shift occurred in politics and the arts, one which found expression in a veritable explosion of *Hamlet* productions.

Hamlets of the 18th and 19th Centuries

Hamlet first appeared in a Russian translation by A. P. Sumarokov around 1748, itself a translation of a French version that was made to Voltairian, neo-classical tastes (Stribrny 27, Morozov 11). This Francophilism was common, given the dominance of French culture and language that had obtained in Russia since Peter the Great's reforms (r. 1682–1725). French cultural influence was still strong at the time of his daughter Elizabeth's reign (1741–1761). Sumarokov's version is full of murderous intrigue and moral speculation, but the plot was altered so that it only partly resembled the Shakespearean text. The central conflict became Hamlet's duty to avenge his father, despite his love for Ophelia, whose father Polonius had killed Claudius. Anthony Dawson writes that the main focus in Sumarokov's version was "the prince's duty to set the citizens free of the tyranny visited on them by Claudius and his scheming henchman [...] Polonius" (186). There is no ghost; rather, Hamlet dreams his father says: "Exact revenge, revenge against the tyrant and set the citizens free!" (quoted in Stribrny 27).

Hamlet's avenging the tyrant and the emphasis upon his popular mandate were not welcome political images in the 18th century. As Zdenek Stribrny comments, the fate of Russia's economically and socially repressed people and the more privileged citizens' duty towards them was to become "one of the central issues of Russian political and literary discourse in the nineteenth century" (29). At the time Sumarokov's translation appeared, its messages were unwelcome and threatening to the monarchy and aristocracy. Victor Borovsky clearly links the play's political relevance to its disappearance from performance after the 1750s (51). The events of 1762 led to the play's absence from the stage that year until 1809 because of an uneasy relevance to court politics and intrigue: Elizabeth's death led to the ascension of Peter III (1761–1762), who was shortly thereafter murdered, most likely with the knowledge of his wife Catherine II, who reigned until 1796 the year of her death. Catherine, though not fond of *Hamlet*, enjoyed Shakespeare and translated and adapted her own versions of several plays. These were notable culturally since Catherine appears to have resisted the neo-classical unities that had been in vogue previously in favor of a more

Shakespearean style of treating high and low themes, humor and pathos and the dramatization of historical time, as did Pushkin later on in his *Boris Godunov*. (Interestingly, Ernest Simmons proposes some comparisons between Catherine and Elizabeth I.) It was generally known that Catherine II was not especially sorrowful over Peter III's death, causing an analogy to be drawn between her and Gertrude, who — although ignorant at best, repentant at worst — is linked to Old Hamlet's murder through her relationship with Claudius. Borovsky quotes 20th-century Soviet critic Bardovsky who wrote, "The real, not the stage tragedy of Prince Hamlet was taking place before the eyes of all Russian society" (quoted on 51). Borovsky goes on to identify Catherine as Gertrude; Orlov, a murderer and schemer of the court as Claudius (who in Sumarokov's play was neither a king's brother nor a king); and Paul I as heir apparent, Hamlet.

Censorship of the play continued under the reign of Catherine's son Paul I (1796–1801), who feared assassination. His fears were proven correct in 1801 when he was murdered and his son Alexander I (1801–1825) assumed the throne. Alexander was a favorite of his grandmother Catherine, who disliked her own son, thereby making Paul I's succession initially insecure. As Catherine O'Neil points out, comparisons between Paul I and Hamlet were quite common during this episode (66–67). Evidently, a pretender to the throne appeared following Paul's father's murder, thus placing Paul in a very Hamlet-like situation in which he was nearly prevented (whereas Hamlet is completely prevented) from claiming his ascension. Peter Holland muses: "The play [...] becomes useless theatrically and politically dangerous, precisely because of the precision of its potential interconnection with the audience's perception of power politics" (319). The play was popularly read during this time, and Holland speculates that its removal from the stage only served to enhance its appeal and increase readers' sense of its correspondence to events at court. Therefore, from its very first appearance in Russia, *Hamlet* served a subversive political purpose and was therefore disliked by the monarchy enough to cause its suppression, even as its popularity grew in response to its topicality.

The year 1810 saw the arrival of another French-inspired translation, with even more plot alterations. What this version shared with its predecessor were several short inserted passages evoking contemporary liberal politics, specifically put into Hamlet's mouth, who, at the time, according to Russian formalist critic Boris Eikhenbaum, stood for the (temporarily) liberal Alexander I (see Rowe 16–17; the Hamlet comparisons would diminish as Alexander became more draconian). Yet the vogue for French Neoclassicism was soon to give way to a German-inflected Romanticism.

Russians re-viewed Shakespeare through German eyes. In 1828 Mikhail Vronchenko presented the first translation of *Hamlet* directly from English. His version of the play, however much it was influenced by Goethe and the German Romantics, was the most direct and faithful to date in Russian. Shakespeare had become important in German letters of the Romantic movement, and *Hamlet* was the most frequently discussed play and title character. The German interpretation cast Hamlet as "weak of will, overactive in intellect, or decadent in character" (Rowe 22). This characterization would eventually develop in Russia into Hamletism, the cultural phenomenon that engendered a veritable battalion of literary counterparts estranged from active life due to an overabundance of melancholy, intellect, laziness, or some amalgam of the three (Rowe 22). In Kozintsev's view, the Germans had decided to use Hamlet the character for ends unrelated to the play or its historical context: "It was as though the center of the action had shifted from the castle of Elsinore to the soul of Hamlet" (*STC* 111). Kozintsev saw the emergence of Hamletism as originating with the German interpretation of the play's central character, especially Goethe's (*STC* 112). The result was a distortion: "Anything that contradicted Goethe's approach was eliminated from the play" (*STC* 112). Kozintsev summarizes the Hamlet of Goethe and German Romanticism:

> The elegiac Hamlet of the second half of the eighteenth century received new and highly important traits. He staggered under the burden that had fallen onto his shoulders. According to this new approach, the main point of the play was that Hamlet could neither refuse to fulfill his duty nor could he fulfill it. The story of the Danish Prince became that of a soul, beautiful and noble, but by nature incapable of action [*STC* 112].

The German Romantic view of Hamlet as passive and ineffectual — an interpretation that influenced not only Russia, but also England by way of Coleridge — came from Goethe's novel *Wilhelm Meister's Apprenticeship* (1795-6). This book was enormously influential in the German Romantic movement; in it, the title character presents a Hamlet who would come to dominate interpretations of the character well into the 20th century. Wilhelm says of *Hamlet* and its titular character, "To me it is evident that Shakespeare meant to describe a great duty imposed upon a soul unable to perform it. [...] A beautiful, pure, noble and most moral nature, without the strength of mind which forms a hero, sinks beneath a burden which it cannot bear and which it must not renounce" (quoted in Diamond 90). Wilhelm's views on Hamlet are solipsistic, transferring onto the Danish prince his own feelings of listlessness and despair.

Kozintsev pondered why the Germans would have been compelled to devise such a Hamlet. He found the answer in the historical situation of turn-of-the-century Germany. Despite the great movements of democracy and liberation in Europe, people were essentially re-enslaved to capitalism and industrialization and lived under more or less the same oppressive system of government as before (*STC* 113). Following Engels' view of Goethe and the Germany of his era, Kozintsev saw the intellectuals and potential radicals of Germany paralyzed by the persistence of oppressive social forces. Kozintsev writes: "Those who aspired to the ideal of free and active man saw that their hopes could not be realized without revolt and the destruction of the bases of the present social order. But there was no real possibility of revolution yet, and furthermore, the thinkers did not have the pure strength of will necessary to rebels" (*STC* 114). Throughout the 19th century Hamlet came to stand as mirror and symbol for the situation of the German nation itself as conceived by its artists and intellectuals: "All this bespoke not only one generation's vice but also the disease of a nation" (*STC* 116). Although "Hamletism seemed to have found a homeland and to have entered its heyday," for Kozintsev the German engagement with Hamlet and Hamletism paled in comparison to its effect upon the Russians (*STC* 116).

The German Romantic Hamlet had a huge influence upon Russian intellectuals and artists, but the Russians did not make a wholesale adoption of this flaccid personality. The Germanic-Romantic Hamletist Hamlet responded to external problems, be they political or personal, by withdrawal: he often analyzed, but seldom acted. Of the late 18th and early 19th centuries Spencer Golub writes "The intelligentsia [of Russia] rejected the part of the European Hamlet that was a purely asocial compositional device but embraced his resolve to reconstruct history, in opposition to state-engineered forgetfulness, or at least to construct a counter history of performative fate" (175). Because of the readings of 19th century literary critics Alexander Herzen and Vissaron Belinsky, among others, the Russian Hamlet was re-imbued with an active, politically-potent energy, even as some other Russians adopted the stance of the more "decadent" Hamletist variant. For Kozintsev (following Lenin), Herzen, although skeptical of the individual's ability to effect social change, brought Hamlet into a new realm, one that anticipated the social forces that led to political reform in the late 19th century and then to revolution in the 20th (*STC* 117). Similarly, Belinsky, inspired by the famous actor Pavel Mochalov's *Hamlet* of 1838, both conjured and rejected the Goethian position and posited instead a Hamlet who was active and effectual. Before Herzen and Belinsky, Alexander Pushkin launched a revolt against the German Hamlet and

Romanticism, and adopted Shakespeare as the model for a new Russian artistic revival, revoking the influence of French neo-classicism.

Alexander Pushkin

Pushkin, Russia's most celebrated and beloved writer, was hugely influenced by Shakespeare, yet was not overly enamored of *Hamlet*, although references to the play and to Hamlet as a character type appeared in his works, commentary and letters (Rowe 30–34; O'Neil 26). What seems, however, to have intrigued and appealed to Pushkin most was Shakespeare's use of macabre, grotesque and black humor in *Hamlet*: for instance, in the ghost and graveyard scenes. Pushkin notes: "sometimes terror is expressed in laughter. The ghost scene in *Hamlet* is written in a joking, even low style; but Hamlet's jokes make one's hair stand on end" (quoted in Rowe 30). Rowe suggests that references to the ghost or the gravediggers appear in several Pushkin works and that they play upon this absurd, dark humor. Just as Shakespeare added humor to scenes that conjured the most disturbing thoughts and imagery — death, violent revenge, decay, loss — so does this juxtaposition appear in Pushkin. The ability to laugh in the face of death, evil and tragedy took on a political aspect in Pushkin's case. As Stephanie Sandler suggests, humor is a tactic for transcending the futility and frustrations of dealing with the problems of earthly power and the inherent meaninglessness of worldly problems (89).

Pushkin was under the direct censorship of Nicholas I as the Tsar's preferences were communicated under the auspices of the Third Department, described by historian Geoffrey Hosking as a "political police" unbound by "formal legal procedure" (265; 271). Throughout his career, Pushkin was concerned by the failure of the Decembrists, a sympathy which would not endear him to the monarchical status-quo, and sought greater freedom and respect for writers, again, in an era of "mutual distrust between the regime and educated society" (Hosking 272). Pushkin's resistance and independence were manifested in his works, and this did not go unnoticed by his patron and censor. Pushkin spent time in internal exile, during which his scrutiny by the authorities was especially suffocating. Many of Pushkin's works were withheld from publication for protracted periods of time, as was the case with *Boris Godunov*, which was composed during his exile and reflects upon his resentments towards the government in that period (see O'Neil 29–30 and the study edited by Dunning).

Pushkin's troubles with the repressive regime of Nicholas I (who ruled after Alexander I, from 1825 to 1855), found expression in many of his works, for example by way of *Hamlet* allusions in the poem "From Pindemonte." This poem was ascribed to pre–Romantic poet Ippolito Pindemonte (1753–1828) and presented as a translation of a nonexistent poem entirely to "hoodwink" the censors into believing his subversive ideas were someone else's, according to Walter Arndt and others (quoted in Rowe 32; Sandler 78–81). Pushkin alludes to Hamlet's discussion with Polonius — "words, words, words"—as the speaker in the poem sarcastically asserts that he does not need the freedoms he lacks.

> I don't much care for those resounding rights
> That take so many heads to dizzy heights.
> I won't complain. I'll just admit, the fact is
> The gods debarred me from disputing taxes
> Or parleying with emperors at loggerheads;
> To me it makes no difference whether blockheads
> Are hoodwinked by an unrestricted press
> Or sharp-nosed censorship snuffs out excess.
> All this, I have to say, is *words, words, words*.
> To rights of this kind I have grown averse,
> Freedom of this kind is to me quite feeble:
> Subject to the sovereign or the people —
> What does it matter? Let it be.
>   To none
> To owe account, to serve oneself alone,[1]
> And please oneself, and breathe without delivering
> One's conscience, thoughts or neck to power or livery;
> To take in Nature's beauties at one's will,
> To feast the eye on highest art, and thrill:
> These things are happiness, rights ... [Wood].

The narrator disingenuously denigrates the importance of free expression in language as subordinate to other privileges. By recalling Hamlet's "words, words, words," Pushkin draws attention to the potency of language and verbal expression. Sandler points out that Pushkin himself added a footnote to the "translation" indicating that this was a quote from *Hamlet* (80). Hamlet was not hiding from action or vacillating: in Elsinore simply uttering the truth was action enough to unleash chaos and violence. Sandler points out several other places in the play in which metaphors suggest that words are violent (80–81). Even Old Hamlet's murder was caused by poison flowing into his *ear*: "[Hamlet] reminds us that his father was poisoned in the ear, as if murder were perpetrated by an abusive speech that could enter its victim's ear and do its damage with the poison of words" (Sandler 81). The ending of the poem suggests that words, poetry, and art are the means of outliving the limitations of both tyranny and death (Sandler 79). Utopia is not only a place to marvel at the glory of Creation, it is also a place to revel in the unrestrained genius of the creations of man.

Translation was a convenient screen to elude the scrutiny of censors. Pushkin, under the patronage and protection of the tsar, needed to cover his real opinions in various ways, such as by ascription of his works to another poet. An artist working under a repressive regime — parallels between the time of Nicholas I and Stalin are numerous and arise obliquely in Soviet criticism and art — can often express many officially unpopular ideas in translation that would not be acceptable in an original work. Another option was to retreat into abstraction, surrealism and absurdity (a version of grotesque humor), as in the case of Gogol, who was also writing under the time of Nicholas I. Ultimately, however, Pushkin was drawn more to other Shakespeare plays, possibly, as Rowe suggests, because the prevailing Germanized views of *Hamlet* did not appeal to him (33). A German-inflected interpretation with an over-intellectual and weak-willed Hamlet was an insufficient vehicle for Pushkin's outrage over his maltreatment at Nicholas I's hands.

Mikhail Lermontov, upon Pushkin's violent and premature death during a duel in 1837 (before his thirty-seventh birthday), wrote a poem called "The Death of a Poet" in which Soviet critic Yuri Lotman found clear references to the relationship of young Hamlet and Claudius, the evocation of which put the blame for Pushkin's death squarely upon Nicholas I, his lackeys and the general culture of duplicity and half-truths he encouraged.

> A poet's dead — entrapped by honour,
> Felled by slanderous rumours spread —
> A bullet in the breast, with vengeful anger,
> He bowed at last his noble head.
> His soul could not endure the legions
> Of trifling insults and their shame,
> He stood against the world's opinions,
> Alone, as always — and was slain!
> [...]
> Deriding, mocking with disdain
> This land, its language and its story;
> He had no mercy for our glory,
> And, at that point of time so gory,
> No thought of what it was he'd slain!
> [...]
> Now why from peaceful bliss and friendship among brothers
> Did he come into this world so envious that it smothers
> The heart's free reign and flaming passion's tears?

Why did he embrace the fools who wrongfully accused him,
Why did he trust the lies of those who so abused him,
He whose insight long surpassed his years!
And taking off the wreath, now once again they crowned him —
A crown of laurels, secretly enmeshed
With thorns, whose needles all around him
Pierced through the noble poet's flesh...
His life's last moments venomously blighted,
By mocking fools' sly whisperings aggrieved,
He died with thirst for vengeance unrequited,
Tormented in his soul by fervent hopes deceived...
[...]
And you, you haughty ones, descendants
Of forebears known for shallowness of trait,
Who trample under slavery's heel the remnants
Of generations scarred by whim of fate!
You stand before the throne, a horde of greedy misers,
Who freedom, genius, honour, seek to kill!
You hide behind your lawyers and advisors,
Before you truth and judgement — both keep still!
But there is a Judge Divine, you playmates of perversion,
There is a Judge Almighty — He awaits,
Your gold for Him is no diversion,
He knows well in advance your thoughts and deeds and traits.
In vain now and henceforth will you resort to vileness:
It will not do you any good,
And you will not obliterate with all your blood of blackness
The poet's true and righteous blood![2]

The poem won Lermontov a sentence to a term of hard labor. In this poem he accuses the tsar of getting away with murder, hiding behind the law by virtue of corrupt power. It also espouses the Decembrist defense of justly usurping the corrupt tsarist system, since progressives and revolutionaries in the audience would, presumably, find Hamlet's murder of Claudius justified. (The Decembrists led a failed uprising in 1825 after the death of Alexander I.[3]) Lotman, writing in the Soviet era, might have read quite a bit into the poem here, thereby revealing his own frustrations as a critic operating under censorship. Whatever the case, his interpretation points to Lermontov's preference for an active Hamlet rather than the Hamletist man of inaction (Rowe 38). Lermontov's other works, when they evoke *Hamlet* (such as in *A Hero of Our Time*[4]), also evidence his preference for an active protagonist against the dominant German Romantic trend (Rogers 1972, 36–39). Nonetheless, the Hamlet of Hamletism reflected an oblique response to the oppression and social changes of the mid-to-late 19th century, even if that response entailed a withdrawal from action.

It was not, after all, an era in which the individual had much real political power or artistic freedom. As in Soviet times, the rights of the individual were seriously limited, and official censorship was *de rigueur*, making protest dangerous and futile, and effective political action nearly impossible. It is also worth pointing out that this poem appears to have had a great influence upon Pasternak whose poem "Hamlet" also contains specific references to Christ and the Crucifixion.

That Lotman was writing during the Soviet era leads one to take a second look at why he would have been so keen to read Lermontov, or even *Hamlet*, through the lens of the Nicholas I era. Lotman, a Jew, left Russia for Estonia in 1950 because the anti–Semitism of the Stalin era prevented his pursuing graduate studies. His work then provides a clear example of the ways in which Soviet literary criticism was made to speak to the politics of its time in an indirect manner. Lotman could write of *Hamlet*, Nicholas I and the Decembrists, while at the same time evoking the problems of his own era. Indeed, the very poem he is reviewing uses an imagined past history, that of *Hamlet*, to evoke Pushkin's own political situation. Like Pushkin and Hamlet, Lotman suffered under oppression just as many Russians did under Nicholas I and his response was to turn to Shakespeare.

Translation, Criticism and Performance in the Middle 19th Century

Around the time of Pushkin's death (1837), another translation appeared, that of Nikolai Polevoy. It was, like its predecessor by Mikhail Vronchenko, a Romantic, Germanic version, influential and popular, no doubt because of its incredibly successful (and very different) stage interpretations by the actors Pavel Mochalov and Vasily Kartygin. The Polevoy translation, however unfaithful to the Shakespeare texts, was also the first to make the language of the play sound like idiomatic, contemporary Russian, which helped to enhance its popularity as well as its topicality (Levin 86). Of this version Peter Holland writes: "the sense, strongly marked in the translation, of an individual's powerlessness in the confrontation with a strong but inert state machine [...] was in itself a political emphasis perfectly appropriate for the Russia of the early nineteenth century" (320). Polevoy's Hamlet famously laments, "Afraid, I am afraid for man!" but ends up quite unable to effect any change on man's behalf. Holland does not miss the opportunity of remarking that this aspect of the translation also brings to mind *Hamlet*'s aptness for presentation on the Soviet stage

(Holland 320). Like Lotman reading Lermontov, Holland looks back upon the translation in its historical context and immediately grasps the similarity of the Nicholas I regime to the Soviet era. Kozintsev too notes that Polevoy turned to translating Shakespeare as a result of his public persecution by the tsar after he wrote a negative review of a theatrical performance in 1834 that the tsar particularly enjoyed: Polevoy's "criticism was equated with rebellion" (*STC* 120). In company with Pushkin, and later Pasternak, Polevoy also sought refuge from harassing censorship in translating Shakespeare, using his plays as a means of covertly critiquing the times.

The Andrei Kroneberg translation appeared around the same time as the Polevoy, but was never as successful because it was widely considered to be "faulty" beyond what even the Russians could tolerate in terms of "loose" translations (*STC* 19). Yet the phrase "the time is out of joint" struck a chord with Russian critics and theater practitioners, being more pointed than the previous translation's: "the continuity of times has been destroyed" (quoted in *STC* 19). According to the translator of Kozintsev's *Shakespeare Time and Conscience*, the Russian word for "out of joint" (*rastroit*) meant a literal dislocation, as of a shoulder or knee joint. Therefore, the juxtaposition of physical injury with the abstract idea of time was "striking" (*STC* footnote on 19). Kozintsev remarks: "dislocated time [...] was accepted by scholarly opinion as almost literally reproducing the English line. It forcibly reminded the reader of physical dislocation and removed him from the world of abstract ideas" (*STC* 19). Later on, however, Kozintsev muses further on Hamlet's historical situation, deciding that the emphasis on the abstract discontinuity of time really is more apt than the idea of a literal physical dislocation: the latter is too metaphorically removed, the former points more directly to the moral vacuum Hamlet faced in Claudius' court. The central problem therefore became one of damages done to spirit and thought, not a physical injury. "Everything proved to be unstable; things found continuation in nothings; no affirmations proceeded from the negations. There was a disunification of the past, of the present, of the future. [...] It seemed to me that the phrase 'the continuity of the times had been destroyed' was the more successful and that 'dislocation of time' was but a mannered metaphor with little real association" (*STC* 20). Kozintsev's perennial preference for imagery that evokes real historical contexts and emphasizes shifts in cultural values is evidenced in his reconsideration of his treatment of this passage. Moreover, he was unaffected by the latest fads in criticism and translation, preferring instead to survey past translations, performances and interpretations to derive his own independent point of view based upon his historical knowledge and commitment to his audience's concerns. It would seem that this shift in emphasis also points to Kozintsev's movement away from a strictly materialist point of view in favor of a more allegorical and abstract one, which would illustrate his resistance to the dictates of Socialist realism. At any rate, the Polevoy translation remained the more popular one until Pasternak's transcended it in influence in the 1940s. Kozintsev preferred Pasternak's translations for all of his productions, despite his extensive knowledge of the alternatives. Indeed, many Russians today know Shakespeare through Pasternak, which is remarkable given the fact that he was so despised by the Soviet regime — perhaps this very marginalization actually led to his popularity in a world in which anything that was underground was likely viewed as more genuine than what was visible on the surface.

The 19th century produced artists, interpreters and critics who were exasperated by the Dane's avoidance of social action, such as Vissaron Belinsky, a critic and well-known radical who believed that art and literature must respond to social and political problems (later, this was to be a central dictate of Socialist realism, the Soviet era's officially-imposed artistic ideology and aesthetic). Belinsky did for criticism what Pushkin did for literature in terms of finally adopting Shakespeare for Russia without the strictures of classicism. Belinsky and Pushkin responded to Shakespearean realism and saw his approach as a model for Russian arts and letters. In his exuberant essay on Mochalov's performance as Hamlet, Belinsky writes, "It [*Hamlet*] is the life of man, it is man, it is you, it is I, it is every one of us!" (quoted in Morozov 15) For mid–19th century thinkers and artists, the Hamlet of Hamletism and the many literary figures who were like him — the superfluous men — were insufferable and came to represent the vicissitudes of the aristocratic, serf-owning classes: "all that was unacceptable to those advocating social concern" (Holland 323). The Polevoy translation and new performances of the play suddenly brought Shakespeare into the political fray and into the hearts and minds of Russians. The choice was between seeing Hamlet's political apathy as a flaw that he could have remedied, or as a tragedy of the age caused primarily by the inhumanity and corruption of those in power; that is, Hamlet as stymied by his own flaws, versus Hamlet as martyr of the political and social conditions of his time. Interestingly, Kozintsev's only non–Renaissance-based film after Stalin's death was a biography of Belinsky, a decision which allied his own vision as artist with that of the deceased critic.

Hamlet, for some progressives, such as Nikolai Chernyshevsky, was of a piece with the superfluous man or "alienated man" of the 19th century:

privileged and intelligent, but selfish and useless. This was the dominant Hamlet of the late 19th century, made famous by actor Aleksandr Lensky in the 1870s and imitated, with much less reverence, by some of Chekhov's characters in *Ivanov* and *The Seagull* (Ostrovsky 229–230). Chernyshevsky rejected Shakespeare as useless to the progressive cause. Nonetheless, it is clear that in performance *Hamlet* was still able to influence and inspire the more civic-minded, realistic artists and intellectuals of the pre–Revolutionary period, even as others rejected Hamlet and Shakespeare as too conservative and "reactionary." Many 19th-century progressives were moved by *Hamlet* and, despite the popularity of the superfluous man figure, the potentially explosive political message was not totally absent from theatrical, literary and critical interpretations of the play in this period. Nor did the dominant reading preclude other assessments of the possible political potency of the play (Rowe 44–49). The movement in arts and letters had already begun to shift from a detached romanticism to an engaged realism, and *Hamlet* (as well as Shakespeare's other works) would not be rejected in its cause. Somewhere between Hamletism and a totally rewritten *Hamlet* (for example, if Hamlet were to kill Claudius in Act 1) lay Belinsky's reading, and, later, the Revolutionary and official Marxist readings of the play: Hamlet became deeply engaged with the problems surrounding him, stymied, not by a character flaw, but rather by the external oppression he faced.

Rowe writes that Hamlet was "an idealist in conflict with a corrupt world" and that this "can be seen to anticipate the Soviet treatment of him as a humanist hero" (48). That this view might be more evident in Belinsky's criticism than in the majority of public discourse and popular art of his era once again lends credence to the theory that under a censorious regime the social reformer must present his message in forms of expression not typically associated with public polemics (Rowe 56). Belinsky's criticism was, not atypically for Russian (and Soviet) commentary and scholarship, influenced by performance, in his case the production of 1837 in Moscow with Pavel Mochalov as Hamlet that used the Polevoy translation. Mochalov's extremely passionate, active, at times incendiary, interpretation of the role overcame the disconnected, disaffected Hamlet evidenced in the Polevoy version. Kozintsev notes that "Mochalov's Hamlet jeered, damned, despised and tormented himself" (*STC* 121). Kozintsev quotes Belinsky's reaction to Mochalov's performances, which, although they gradually gave way to sadness and melancholy from their initial vigor, by most accounts, were always punctuated by "volcanic moments": "evidently, the actor found deep unity with the author [Shakespeare] during these instants.

[...] And at these times, the actor possessed — and conveyed to the audience — the tragic sense of an imminent catastrophe that threatened mankind" (*STC* 176). Levin comments, "criticism of *Hamlet* in Russia eventually developed into self criticism," in as much as the Hamletist Hamlet was a critique of the intelligentsia's own limitation, fear and despair. Yet there was simultaneously an underlying surge of a will to action, the reaction to that "imminent catastrophe." The political climate of the time, following the thwarting of the Decembrist movement, and amidst the revolutions occurring and brewing around Europe, found expression in Mochalov's characterization of, and in Belinsky's commentary on Hamlet (Stribrny 45; Dawson 186). Dissatisfaction with Hamletism and the superfluous man reflected frustration with artists and intellectuals who hesitated and cogitated but failed to take real action.

Like Belinsky, Kozintsev preferred the anti–Romantic Hamlet as first personified in performance by Mochalov. Interestingly, and in keeping with his demonstration of extensive knowledge of Shakespearean scholarship and performance history, Kozintsev examines the theatrical debate over Hamlet's characterization with Edmund Kean and Mochalov on one side and Charles Kemble and Karatygin on the other. The English Victorian Hamlet was also popularly conceived as effete, romantically gloomy and generally ineffectual — this was the Hamlet of Kemble and Kartygin. Kozintsev expands upon audience's reactions to these four actors, as well as their legacies:

> The several contemporary critical reproaches regarding "the ignoble manner" and "the absence of greatness": did not concern the natural qualities of the actors at all, but their interpretation of the role. These artists sought strength, acuity, and a rebellious spirit in their hero. Both Kemble, the celebrated performer of "noble Romans," and Karatygin, the tragedian of the palace guard, played with a full measure of beautiful manners and courtly elegance. *Theirs was not the victory* [*STC* 142, emphasis mine].

The victory, according to Kozintsev, went to the active Hamlet of the people as personified by Kean and Mochalov. For Kozintsev, it was impossible that Shakespeare would have intended a figure so removed from the majority of his audience and their milieu, as well as that of the Globe itself, since it stood in a rough, seedy locale, competing with taverns, bear-baiting and other "crude" amusements: "London apprentices, draymen, sailors on leave, and farmers in the big city all laughed at Hamlet's jokes and sympathized with his feelings. This was a character who was understood and appreciated not only by the connoisseurs but by all those who stood on the three sides of the Globe stage" (*STC* 142). Many of the translations and performances Kozintsev decried cut out large chunks of the text and made significant alterations to the plot. Looking at the totality of the play, Hamlet's language itself speaks to a man of the real world: "The poetry of Hamlet grew out of everyday prose, stripped of ornament, often coarse and cruel as well as merely severe. Hamlet is a popular figure of a man who speaks truth in 'words like daggers'" (*STC* 142). Again, the use of language that does not aspire to the realm of the overly poetic is compelling to Kozintsev precisely because it can transmit meanings across time and space.

In *Shakespeare: Time and Conscience*, Kozintsev emphasizes a watershed moment in the middle of the 19th century: the silencing of the voices of opposition that dominated the 1830s gave way to "a rebellious human voice" with *Hamlet* as its mouthpiece. The laughter that had so struck Pushkin cut through Hamlet's sadness: "the idea of a man who is able to laugh in a moment of sorrow revealed new characteristics in the image of Hamlet. His laughter echoes through the silence" (*STC* 123). Kozintsev later adds: "it is useless to equate a man with a flute [...]; it is possible [...] to laugh with startling energy at everything strong — to laugh from hatred and sorrow" (*STC* 123). Hamlet "proved that is was possible to break away from the system, disobey the command, tear off the suffocating uniform, and refuse to be silent" (*STC* 123). In short, "the gag had fallen out" (*STC* 123). The 1850s ushered in a violent reaction against Romantic, decadent, strains in arts and culture; social agitation was growing, which demanded either rejecting Hamlet altogether or reforming him in a new mold. Kozintsev saw Hamlet and Shakespeare as most aptly being carried into the new era of rebellion, even as others branded them anti-realistic and irredeemably reactionary, accusing Shakespeare of preferring the interests, values and language of the aristocracy to those of the people. Whatever the case, the Hamletist Hamlet was antiquated and no longer spoke to the times. Through figures such as Pushkin, Belinsky, Herzen, and then the influential writers and thinkers of the later 19th century, such as Ivan Turgenev, Anton Chekhov, Lenin, Marx and Engels, "Shakespeare was a contemporary author again, one who, in speaking of the prison that was Denmark, spoke against all states that were jails" (*STC* 124).

Ivan Turgenev

Hamlet, as a person of conscience and an emblem of resistance to oppression, came into fellowship with his fictional peer, another Renaissance hero, Don Quixote. The positive comparison between the two will appear later in the Soviet context through Kozintsev's works: his own cinematic version of *Don Quixote* (1957) appeared in between his staged *Hamlet* of the mid–'50s and his *Hamlet* film (1963). Such convergences illustrate how closely allied the two figures are in the Russian imagination. Turgenev, in his 1860 essay "Hamlet and Don Quixote," presented the two figures as not exactly diametrically opposed, but more like complementary opposites. His consideration of Hamlet transcended an easy declaration of type, even though this essay is usually cited in the context of simplistic definitions of Hamletism.[5] Turgenev's final estimation was that Hamlets are socially and politically useless, and what was needed was a more active response to social ills more like the actions of Don Quixote, although he too was a tragic figure, doomed to be beaten down by the power of the *status quo* (Rogers 1972, 27–28). The point was to take action no matter the consequences for the sake of righteousness.

Turgenev was nearly obsessed with Shakespeare — like Belinsky, he had seen the Mochalov performance as a young man and was very much moved by it — he maintained that Shakespeare was uniquely suited to Russians, especially *Hamlet*: "is not the picture of Hamlet closer and more understandable to us than to the French, let us say more — than to the English?" (quoted in Rowe 65) Don Quixote acts fearlessly, creatively and decisively from an inner faith, one that is unshakable, while Hamlet questions his faith frequently enough to make fear and doubt overwhelm his ability to create or act. Turgenev's short story "A Hamlet of the Shchigrov District" features a Hamlet who fits the Hamletist description, as do most of Turgenev's other Hamlet-like characters. Turgenev's Shchigrov Hamlet is a *malenkii chelovek*, a little man, a man of the "provincial nobility" whose petty concerns, weaknesses and affectations are exposed to ridicule in the story (Diakonova 103–105). The aim of using Hamlet became a pointing outwards for Turgenev; the larger problem was the lack of Don Quixotes in Russia and the predominance of Hamlets: "in our day [...] the Hamlets have become far more numerous than the Don Quixotes" (quoted in Holland 323). Turgenev's discussion of Hamlet and Don Quixote should be understood as only partly a matter of literary interest: Nina Diakonova writes, "the underlying concept is defined by specifically Russian conditions, political and social" (99[6]). As ever, the literary critic speaks politically. The collection in which this story appeared led to Turgenev's "home arrest" in 1852 because of its depiction of oppression, especially of the serfs, who were, ironically, freed by government decree less than a decade later. Turgenev was arrested and sent into internal exile for over a year in part because of his support for the end of serfdom and also for simply the act of speaking out freely (Stribrny 45).

Turgenev's Hamlets, as with the aristocratic (hence wealthy and [over]educated) little men, "are really useless to the people; they give it [*sic*] nothing, they cannot lead it anywhere. [...] Moreover, the Hamlets detest the masses" (quoted in Holland 325). Although, as Holland suggests, Turgenev was not advocating a violent revolution (as other radicals of the late 19th century certainly were), he was using the Hamlet figure as a negative example to try to remedy the ills of an inert, complacent aristocracy and intelligentsia by calling them to real action and engagement with social problems. The "masses" required help from above and those above were morally required to provide it. That later Marxist and Soviet critics will turn to Laertes as the hero of the drama is anticipated here: it is Laertes who returns to Elsinore with the support of the people, who are otherwise conspicuously absent from discussion in *Hamlet*'s world. Soviet staging favored depicting the masses, especially in Laertes' return and occasionally with Fortinbras as well. Kozintsev's film places the common people in many scenes, thereby aligning them more closely with Hamlet himself—overall, for Kozintsev, Laertes seems the more isolated man: while he may summon armies, it is Hamlet who has a spiritual and temperamental connection to the common man. Kozintsev says of the moral imperative facing Russia in Turgenev's era: "the tragedy of Elsinore could not repeat itself in the land-owners' Russia of the 1880s"; the quest for justice had to be successful (*STC* 127). Turgenev's contemporary M. A. Zagulyaev comments on his own 1861 translation of Hamlet: "all of us behave exactly like Hamlet [...] when we should take action, we give ourselves over with self-indulgence to philosophical reflections" (quoted in Rowe 85). Diakonova writes of Turgenev's condemnation of Hamlet: "in harshly criticizing Hamlet's weakness and demonstrating the superiority of Don Quixote's naïve heroism [...] Turgenev was also being self-critical" (100). Artists and critics did not merely create Hamletist, superfluous characters as scapegoats; rather, they were themselves reflected in such characters. Their ostensibly outward censure and despair was often also reflexive. Therefore in order to change themselves they also needed to change their fictional characters.

Fyodor Dostoevsky

Dostoevsky was exceedingly concerned with the growth of materialism and the rise of violent, nihilist, relativistic and atheistic movements in Russian politics and culture. An ardent Orthodox Christian and Slavophile, he wished to see progress and reform take place in the context of a renewal of faith and adherence to traditional Russian values as distinct (to his thinking) from European influences. Dostoevsky was impressed in his earlier years by Pushkin's and other mid-century writers' adoption of Shakespeare as a model for the revival of a truly Russian literary culture, throwing off the yoke of the Petrine preference for French neo-classicism that had led to the denigration of domestic culture. Later, like Belinsky, Turgenev, and others, Dostoevsky would also reject the Romantic Hamlet of Hamletism, lampooning such figures in several of his works.

The influence of *Hamlet* and the question of Hamletism shows itself in many characters and themes in Dostoyevsky, such as Stavrogin in *The Possessed* (also known as *Devils* or *Demons*); the central character in "Notes from the Underground"; and especially throughout *The Brothers Karamazov*, which contains the most numerous direct references to *Hamlet* of any of his works (Stribrny 47–48; Levin 90–91; Rowe 83–93; Rogers 1972, 43–46 and, to a lesser extent, Cooperman's article, give examples of Shakespearean influence in Dostoevsky). Dostoevsky reacted against Hamletism, choosing to see Hamlet, and Shakespeare's works in general, as representing a more responsible and realistic view of the human condition. His personal view of Hamlet was that he is "the embodiment of mental anguish, despair, noble suffering," a victim of his external circumstances; therefore, Dostoevsky's "true" Hamlet was somewhere between the Hamletist superfluous man, who merely adopts the guise of deep feeling and noble suffering, and the active, revolutionary Hamlet who will come into full flower in the 20th century (Rowe 84). Certainly, such interiority makes sense in the context of Dostoevsky's *oeuvre* and worldview in as much as he was a religious man who was largely concerned with the personal realms of conscience, integrity and compassion. Still, outward actions are born of inward change, so there is much to be said for characters on their way from Hamletism to heroism.

Anton Chekhov

Anton Chekhov was an ardent admirer of Shakespeare, especially *Hamlet*: David Magarshack quips, "*Hamlet* seems to have been one of Chekhov's obsessions: he couldn't help bringing it in even if he had to make a grandiloquent ass quote the tritest passage from it" (146). Of course, the fact of an ass spouting Shakespeare shows how fully the works had been integrated into Russian culture since their first appearances. As with modern-day English and American culture (and beyond), Shakespeare quotes, characters and themes are so ingrained that one often finds them in the seemingly unlikeliest of places. Many of Chekhov's plays contain references to *Hamlet* that range from random quotations, as in *Platonov*, to entire thematic structures, as in *Ivanov* and *The Seagull*. Amusingly, at the end of at least one of his letters, Chekhov signs himself "your Schiller Shakespeareovich Geothe," thus designating himself Shakespeare's son,[7] as well as illustrating his knowledge of German letters and the German influence upon Russian concepts of Shakespeare's works ("Chekhov's Letters," Senelick, Ed., 385).

Kozintsev admired Chekhov's sense of humility and his lack of pretension. In this respect he saw Chekhov and Shakespeare as kindred spirits: both were men who eschewed any trappings of the "Artist" in the distortedly elevated romantic sense. Shakespeare was a businessman who lived in the real world of Elizabethan commerce and politics. Kozintsev mocked with gentle irony the fancy portraits and statues of the writer that he saw in his trip to England. The finery with which this idolized Shakespeare is dressed and accessorized annoyed Kozintsev. He imagined Shakespeare's reaction to it would be similar to that of Chekhov in this anecdote: "when the gentle, patient Chekhov was presented with a silver pen on an anniversary, he quite seriously got angry. The gift struck Anton Pavlovich as an insult" (*STC* 16–17). An exalted, refined image of the artist struck Chekhov and Kozintsev as absurd, and this in turn informed their interpretations of Shakespeare's works and characters, as well as their ideas about Shakespeare the person. Chekhov and Kozintsev resisted the prevailing image of Hamlet as a refined intellectual or effete artist as ludicrous: if an artist or intellectual was to have any credibility, he must also be a real human being, otherwise his output would fail to have any meaningful or lasting impact on the world.

The only review of a Shakespearean production that Chekhov wrote was in response to a production of *Hamlet*. Chekhov loved the play, but clearly hated the interpretation, especially that of the central character as played by actor Mitrofan Ivanov-Kozelski. In Kozintsev's framework, Chekhov's negative reaction not only spoke to the revolt against Hamletism, but also to the need for a Shakespeare made relevant to its audience. Mochalov's performance had stirred Belinsky, but Chekhov could not abide Ivanov-Kozelski's "'hiss[ing] like a silly country gander'" and he "was exasperated with his weeping" (quoted in *STC* 128; 224; see also Rowe 108; Winner 103–104; Magarshack 27–29 for more on Chekhov's reaction to

Hamlet). Evidently, an over-emotional Hamlet was detestable. Chekhov's preferred interpretation of Hamlet clearly informed Kozintsev's development of the character in his preference for a strong, masculine and emotionally-reserved man. All the trappings of grandiosity and pretense were stripped from Hamlet: "the acting, the melodrama, becomes banality. Chekhov's idea — that when a man suffers, he does not grimace, but is silent or jokes and whistles — is true here" (*STC* 227). Kozintsev expands upon this, saying: "the difference between these actors [Mochalov and Ivanov-Kozelski] consisted not only in the degree of their talent but also in the relevance of their Hamlets to reality" (*STC* 128). As is continually expressed in Kozintsev's writings, making Shakespeare real and relevant to his audience was paramount in the director's vision. If *Hamlet* was to resonate with the audience, then Hamlet must be a real person who acted and reacted as someone in the audience might in real life, therefore bringing to mind contemporary events and circumstances. Realism in this case could not be a man who openly falls apart, but rather one who tries to keep it together. Despite Chekhov's disdain for the Ivanov-Kozelski production, he still shared Pushkin's enthusiasm for Shakespeare, seeing his works as necessary to revitalize the Russian stage: "Shakespeare must be played everywhere for the sake of letting in fresh air, if not for the sake of instruction or some other more or less lofty purpose" (quoted in Magarshack 28). Many Soviet artists, especially Kozintsev, came to carry out this Chekhovian mandate. Later, Shakespeare once again brought "fresh air" into the increasingly suffocating climate of Stalinist and post–Stalin arts and letters.

References, parallels and direct quotations from *Hamlet* are strewn throughout Chekhov's works. Two of Chekhov's "sketches," "The Baron" (1882) and "In Moscow" (1891), confront the Hamletist Hamlet of Turgenev, in both cases suggesting the inaccuracy and bankruptcy of the prevailing characterization of Hamlet and its negative influence upon the identities of many self-styled superfluous men of the later 19th century (Rowe 108–109; Shakh-Azizova 157–58). Laevsky in *The Duel* (1891) and Platonov of *Platonov* (circa 1880) are heroes who identify themselves as Hamlets and as such are meant to be read as stymied, weak-willed and self-sabotaging in their pose of romantic genius and chronic malaise (Rowe 109–110). Kozintsev's styling of the playwright as "gentle Chekhov" is important to remember — Chekhov had great sympathy and affection for his heroes, however much he used them to satirize the dominant culture. Rowe writes, "in Chekhov's best work, there is always a balance, an objectivity; the author imposes no easy value judgments. We do not feel that Laevsky is to be ridiculed for identifying himself with Hamlet, though clearly it is an identification to which Chekhov grants little or no objective validity" (110). There is no reduction of characters to easy typology; they are real, no matter how wrongheaded. The sum total of Chekhov's "gentle irony" in his treatment of his Hamletist heroes ultimately equals a sadness over the pernicious influence of Hamletism and the cult of the superfluous man upon a certain generation and stratum of late-19th century Russian society. In this respect his satirical humor was also tragic. Chekhov had plans to write a short "vaudeville" play titled "Hamlet, Prince of Denmark," in collaboration with another writer. In Chekhov's letters, it is clear that he intended, much like Hamlet in his addresses to the Players, to critique the "prevailing conditions of the stage" (quoted in Magarshack 55). Realism was the remedy preferred by Chekhov and his like. The distance between the stage and the audience's lives had to be bridged and realism was the material for such building. It is important to bear in mind the extent to which Chekhov's treatment of *Hamlet* and its central character are part of his ever-present tendency towards using humor, irony and satire in his works, gently, but pointedly, illustrating the foolishness of his era, but with a tragic sympathy and lament for the apparent loss of a generation of men to the Hamletist cult of the superfluous man.

In *Ivanov* (1887), the titular character resists the temptation to label himself a Hamlet or a superfluous man. He says "there are pitiful people who are flattered when you call them Hamlets or superfluous men, but for me that is a disgrace! It disturbs my pride, shame oppresses me…" (quoted in Rowe 111). Kozintsev saw the nature of Chekhov's antagonism towards anyone who styled himself a Hamlet or superfluous man as evidenced in Ivanov's voice. He writes, quoting *Ivanov*: "Hamletism is now an act, a pose, Ivanov is an intelligent, noble person, and pretense is repulsive to him. Yet there are a number of people who, when they find themselves in an analogous position, have no objection to being 'a sort of Hamlet [...] a superfluous man'" (*STC* 127). Rowe comments "[Chekhov's] hero refused to mask his inner emptiness with the Turgenevan cliché which had come to stand for the image of Shakespeare's hero" (111; see also "Chekhov's Letters," Senelick Ed., 395). Unfortunately, Ivanov could not find a fruitful alternative identity or life plan for himself, so, like Treplev in *The Seagull*, but unlike Hamlet, he committed suicide (although we know Hamlet thought about suicide). Zdenek Stribrny points to the political and cultural context of the play as part of Chekhov's underlying paean to the loss and despair facing artists, intellectuals and would-be reformers of the time. Stribrny writes that Ivanov "appears as a striking example of the 'superfluous man' of [...] the second half of the nineteenth century when the emancipation of the serfs did not stir the expected initiative among them, while radical movements among the intelligentsia were stifled and then crushed after the assassination of Tsar Alexander II in 1881" (48–49). Tragically, Ivanov only blames himself for his woes and is unable to see how external circumstances might have led to his sorry state and his lack of options for growth and opportunity. He laments, "my conscience aches day and night. I feel that I am profoundly to blame, but just how I have done wrong I do not understand" (quoted in "Chekhov's Letters," Senelick Ed., 396). Stribrny observes that "the whole play shows objectively in what an empty, shallow, and disgusting world he has to live. Russian provincial life is represented in all its alcoholic stupor, its addiction to gambling, the incompetence of the degenerate and impoverished aristocracy, the greediness of the *nouveaux riches*, and the laziness of the bureaucrats. There are no prospects opening before the young generation, there is nobody to respond to Ivanov's 'dying voice'" (49–50). Therefore, the Turgenevan Hamlet and superfluous man stereotypes were taken to their furthest, most self-destructive extremes and served as Chekhov's warning to his audience. Shakespeare's Hamlet did not resign himself, blame only himself, or kill himself in lieu of fighting the external forces acting to thwart him. Moreover, his dying voice was heard by his ally Horatio. Kozintsev's restoration of the true Shakespearean Hamlet was an answer to, or extension of, Chekhov's use of the figure and his call for the death of the weak-willed Hamlets. Tatiana Shakh-Azizova quotes Chekhov: "I cherished the audacious dream that I might sum up all that had ever been written about moaning and melancholy people, and with my 'Ivanov' put an end to this sort of writing" (quoted on 159). Film director Kozintsev and playwright Chekhov both faced times of transition and oppression that demanded resistance, not self-defeating resignation, and they both used *Hamlet* to express these imperatives to their audiences.

Chekhov called *The Seagull* (1895) a comedy. Many allusions, parallels and quotes from Polevoy's *Hamlet* make this the most frequently discussed play in terms of Shakespearean influence upon Chekhov's works.[8] Treplev, the hero, is associated with Hamlet, his mother Arkadina with Gertrude (Rogers 1972, 47–48). Treplev's love-interest and fellow artist, the actress Nina, is associated with Ophelia, as is the other woman, Masha, whose love Treplev spurns (Stroud 370). Treplev himself identifies his nemesis Trigorin as like Hamlet, and, indeed, Trigorin is a sort of double for Treplev, embodying achievements and characteristics he wishes for himself, as well as being his competitor for Nina's affections. T. A. Stroud suggests that Trigorin, as rival for Arkadina's affections and usurper of the literary kingdom Treplev aspires to be a part of, is also like Claudius (368). There is also a parallel in Treplev's staging of his play to the play-within-the-play directed by Hamlet to entrap Claudius (Rowe 112–113; Winner 105–111). In keeping with his sense of irony and tendency to satirize, Chekhov ultimately inverts the associations he invokes. Treplev's play is a failure, although it does appear to cause Arkadina to make the connection to *Hamlet* and to see her son's attempt to stir her conscience; however, she does not take him, his art or his accusations seriously. Thomas Winner comments, "the obvious echoes of the *Hamlet* 'play-within-a-play' only help in pointing to Treplev's impotence, which becomes increasingly clear during the course of the play" (108). Of course, by implication this suggests, encouragingly, that most people see Hamlet's play as inherently effectual. Treplev does not act heroically; rather, like Ivanov, he kills himself in a brutally ironic, anti-climactic, off-stage moment. Nina, unlike Ophelia, does not succumb to despair, but soldiers on, actively committed to artistic expression and hope. Winner writes, "Nina, far from being an unhappy Ophelia, who is destroyed as the unhappy bird [the seagull Treplev shot] was destroyed, is actually the only one in the play who has had the strength to realize her convictions and the achieve the aim for which Treplev has suffered: true art" (110). In the end she declares "I am not afraid of life" (quoted in Winner 110). In contrast, Treplev "*is* a coward who poses as the bearer of Hamlet's indecision to hide from himself his inability to act in the creation of the new art which he craves" (Winner 111). As in his sketches and *Ivanov*, Chekhov evokes popular interpretations of Hamlet in order to subvert them, continuing his resistance to Hamletism and expressing his sorrow over the lives and contributions lost in the name of its cult.

In his final play, *The Cherry Orchard*, also called a comedy, Chekhov once again brings in *Hamlet*. In this instance, the thwarted relationship between Lopakhin and Varya is compared to that of Hamlet and Ophelia. Instead of calling Varya Ophelia, he calls her "Okhmelia," a play on drunkenness, and a vulgar one in its context, and misquotes Hamlet's line "Oh nymph, in thy orisons be all my sins remembered" as "Okhmelia, O nymph, remember me in your prayers" (Magarshack 278–9, Golomb 81–82, Rowe 113). It is probable that the play on the word for drunkenness in "Okhmelia"—*okhmelet* or *khmel* (Golomb 81, Rowe 113)—influenced an important Soviet staging by Nikolai Akimov in his characterization of her character as an alcoholic. In his play she dies from drowning due to being over-intoxicated in what appears to be a nod back to Chekhov. Chekhov's vulgarizations and misquotations of Shakespeare point to Lopakhin's status as ignorant and uneducated, but also to the prevalence of *Hamlet* in Russian culture, which was so pervasive that even a peasant such as Lopakhin would be familiar enough with the play to think of it, even though he misquotes it.

Kozintsev's *Hamlet* productions pay homage to Chekhov's *Seagull* in visual imagery, and respond thematically to Chekhov's critique of the romantic, decadent *Hamlets* of the 19th century. Chekhov killed off his weak Hamlets because "a conscious life lived without any definite world outlook is not life, but a burden, a horror" (quoted in Shakh-Azizova 159). Kozintsev resurrected this Hamlet anew as courageous and active. For both artists, in *Hamlet* "the drama of a generation that has been deprived of its former faith, and longs for a new faith, emerges in its entirety" (Shakh-Azizova 160). The courageous and active Hamlet was what the times demanded, for Chekhov's audience at the turn of the century, and for Kozintsev's in the aftermath of Stalinism. Furthermore, the writer and the director converged in their concern with Hamlet as representative of the artist and the relationship of the artist to his cultural situation. Kozintsev's emphasis upon Hamlet's directorial role, especially in the "Mousetrap" scene and in his interactions with the Players, picks up the threads of Chekhov's concerns over the efficacy and agency of art and artists. Kozintsev insisted upon realizing Chekhov's hopes for a vital, influential relationship between the artist and his culture.

Hamlet was being drawn along in the currents of late and turn-of-the-century thought in Russia. Hamlet was presented so as to shame his detractors into taking action, in as much as he reminded them of their own failures. Soon the fashionably disenfranchised Hamlet would become a figure of the past. Revolutionary, progressive stirrings were growing, along with a great flourishing of artistic, intellectual and theological debate and development, all of which would lead inexorably into the dramatic events of the early 20th century.

Leo (Lev) Tolstoy

Tolstoy's essay "On Shakespeare and the Drama" (composed in 1903, published in 1906), touches upon *Hamlet* in a more general discussion of Shakespeare's plays as they "correspond to the irreligious and immoral frame of mind of the upper classes of his time and ours" (Tolstoy quoted in Stribrny 52). Tolstoy's main objection seems to be against the almost universal reverence of Russians towards *Hamlet*, its central character, and to Shakespeare in general: "in connection with none of Shakespeare's works do we see so strikingly displayed that blind worship of Shakespeare" (quoted in Stribrny 52). Certainly, Tolstoy's extreme religious views, coupled with the events of his later life, influenced his bitter tirades against a writer whose moral framework is arguably obscure and ambivalent, at least as it manifests itself in the plays, and against a dominant popular culture he saw as on its way to total moral ruin (Sokolova 140–141). Tolstoy maintained that drama should serve a moral purpose within a Christian framework, should be intelligible to all persons and should take the side of the common people. He saw only elitism, immorality, amorality, unnecessarily flowery and inflated grandiose language, ridiculously convoluted and implausible plots and poor characterization in Shakespeare's works.[9] Philip Rogers's fascinating article analyzes Tolstoy's marginal notes in his personal copy of *Hamlet*. For the most part, these notes reveal Tolstoy's revulsion over the use of poetic and highly rhetorical language and the lack of realism to which these devices contribute, at least in his estimation. Although Tolstoy was not one of the political progressives, his attitudes converge with skeptics such as Chernyshevsky, who also saw Shakespeare as an elitist and his plays as too contrary to realism and divorced from the lives of common people to be useful for Russia (Donskov 130). Yuri Levin's "Tolstoy and Shakespeare" considers other anti–Shakespeareans of the late 19th century, including such diverse figures as the progressive Chernyshevsky, the playwright Alexei Tolstoy and the conservative Druzhinin, who all engaged with Shakespeare in their considerations over the proper direction for Russian culture and politics.

Kozintsev seems to have had some sympathy for Tolstoy's point of view in as much as it met with his ideas about Hamlet's characterization and the need to make Shakespeare relevant to all potential audiences. Tolstoy's objection to Hamlet found an echo in Kozintsev's rejection of the Hamletist Hamlet. Tolstoy writes: "and, lo and behold, profound critics announce that in this drama, in the person of Hamlet, a perfectly new and profound character is most powerfully presented: consisting in this, that the person has no character; and that in this absence of character lies the achievement of genius — the creation of a profound character!" (351[10]). One could envision Kozintsev agreeing with the error of a characterless Hamlet. Perhaps it was simply impossible for Tolstoy to get the Hamletist Hamlet out of his mind when he encountered the play. Kozintsev paid special attention to what he considered Tolstoy's central problem, which is that he failed to appreciate Shakespeare's poetry. Kozintsev compared this to Tolstoy's description of the opera in *War and Peace* in which the opera is described without reference to the music and therefore seems as ridiculous as describing the plot of *Hamlet* or *King Lear* without considering the poetry and its meaning. Of Tolstoy's analysis Kozintsev writes "the words of poetry lost their meaning in the prose retelling, and the action became incidents, and improbable ones at that" (*STC* 55). Kozintsev, characteristically, considers Tolstoy's historical situation and its influence upon his rejection of Shakespeare:

> Tolstoy, who well understood music, feigned deafness only to demonstrate that art deprived of an ethicoreligious idea is not necessary to people. In a period of passionate enthusiasm for this notion, Tolstoy compared a man who wrote verse to a ploughman who had decided to follow his plough dancing childishly. At this time, poetry struck the novelist as no more than unprincipled mischief-making [*STC* 55].

Kozintsev's attitude was that Tolstoy's ideals and intentions were not only in keeping with the prevailing social and political concerns of the times, but also illustrated an admirable commitment to the *narod* (the people, or the masses) and to keeping art vital and relevant. The terminal problem with Tolstoy's point of view was that poetry and music were not destined to be eliminated by the Bolsheviks, nor was Shakespeare. Marxist artists and critics "rehabilitated" Shakespeare for the masses, maintaining that he was indeed of the people and that his poetry did not in any way diminish this fact. For the promise was that under the Bolsheviks the ploughman would be encouraged to dance behind his plough after all.

CHAPTER TWO

Kozintsev's Contexts 2: Soviet *Hamlets* from the Revolution until after Stalin's Death

As the end of the 19th century drew near, the political rumblings became louder and the critique of *Hamlet* (and of Shakespeare in general) came to reflect the larger preoccupations of Russia and its movement towards the Bolshevik Revolution of 1917. Between 1878 and 1900 eight new translations of *Hamlet* were offered, as well as a complete works collection in 1904. The Gordon Craig and K. S. Stanislavsky production of 1911 is still known as "the Moscow *Hamlet*," indicating that the play's resonance with contemporary life and thought only accelerated at the turn of the century. Significantly, this production went against the grain of Hamletism in Russia and Europe, presenting, in Craig's words "the first STRONG Hamlet the world has ever seen" (quoted in Sokolova 143). Despite attracting a great deal of negative official criticism for its religious and "mystical"[1] associations, the production remained part of the Moscow Art Theater through the 1920s and was performed abroad during the Civil War. Kozintsev devotes a chapter to this version in his book on *King Lear*—it would appear he includes it because Craig died in 1966 and this book appeared in 1973; therefore, Kozintsev was writing about Craig during production of his *Lear* film in the late 1960s. The chapter gives an impressionistic and affectionate review of the 1911 *Hamlet* and a loving portrait of Craig (*KLST* 133–58). That Kozintsev was well aware of his position along the continuum of artists tackling *Hamlet* cannot be forgotten.

The years leading up to the Bolshevik Revolution of 1917 saw the consolidation of a new vision of Shakespeare and his works: yet again, they were adapted to speak to the new political climate by way of new interpretations in criticism and performance. The Tolstoyan attitude towards Hamlet and Shakespeare's politics, which saw both figures as reactionaries who despised the masses and served the interests of the monarchy and aristocracy, had to give way under the dominance of Marx and Engels' writing on the subjects of history and Shakespeare in order to survive the Bolshevik Revolution (Holland 333; see also Gibian 27–28 on the influence of critic Vladimir Friche in the late 19th century). Hamlet would not die like the Tsar; rather, he was adopted by Marxism and became, as Rowe asserts, an emblem of the "conflict between new and old ideas and social systems" (119).

Essentially, the play, and Shakespeare's works more broadly, came to illustrate the class struggle and political and cultural upheavals of the Elizabethan Renaissance period as understood from a Marxist perspective. Between the residual and declining feudalism of the Medieval age and the newly emergent bourgeois capitalism of the Renaissance period, stood Hamlet (and Shakespeare), the lone "humanist" battling it out at the site of struggle over who would win out in a period of shifting values and circumstances. Amongst Marxist critics, it was not always Hamlet himself who was cast as the true hero of the work until somewhat later into the Soviet period. More often it was Laertes (or occasionally even Fortinbras) who served as the people's spokesman; his return to the castle was treated by critics and directors as a rebellion or attempted coup (along the lines of the Earl of Essex's revolt in 1601), evocative of the 20th century situation in Russia, especially after the events of 1905 and 1917 (for example, see Sokolyansky 221). Of course, the downside in the play is that Laertes' rebellion is quickly subdued under the king's duplicitous and autocratic control. Therefore his revolt could stand for a righteous but thwarted revolution in the context of which Laertes became a victim of historical circumstances that were, from a Marxist perspective, not yet set up to enable such a coup to succeed. Kozintsev saw Laertes' attempted coup as a minor distraction and easily subdued by Claudius: "The revolt of Laertes is a court squabble with a little throat-cutting. [...] Shakespeare did not bother to mention the suppression of it. The mutiny itself came to nothing when Laertes ran to the royal chambers" (*STC* 241). For Kozintsev, Laertes is pathetic, ridiculous when places against the full power of the state.

Depending upon the climate and the particular Marxist critic or interpreter in question, there was a choice among several true heroes in the piece: Laertes, Hamlet or Fortinbras. Fortinbras could be a throwback to feudalism's brute force, a representative of Elizabethan and Jacobean repression (the Renaissance era was generally known in Russian and Soviet Marxist criticism for its monarchical oppression and economic inequality), or he could be cast as the liberator come to sweep away the corpses of the failed regime, to honor Hamlet's struggle as Horatio relates it, and presumably to set up a better world from his position as usurping ruler. Instead of a new tsar he could be a revolutionary hero. Whatever the particular construction of Laertes and Fortinbras and their potential as proto-Marxist heroes, Hamlet was still the most significant character of the play and he required a definition in Marxist terms. In the pre- and post–1917 Revolutionary era his vacillations and gloominess finally and definitively gave way to a much more action-oriented emphasis. Hamlet's failures were no longer blamed upon his Hamletist weak will; instead, he took whatever action he could and strove for humanist ideals, but was, like Shakespeare himself, in the wrong place at the wrong time to effect any permanent, lasting changes. History had not yet reached the point at which a "humanist"[2] society could emerge. From a Marxist historical perspective, Socialism could not occur until much later because capitalism had not yet run its full, destructive course. Hamlet provided a beacon, a light in the darkness, but he was doomed to fail because of forces outside of his control (this is similar to Kozintsev's reading of Laertes, as quoted above). Hamlet's fatalism departed from a negative, passive brand of romantic decadence (Hamletism) into the pressure-cooker of historical contingency: Hamlet's political martyrdom in the Russo-Soviet 20th century interpretation was characterized by an heroic, not an accidental, death. Laertes and Hamlet were no longer opposites, but both virtuous humanists crushed by the forces of a corrupt era. This revolutionary Hamlet reflects — at least in this early phase, before the promise of the events of 1917 died under Stalin's tyranny — a shift from the political futility of the superfluous man, the individual beaten down by the powerful, or by his own personal weaknesses and character flaws, to the idea that the people, the masses, ordinary individuals could, must and would rise up to overthrow their oppressors and reorder and redirect their societies. What Hamlet failed to do the new revolutionaries would carry out.

Mikhail Chekhov in the MAT2 *Hamlet* of 1924

The somewhat brief period of political and cultural optimism at the start of the 20th century was reflected in many aspects of early Soviet culture. From the late 1900s until the mid–1920s, there was a great flourishing of new, iconoclastic and experimental art.³ This spirit of experimentalism touched all the arts, including theater and the bourgeoning film industry.⁴ There was a sense among the people that free expression would be allowed now that tsarist censorship had been cast aside. An eclectic production of *Hamlet* starring the actor Michael Chekhov, produced by the Second Moscow Arts Theater (MAT2) in 1924, was greatly influenced by symbolism, expressionism and the more esoteric aspects of the 1911 Moscow *Hamlet*, and as such belonged more to this time of experimentation and artistic freedom than to the repressive period to come. The mood of the country had changed since the '00s and '10s and Chekhov's production was derided by Party critics as "decadent" and "reactionary" (Stribrny 79⁵). At issue, among other things, was the Party's desire to eschew Western influence. The production's mystical and religious imagery and themes attracted tremendous criticism; yet this religious influence would resurface and be felt again in later adaptations, such as Pasternak's translation and Kozintsev's productions. Religion and spirituality had no place in the materialist worldview of the Bolsheviks. The great era of experimentation and artistic freedom was over by the mid–1920s, when the Soviet culture apparatus had already begun to constrict free expression in the interests of solidifying Party propaganda across all forms of public discourse. Thus began anew the artists' need to employ he techniques of double-voicing. Theater historian Spencer Golub writes of Chekhov's production, "Hamlet's staging of the truth in a world of empty appearances affirmed the truth of his being. He went out to meet his fate rather than passively await its arrival. Chekhov's *Hamlet* validated the inner man in an era of social masking" (178). The consolidation of Bolshevik power required a uniformity of message that was to become part of the wider propaganda effort and led to a culture of "social masking" in arts, politics and daily life: it was no longer safe to trust anyone with one's true opinions or to express oneself freely. It had already been proven since the Bolshevik Revolution that the only views to be expressed openly were those that were officially acceptable. Public messages, under the dictates of Socialist realism, had to be unambiguously positive, progressive, clear and intelligible to all.

Mikhail Chekhov felt compelled, like so many artists and intellectuals in the 1920s, to flee Soviet Russia in 1928, allegedly the day before he was due to be arrested (Leach 318). He wrote: "external influences of a tendentious system of inspection and the narrowly propagandistic demands of the censorship in Russia have deprived the artist of freedom in the area of his creative activity" (quoted in Stribrny 79). Chekhov's depressive, brooding, almost nihilistic, yet also active and violently passionate Hamlet moving about in an abstract and terrifying world would not be part of the official Revolutionary message. As Arthur Mendel puts it, "Stalin liquidated Hamlet: there was no place in the closed society for one who questioned and vacillated" (734). Under Stalin's cultural overlordship, interpretations of *Hamlet* would have to follow the Party-line or, as appears to have been most frequently the case, simply cease altogether. After the Civil War and into the Stalin regime, certain performances of *Hamlet* were criticized, relocated or tacitly banned. Some scholars will overstate the case and claim there was an outright ban on the work, but this is not true, as the performance history bears out. Moreover, the Soviets usually tried to avoid making laws prohibiting free expression in order not to appear in a bad light to the rest of the world—they could only keep the West and the rest of world just so far away. The existence of legalistic and specific code for censorship would have implied that there were people around who were opposed to the status quo, and the Soviet propagandists' message was that no such people existed, at least not in significant numbers. Stalin seems not to have favored banning specific plays by an explicit legal prohibition, but certainly a particular theatrical version could be shut down if it seemed too threatening, as in the case of Akimov's 1932 production. It was commonly known that Stalin disliked the play and that was enough to limit its appearances. Mendel cites Chushkin's mention of an "offhand remark" made by Stalin regarding a production in rehearsals in 1941, which effectively derailed it entirely (733). Themes of regicide were not welcome, for obvious reasons, and although Stalin's full opinion on the matter is not known, one can speculate that the play's treatment of politics, spying, exile, imprisonment, death, fate, suicide, etc. held up an unflattering mirror to the world of the "Great Leader."

Due to the changing landscape of Soviet arts and letters, Hamlet would yet again have to change to suit the times. Despite the predominance of the revolutionary-zeal *Hamlets*, in the undercurrent of critical and interpretive possibilities Hamlet became something more than the proto-Socialist revolutionary—although he usually maintained this disguise when inside the Soviet Union in order to appear of the Party. He also grew into a dissident, an artist and intellectual who tried to remain true to his conscience, morality and inner being in a world perverted by tyranny, violence, surveillance and hypocrisy. His guise of insanity and his weird jests spoke to the people of the new era of social masking. Productions and criticism of *Hamlet* during the Stalin years reflect a tendency to see Hamlet as struggling not only against Elsinore and Denmark, or acting as Shakespeare's allegory for England's problems, or as Decembrist or Bolshevik, but as a man coming to terms with the trauma and aftermath of the Civil War, and the apparent failures of the post–Revolutionary decades, which brought famine, disease, and ideological dislocation under Stalin's systematic despotism, repression and violence. Hamlet gained yet another persona on top of the superfluous man and proto-revolutionary humanist: he was also a political dissident.

The *Hamlets* of Nikolai Akimov, 1932 and Sergei Radlov, 1938

One of the most controversial Stalin-era *Hamlets* was a 1932 Moscow production directed by Nikolai Akimov, which was both farcical and politically bold. Mikhail Morozov, a Soviet critic writing just after World War II, praises this production for getting Russian *Hamlets* out of their "rut"— perhaps a covert comparison to the Craig-Stanislavsky and/or MAT2 *Hamlets*— and eschewing "conventions" in presentation of the Dane: "Instead of the 'velvet prince' we saw a Hamlet who was the last man to be worried by any brain storms. The whole play degenerated into a conflict for the throne of Denmark" (41). Rowe describes the production as a "zany story of political intrigue" (128). Akimov turned the question "to be or not to be" from a musing upon life or death into a question of whether or not Hamlet should try to take the throne from Claudius (Rowe 129; Golub 178). The ghost was a fabrication of an ambitious Hamlet and Ophelia's death was linked to her alcoholism (as in Akimov's characterization). An undoubtedly ironic line was inserted into the play: "Oh century! Thought is awakening, the sciences are blooming, what a joy it is to be alive!" (quoted in Rowe 129). Among other recent events and problems, 1931– 1933 saw widespread famine, due in part to the massive collectivization and de-*kulakization* plans enforced under Stalin, who had, by the late 1920s, consolidated his power and begun to implement his five-year and ten-year plans. In 1932, the Writers' Union was formed as the sole organization governing literature and letters, in place of numerous others that had existed before (Hosking 479). Awakening thought and blooming sciences indeed.

Dmitri Shostakovich, who would in just a few years get into trouble with Stalin over his *Lady Macbeth of Mtsensk* opera, produced music for this play to augment its irreverent tone. Rowe refers to an historian of the arts under Stalin who described an episode during the scene of Hamlet's questioning by Rosencrantz and Guildenstern: "in order to ridicule the proletarian composers, Shostakovich had Hamlet press a flute to the lower end of his spine [i.e., his buttocks ... and] played the shrill, false notes of a proletarian song" (Rowe 130). The play was extremely popular with audiences, but after a negative article in *Pravda* penned by Karl Radek, who was speaking for the Party, the production had to move from the capital to Leningrad. Instead of the government's explicitly banning or closing productions, they were often simply "exiled" from Moscow — again, an outright destruction might look bad, moving could always be justified benignly for this or that reason. Mikhail Morozov's 1947 overview of *Hamlet* performances gives the impression that Akimov's was the last Moscow production of the play until after Stalin's death. It seems to have only been played in theaters removed from major centers of political life. In this case, however, as Stribrny reports, the move to Leningrad was in itself part of high-powered political struggles in the Party. The Leningrad Party secretary was Sergei Kirov, one of Stalin's rivals, and it would have been Kirov who approved the production's reappearance in Leningrad. The story gets even more interesting as ghoulish parallels emerge between Kirov's and Hamlet's stories. In 1934 Kirov was assassinated; Stalin's involvement was suspected, since this was a time of purges in which Stalin eliminated, in one way or another, all enemies of his power. Stalin went to the funeral and kissed Kirov's corpse, much like Claudius falsely mourning Old Hamlet's "accidental" death (Stribrny 84–85; Hortmann 224). These events, and the tacit ban on the play due to Stalin's evident dislike of it, bring to mind the 18th century prohibition of the play because of its correspondence to contemporary political events surrounding Tsarist succession. In both cases, the resistance of those in power to *Hamlet* serves to make its allegorical relevance only that much more apparent.

Morozov, as a Soviet critic apparently trying to avoid getting into trouble himself, downplays the popularity and controversy of the Akimov production, saying only that "it occasioned a flare-up of criticisms in the press" (41). Yet he credits the production, in the purposefully vague language characteristic of so much Soviet critical prose, with "making Shakespeare's tragedy the center of a heated controversy among our dramatic critics and also heated arguments among our Shakespearean scholars as to the meaning of individual passages in the text, the various conceptions of tragedy, and so on" (41). Soviet critic Alexander Anikst also recalls the production as influential enough to cause a renewed interest in the play among scholars and performers intent upon recasting Hamlet as "a humanist on a horse," that is, closer to the people than the aristocratic Hamlet of the 19th century (Rowe 132; Gibian 31). That it is this particular production

Anikst refers to points towards a multiplicity of interpretations of Hamlet as "humanist." Anikst is, after all, not citing a "safe" production — he is citing one that was explicitly *avant-garde* and farcical in a time when that was no longer allowed. The Akimov production was politically outspoken at a time when that was extremely dangerous. A revolutionary, humanist Hamlet after the 1930s was no longer fighting against the Tsar, the aristocracy, or the advance of capitalism, he was also (or instead) fighting against those who usurped the Bolshevik Revolution and perverted its true course. Here, as elsewhere, we begin to find Soviet critics intending a double meaning for many of the common Soviet critical buzzwords. The scare quotes are not there, but the implications are clear enough.

It is important to stress that there is no reason to suspect that the Soviet critics or artists cited in this study were all fundamentally against Socialism or communism; in fact, they largely seemed committed to forging a new society along Marxist lines, but saw their aspirations squashed by tyranny and censorship; Kozintsev is decidedly within this group. The fact that their disappointment and horror is expressed "under the radar" is due to the fact that the "people"— artists, intellectuals, teachers, citizens, etc.— had lost any freedom to participate in their government by means of pointing out its errors and shortcomings in free public discourse. The use of Shakespeare's plays as allegories for the current situation proliferated, since they offered a useful screen. Shakespeare was an artist admired by Lenin, Marx and Engels, who had been rehabilitated in Soviet criticism; therefore, most of his works were fair game and criticism of Shakespeare flourished. As the official critical response to and relocation of the Akimov production illustrate, a great deal of effort was being made to reclaim *Hamlet* for the Party and, at the same time, to use it to point out the government's and the people's problems. All the while, artists were operating under the mandate of Socialist realism, which was the dominant paradigm from 1934 onwards, entrenched by the institution of single, centralized unions to oversee all branches of the arts in 1932 (Gillespie 3). Sometimes the best policy was to be obscure, no matter what the prevailing winds — they could change at any time. This in itself must have been a great source of frustration for artists and intellectuals; yet one which, in turn, only increased their motivation to speak out.

The struggle to recast and reclaim *Hamlet* continued in the form of a production by Sergei Radlov, featuring music by Prokofiev, in 1938 in Leningrad, at the height of the "Terror" period. The Radlov *Hamlet* was yet another politically-charged production, albeit one that, in keeping with the times, downplayed its relevance to contemporary events in order to avoid trouble: for instance, by keeping the play in Renaissance dress and using Elizabethan-style music written by Prokofiev (Golub 179, Morrison 84). According to Simon Morrison, the fallout from the Akimov and Chekhov *Hamlet* productions, both of which met with official critical censure, meant that Radlov "was forced to stage *Hamlet* along party lines," or to at least be very careful to appear to do so (82). Nonetheless, there were elements of ambiguity that complicate reading the production as simply Party line. On the one hand, the casting of the same actor as both the ghost of Old Hamlet and Fortinbras emphasized "that order has been restored in Denmark" (Morrison 84). Yet, on the other hand, "the discord that Prokofiev builds into the march comments on the terrible cost of this restoration" (Morrison 84). Perhaps in order to avoid ending on an ambiguous or negative note, which might have drawn critical ire and Party censure, Prokofiev's music culminates in a triumphant major key, ultimately indicating a positive victory. Morrison downplays the potential subversion here, avoiding seeing in the juxtaposition of theatrical events and musical styles a Shostakovich-like irony. However, Prokofiev's collaborations with Eisenstein on *Nevsky* and the *Ivan* films indicate that he was not averse to working on politically-charged material that pushed up against the preferences of the state. Also, like Shostakovich, Prokofiev was frequently on the list of artists whose work made him an enemy of the people, especially the infamous Musicians' Union "blacklist" of 1948. Indeed, Radlov and Prokofiev's triumphant ending could very well have been deliberately mocking the mandates of Socialist realism, just as the "monumental portraits" of Claudius in the production that "threatened to crush Hamlet from above" could have been intended to conjure the threat of Stalin's "cult of personality" (Golub 178–179). The production clearly incorporated the sights and sounds of Soviet Russia to encourage the audience to project itself into the action on the stage.

To give a fuller historical backdrop for this period, Stalin's "Terror" of the late 1930s refers to his violent consolidation of power and unification of culture and propaganda, which was accomplished through show-trials, false imprisonments and arrests, internal exile and displacement and even murder and assassination (as in the Kirov example above). It is estimated that between 1937 and 1938 1.6 million people were arrested, 87 percent for "political crimes" (Hosking 468–9). Outside of the prison system, things were not much better: by the end of the 1930s, approximately 10 million people had died from famine-related illness and starvation (Hosking 468–9). The situation was so dire that there are even accounts of cannibalism, with photos and reports surviving of people actually selling human flesh as food (Khlevniuk 54, 65). This context clearly illustrates why Radlov would have had to be very cautious and very clever in his production in order to avoid becoming yet another victim of the Terror, and it also provides ideas about his possible motivations in encoding a degree of political subversion on behalf of the Terror's victims. Unfortunately, events would ultimately conspire to effect Radlov's designation as a *persona non grata* some years later.

During the World War II Leningrad blockade of 1941–44, the Radlov production was moved to the Ukraine and then into Germany, where it was performed for German workers (Rowe 134). Speculation about Radlov's fate after that requires a look at the wider war and post-war era during which many citizens or soldiers who had been abroad for any reason (e.g. as prisoners, temporary exiles or those who lived in occupied areas, of which there would have been tens of thousands) were sent to prison labor camps. Despite the incredible surge in patriotism and energy throughout the country in response to the war effort, as well as a relative loosening of censorship, religious prohibitions and other cultural regulations, arrests and labor or death sentences continued and actually increased after the war as Stalin set out to rein in the temporary increase in freedom of expression and to firmly reconsolidate his power.[6] By 1953, the year of Stain's death, it is figured that 5.5 million people were prisoners and 786,000 had been executed for "political crimes" (Hosking 468–9).

Rowe cites various official histories of the theater written in the '50s and '60s that make no mention of the Radlov production and that have no information about him from between roughly 1939 and 1953. This is because, like almost everyone else who found themselves abroad or in occupied territory during the war, Radlov and his wife were sent to prison camps upon their return home from Germany (Rowe 133–34). Kozintsev also avoids mentioning Radlov or Prokofiev, the reasons for which are inscrutable, given the fact that Kozintsev freely mentions Meyerhold, Pasternak and Shostakovich, who had serious troubles during and after the Stalin era. It is implausible that Kozintsev would not have known about Radlov and his productions — Golub suggests that Radlov's production "prefigured" Kozintsev's depiction of Claudius as Stalin-figure (178). Unfortunately, "black holes" such as these appear frequently for anyone studying the Soviet period, during which silent and unaccountable omissions were commonplace — it might very well be that Kozintsev was protecting Radlov at his own request. Radlov's year of release from prison is significant as it was the year of Stalin's death, 1953. Radlov died in 1958, his wife died earlier while still in the Gulag.

Post-Stalin *Hamlets*

Stalin's death precipitated a wave of prison revolts, which led to many of the post-war inmates being released and "rehabilitated." For a few years at least, there followed a huge wave of expression, both of bitterness and pain, and of a guarded hope, or at least optimistic doubt, about the future. This period, under the new leader Khrushchev (who famously denounced Stalin and his "cult of personality" at the Twentieth Party Congress of 1956 in a not-so-secret secret speech) was known later as the "Thaw," a nickname drawn from the title of the 1956 book *The Thaw* by Ilya Ehrenberg. It was as if the action at the end of *Hamlet* were playing out — was Fortinbras, i.e., Khrushchev, the savior come to set the kingdom aright, or was he merely another in a long line of tyrants? Did Hamlet fight in vain, or would his legacy actually help to rescue future generations from experiencing the same horrors? *Hamlet* spoke to this time as it had not done at any other; there was a veritable mania for the play, with performances and criticism flooding public discourse. Given the number of dead and imprisoned cited above, coupled with the fact that the war had raged on Soviet soil, there were probably few people who had not been affected by personal tragedy and suffering. Historian Geoffrey Hosking writes: "there must have been few families, especially among the peasantry and the intelligentsia, who did not have at least one member behind barbed wire or in danger of disease, disablement and death. If one imagines the worry, grief and physical suffering which lie behind these figures, then one has to see the Soviet people [...] as a population in torment" (469). In the post–Stalin era there had to be, finally, an outlet for the pain so many had to silently endure. For some, *Hamlet* provided that outlet.

Nikolai Okhlopkov's 1954 *Hamlet*

Stalin died in 1953. Nikolai Okhlopkov's *Hamlet*, using Pasternak's translation, opened in Moscow in 1954. Okhlopkov's writings on the play and the production appeared in the journal *Teatr* (theater) in 1955. Both the production and the director's writings served to illustrate the ways *Hamlet* was being used at the time. The fact that the production would end up being removed from the Moscow stage reminds us that public discourse was still fraught with danger and the censors were still vigilant — for many years to come there would be a constant tug-of-war between the Stalinists and the reformers (Rowe 135–137; Stribrny 100). Of this production Spenser Golub writes, "Okhlopkov's *Hamlet* depicted humanism's victory over tyranny, the spiritual rebirth of Mother Russia embodied in an activist but non-ideological Prince" (179). The fact that this Prince was an "activist," but a "non-ideological" one, bolsters the assertion that a "humanist" Hamlet in this period need not be understood in simplistic Socialist or Marxist terms; rather, artists who had been force-fed official dogma were trying to reclaim through *Hamlet* a sense of their own unique personal truths independent of any organized political ideology. According to Holland, the line "something is rotten in the state of Denmark" prompted huge applause from Soviet audiences; he suggests that this is not because of the audience's investment in Danish politics (334). Okhlopkov, who once remarked that "theater is not a museum," took as his central metaphor Elsinore as a prison: his stage was dominated by an enormous grate extending from the bottom to the top of the stage that suggested prison bars (quoted in Rowe 137). A second set of bars was lowered at the front of the stage during Laertes' return to the castle with his mob. The production became known as the "Iron Curtain" *Hamlet* (Stribrny 100). The image must have been striking to the viewers, and their reactions indicate that the production effected a successful catharsis of the audience's trauma.

Material on contemporary responses to the production is not overly abundant, although it was immensely popular in its short run. Soviet critic Sofia Nels, who, although writing in response to the production for official publication, managed to be unusually outspoken in her reports despite the limitations placed upon her by censors. Nels writes that the production, instead of focusing on philosophical questions, developed "social content, deep and significant," and adds, "in order to free man, you must free his thoughts" (quoted in Rowe 136, 135). Okhlopkov's own essay on the play is densely packed with material that, much like the work of his peer Anikst, illustrates the various ways in which Shakespeare criticism in the Soviet era was subtly manipulated to speak to the critics' present circumstances. Audrey Carmelli cites the criticism of a "conservative" panel of critics at a 1956 conference who condemned the production for being "formalist," (a common Soviet ideologue's buzzword for nearly anything that strayed from the Party's tastes or ideology and that smacked of Western influence), and noted, as a negative example, its "illustrativeness and allegorical nature, which substituted for the profound revelation of Shakespearean meaning" (quoted on 59). The resistance to Okhlopkov's allegory illustrates the fact that the play was read by conservatives and dissidents alike as a commentary upon the current Soviet situation. The objections over allegory mean that the comparisons evoked were clearly comprehensible. Presumably, the "profound revelation of Shakespearean meaning" had been determined once and for all by the Marxist critics — case closed. *Hamlet*, as it had been many times before, was being performed on the front lines of yet another culture war: this time the struggle of the people and the nation to find voice and direction after Stalin's death.

There are quite a number of veiled references to events of the Stalin era in Okhlopkov's essay and several passages in which he appears to be praising Hamlet as a dissenter, all the while drawing various analogies to the USSR. For example, of Hamlet as dissident he says: "Hamlet has discovered (alas, all too late) the first rule of life: the absolute necessity for unyielding struggle against all that is evil" (189). Of the difficulties inherent in speaking out Okhlopkov writes: "the least sound or whisper from those who venture to look at the world anew and harness all the fire of their minds to breaking down the walls of the prison merely produces still more savage opposition from the jailers" (192). Not surprisingly, when he writes of "Claudius," we could read "Stalin" instead: "in the 'world of Claudius,' man may not stand erect, may not breathe freely and, for this reason he is full of an insatiable desire for liberation [...] of all honest men from the swarms of traitorous two-faced and predatory masters of the 'prison world'" (184). Carmelli points out that Okhlopkov consistently puts these phrases — "world of Claudius (or Elsinore)" and "prison world" — in quotation marks, perhaps to draw his readers' attention to their use as verbal decoys, markers to cue the audience to look for buried meanings. Other references in the essay bring to mind religious persecution, the Hitler-Stalin pact, the Civil War, some of the famous suicides of victims of the regime (for instance Meyerhold's wife's probable suicide in 1939, and perhaps even Stalin's wife Nadezhda in 1932), the show-trials of the Terror period, the seizure of lands in the country, the program of de*kulak*ization, the wave of prison riots, and the mass release of prisoners following Stalin's death. The essay reads as a giant exhumation of decades of trauma, both personal and collective, yet all in the guise of an historicized analysis of *Hamlet*.

Okhlopkov's summation of the play becomes even more pertinent (and, not insignificantly, more poetic and hence less explicitly overt in meaning) towards its close. He draws his readers in by unexpectedly shifting into the plural first-person, "we," as if to enter into an historically real Elsinore with a flesh-and-blood Hamlet: "in this 'prison-world' we understand from the mighty echoes of the struggle with the jailers that man is alive, that the earth is not a gathering of petty and malicious human souls, but is also a fair garden of human dreams and daring" (200). The action of the play boils down to the will of the tyrant to imprison and the will of Hamlet to break out of the prison. Okhlopkov universalizes this, seeing the struggle as collective and by the very fact of one's awareness of that collective effort, once becomes even more encouraged. Unfortunately, in the action of the play "the victory goes to the captors" (Okhlopkov 202). True to his Socialist idealism and Marxist view of history, Okhlopkov transcends dramatic terminality and looks with hope to the future: "the lessons of Hamlet's life and struggle will instruct others"; "beyond his death, beyond his private defeat lies the historical victory of humanism" (203). Thus the play became a locus for the aspirations of a better life after Stalin, as well as an opportunity for purging grief and bitterness, but at same time with a healthy skepticism that the moment of possibility would really end with positive change.

Golub remarks, incorporating a quote from Soviet critic Alexei Bartoshevich, "The Soviet Hamlet at the beginning of the Thaw period was [...] a generally unphilosophical 'rosy youth, whose sudden discovery of the cruel truth of the world [...] cracked his child-like faith'" (179). Both of Kozintsev's *Hamlet*s, one on stage one on screen, exhibit this inner tension: hope in an improved future, effected by a commitment to truth and integrity, set against the realities of an evil world and the fear that the best strivings of humanity would never accomplish its higher aims under the government of the USSR. The Hamlet of 19th century and Marxist-Leninist Hamletism, as well as the progressive's "reactionary" Hamlet were both outdated by the end of the Stalin era. Hamlet, the character and the play, became part of a new movement in artistic and political culture, one which would, as much as possible, actively resist the force of the State against free expression. Kozintsev's writings and works continually emphasize an active, brave Hamlet who represents artists and intellectuals who would not be cowed by fear and external limitations, but who would risk all to speak the truth.

In keeping with the post–Stalin zeitgeist, Kozintsev's Hamlet, in both his stage and film versions, was diametrically opposed to the Hamletist, Romantic, "decadent" Hamlet—Kozintsev's writings on *Hamlet* deal directly with his departure from and dismissal of the Hamletist character. On the one hand, this rejection fits in with the Bolshevik, Marxist Partyline, in as much as Hamlet, in a Marxist reading, had to become either a reactionary aristocratic villain or an active participant in resistance to monarchial oppression. On the other hand, however, Kozintsev's active, crusading Hamlet also subverts Soviet tyranny, especially that experienced under Stalin, thereby wresting historical-political agency from not only a pre–Revolutionary monarchy, but also from Soviet-style "state-engineered forgetfulness" (Golub 174). In essence, the 1917 Hamlet became a post–Bolshevik, post–Stalinist Hamlet, who was ready to move into yet another manifestation, one that was not supportive of the changes that had swept over Russia in the first part of the 20th century.

1953–54: Kozintsev's Staged Hamlet

Kozintsev was active in the *Hamlet*-mania following Stalin's death, offering a theatrical presentation of the play in Leningrad using Pasternak's translation, a translation that had been somewhat edited and corrected by Pasternak for this production since he had first written it for Meyerhold in the late 1930s, just prior to Meyerhold's arrest in 1939 and his murder in 1940. Mendel writes that "under Kozintsev's direction, Hamlet became a "brother-in-arms" [...] in the arduous and torturous efforts of Soviet society to liquidate Stalin" (734). The allegorical nature of the play and Kozintsev's commitment to making the story relevant to his audience are revealed in his notes for this production (found in *STC* 212–225) and for his later filmed version: at many points he stresses the uselessness of "costume" drama; that is, any presentation that insists upon situating a work in a distant time and place. Often, Soviet productions were done with period costumes so that correspondences with contemporary events could be downplayed in order to elude censorship. Kozintsev was most concerned with the issues of justice, ethics and conscience in the play that could be highlighted and communicated in a vital, visceral way to the Soviet audience, of whom he writes, "they understand Shakespeare perfectly, and they do not like it when his sense of justice is considered rhetorical" (*STC* 212). This is a striking statement in a world in which propaganda dominated public discourse — propaganda which was almost always rhetorical (in the negative sense) as opposed to substantive. Kozintsev felt that his audience depended upon him to speak to them about their own lives, to make his art relevant, and he expected that despite his use of costuming or sets that suggested a distant past they would be looking for what he was trying to say about the present.

The relationship of the audience to *Hamlet* and to Hamlet's situation is not an academic, removed experience for Kozintsev: "a very great misunderstanding — the solitude of Hamlet. How can he be alone if all of us in the house are with him? He speaks for many people, and defends their dignity and their idea of good and evil. But he is alone in the court of

Claudius. Each one of us would have been alone in Elsinore" (*STC*, 213). Like Okhlopkov above, the struggle against the jailers is a collective one, wherein lies its true power. Hamlet's loneliness is not some Romantic self-withdrawal; rather, it has been forced upon him. In order to prevent people from taking effective political action they must be divided, prevented from organizing or even from trusting each other — this was effectively done in the Soviet era during which private meetings of groups of people were difficult to arrange and difficult to keep truly under the radar. Collective living arrangements made ordinary citizens into spies and rendered the experience of a private or independent existence nearly impossible. Kozintsev, in keeping with Akimov, Okhlopkov and others, had rejected the romantic, decadent Hamlet of the later 19th and early 20th centuries in as much as this Hamlet usually withdrew himself from fellowship and social groups. Hamlet's isolation, like that of every Soviet audience member, was not absolute; in fact, the common experience of alienation was yet another thing that linked people to each other and to Shakespeare's play. In the early post–Stalin period the silence and isolation so many Soviet citizens felt "in the court of Claudius" was, for a time, alleviated. People became aware that their guarded inner thoughts and hidden painful memories were shared by their comrades.

Kozintsev, who wrote in keeping with a Marxist interpretation of history (sometimes perhaps as a screen, other times likely in earnest), offers a chapter reflecting upon Hamlets that charts a progression from Hamletism to modernist decadence, all of which point to a Hamlet who refuses, for one reason or another, to take an active role in the world (*STC* 105– 133). Kozintsev reclaimed Hamlet from these distortions of his character, as he perceived them to be, frequently showing evidence that his interpretation of *Hamlet* was based upon a careful and complete reading of the play rather than simply plucking Hamlet out of it and fashioning him to suit some other, unrelated, context and purpose. Kozintsev's reading is textually faithful, historically influenced (he shows a thorough knowledge of Shakespeare's era), and also lends itself with renewed relevance to the Soviet present. Kozintsev's historicism is committed to both acknowledging the original context of the play and to exposing the possibilities it offers for presentation in new contexts.

> The problem is not that this tragedy is a reflection of life and that it is up to the director to translate reflection into reality. The Elizabethan period is well enough known. *Hamlet* is not a mirror but a mine detector: old shells not yet deactivated are concealed in the flesh of every century, and, in thoughts concerning this tragedy, they reveal their presence [*STC* 218].

The mines buried in the Stalin era were exploded by Kozintsev's stage production of *Hamlet*, and many others were going off all over the USSR during this time. Kozintsev's attraction to the play, like Okhlopkov's, went beyond fondness for some sort of "museum piece." "Conscience" was a key term for Kozintsev, so too "thought": the inner world of Hamlet as revealed by his words. "Words" are also a major theme in Kozintsev's interpretation, and are lent a special resonance in an era in which giving words to the thoughts raised from one's conscience became a dangerous act. Hamlet's tendency to analyze and discourse upon truth and morality was no longer a sign of his idleness or dissipation; rather, it was the very core of his challenge to the toadying, spying courtiers in the tyrannical court of Elsinore. Words were his weapons, his "landmines." In the 1953-54 production the problem of Claudius' tyranny was perhaps more pressing than Hamlet's inner world, but later, in the 1964 film version, the problem of giving voice to thoughts was even more relevant as the "Thaw" gave way to newly-revived efforts on the part of the government to prevent free expression — to once again disunify the people by constraining them to a fearful silence.

Despite the fact that Kozintsev used Pasternak's translation of *Hamlet* for both his stage and filmed versions, he and Pasternak had several differences in their understanding of the play.[7] In the case of the post–Stalin stage version, Kozintsev kept to his original urge to alter the Shakespearean ending. Correspondence between Pasternak and Kozintsev reveals Kozintsev's alteration of the ending of the play, in which he replaced Fortinbras' arrival with the Pasternak translation of Sonnet 74. Rowe suggests that the alteration of the ending was deliberately political on Kozintsev's part. The play's original ending ensures that there is always a powerful ruler on the throne. Kozintsev attributes this to Elizabethan censorship (Rowe 153–53). The continuity of power was a huge problem under Elizabeth I; *Hamlet* appeared on the stage around the time of her death and James I's assumption of kingship. Kozintsev wished to eliminate the image of the arrival of another strong ruler in favor of the Sonnets' revelation of "the force of noble human aspirations, the force of poetry which refuses to make peace with the baseness and degradation of the era — these will outlive the emblems of potentates and the thrones of Tsars" (quoted in Rowe 153 and Stribrny 99). Thus, Kozintsev wished to eliminate the Fortinbras ending, which felt too much like a prediction of Stalin's return from the dead in the person of a new dictator. The new "ruler" at the end of the play is art itself: truth deposes Claudius' reign of lies. Once Claudius/Stalin was killed and "dragged like carrion" from the stage, there could be no ruler to take his place, since he would inevitably seem like just another tyrant sliding into his predecessor's throne (*STC* 223). This was an eventuality too bleak for the traumatized Soviet audience of 1953–54 to entertain; therefore Kozintsev chose a different ending, the Sonnet.

> But be contented: when that fell arrest
> Without all bail shall carry me away,
> My life hath in this line some interest,
> Which for memorial still with thee shall stay.
> When thou reviewest this, thou dost review
> The very part was consecrate to thee:
> The earth can have but earth, which is his due;
> My spirit is thine, the better part of me:
> So then thou hast but lost the dregs of life,
> The prey of worms, my body being dead,
> The coward conquest of a wretch's knife,
> Too base of thee to be remembered.
>   The worth of that is that which it contains,
>   And that is this, and this with thee remains.

Kozintsev's choice of Sonnet 74 was loaded and complex. Perhaps it was chosen partially for its elegiac quality, in that it could be read primarily as even a sincere homage to Stalin, while at the same time a covertly sardonic screen for its secondary, underlying lament for his victims, a double-voicing move thereby avoiding negative attention from the Party. Despite the clear relevance of *Hamlet* and the Stalin/Claudius analogy, this correspondence was never directly stated by anyone because it was at no time safe to do so, even in a private letter such as the ones later reproduced in Kozintsev's book, which never mention Stalin or any other politicians directly. One never knew when one's documents might be intercepted or later taken possession of by the authorities. The Sonnet is a statement of the survival of the human spirit in art. As Stribrny writes, Kozintsev's choice of ending "implied a resolute condemnation of the dead dictator who had been chiefly responsible for imposing the worst methods of Tsarist tyranny on the Soviet Union and its satellites" (99). The poem asserts the immortal power and resilience of the human spirit, especially as it manifests itself in the fruits of imagination and creativity, against the powerful who would try to kill or imprison it. The post–Stalin *Hamlet* reasserted the agency of individuals and diminished the specter of the tyrant or anyone who would replace him and replicate his methods.

Kozintsev made other departures from traditional Marxist *Hamlet*s in his theatrical production: whereas Laertes' arrival had been treated before (as well as in some of the other post–Stalin productions) as an heroic act of resistance along the lines of the attempted, but aborted, revolutions of 1825 and 1905, Kozintsev recast it as nothing more than a disguised return to the Imperial past, or even a controversial reference to the carnage of 1917, that is, to the ugly side of Bolshevik Revolutionary zeal. Kozintsev comments, "the revolt of Laertes is a feudal rebellion. A mode of the insanity of family vengeance. A heavy medieval sword in his hands. Madmen converge on one corner of the eye. A raucous deranged voice. A bloody bandage on matted hair" (*STC* 219). Here, Kozintsev rejects the traditional Marxist interpretation of the Laertes episode, while using the same terminology, but with double meaning. "Feudal" was a common term used in Soviet Shakespeare criticism to refer to what was reactionary and against "humanism," which represented a proto-Socialist view. "Medieval" basically functioned the same way as that old chestnut "feudal," yet both terms were used by more independently-minded critics to refer obliquely to systems of tyranny and oppression, including that experienced under Stalin and the Soviet government. The Aesopian double-voicing of theater and film has its counterpart in Soviet literary and artistic criticism.

Kozintsev's director's notes from the theatrical production, as reproduced in the appendix to *Shakespeare: Time and Conscience*, include a letter to the actor playing Claudius, which offers insights into Kozintsev's understanding of the correspondence of the king to Stalin and the way the play spoke to the Soviet Union upon the death of the "Great Leader." Claudius had tricked his own conscience and had employed various devices to maintain power and the illusion of worthiness. "This is both tragic and grotesque. The King is an orator able to wield the most subtle sophistry. He tries to convince us of his righteousness by casuistry, oratorical fire, threats and flattery" (Kozintsev *STC* 222). Here we find a summation of the so-called "cult of personality" embodied by Stalin. Like Claudius, he was somehow charismatic enough to get away with all sorts of evil almost in spite of everyone's better judgment. Like Laertes, the potential rebellion of subjects can be subdued by "casuistry." The play then became part of the post–Stalin effort to judge what had happened, what had gone wrong and how it could be set right again: "Is there a court to judge the deeds of man, and does it have full punitive power? The court of man over man. No one can refuse to place himself under its jurisdiction. [...] The judge is silent. He is not there; he is inside of man. There is a horror to this" (*STC* 222). Kozintsev's inclusiveness here speaks to that cultish enslavement of so many Soviets who became actively or passively complicit in Stalinism.

The "horror" was that Claudiuses still existed even after the Bolshevik

Revolution and, although they had consciences (or at least awareness of their own wrongdoing as Claudius exhibits in the prayer scene), they could still give themselves over to evil while appearing convincingly righteous. For Kozintsev the most horrible thing about Claudius was his smile, which is frequently mentioned in the Shakespearean text: "it is not the bared fangs of the murderer which persecute Hamlet, but his smile. Shakespeare emphasizes Claudius's gift of seduction. His figure strikes me as a perverted unity of something heavy, powerful, bullish and at other moments affectedly refined" (*STC* 222). The similarities to descriptions and depictions of Stalin conjured here would be obvious to a Soviet citizen. Stalin was dark, not very tall and had rough skin; his pictures, like those of Mao in China, were ubiquitous and often showed him smiling, although he was known to be difficult and was generally disliked by the Party officials who knew and worked with him. Lenin, before his death, warned of the dangers of letting Stalin get too powerful — the signs of his disordered personality were clear early on. He is described in historian Geoffrey Hosking's account as "boorish" and "paranoid" (461); having a "crude but lucid mind," which tended to see things in "unambiguous dualities" (462); the Yugoslavs who visited him after World War II were repelled by his "duplicity, cynicism and arrogance" (511).

Looking over this short list of Stalin's physical and temperamental qualities, one can readily find Claudius described. Kozintsev is even more pointed in his comparison here: "for a lifelike situation, it is important that Claudius is a murderer. This is a natural road to power" (*STC* 217). Stalin was not above eliminating anyone who appeared to pose a threat to him by imprisoning, exiling, or killing them under false pretenses or no pretenses at all. Claudius sent Hamlet away to England with a death warrant, ostensibly because he killed Polonius, but really to silence him as a political opponent and a sort of journalistic voice. Stalin assassinated rival Party officials, such as Kirov, much like Claudius poisoned old Hamlet to gain the throne. Stalin was every bit the leader whose road to power was strewn with corpses.

The Thaw period following Stalin's death was not only about exposing his crimes, but was also a time for reasserting the dignity and agency of individual human beings, from prisoners to artists. For Kozintsev, the scene in which Hamlet confronts Rosencrantz and Guildenstern served a central thematic function. Kozintsev's letter to the actor playing Hamlet states "your success with the monologue about the pipe invariably delights me — it seems to me to be the most important passage in the tragedy" (*STC* 224). Kozintsev read this episode as a violent clash between totalitarian oppression and individual freedom: "no play of Shakespeare's has so many frank speeches as *Hamlet*. Here, there is uninterrupted teaching, preaching and instruction. Elsinore is represented in the fullness of its ideology. In answer to it, there is the passionate propaganda of the monologue about the 'pipe.' This is what has 'to fire'!" (217). Anna France, in her analysis of Pasternak's translation observes that, in a translation marked by its somewhat free and flexible adaptation of language and imagery, Pasternak is in this episode fairly diligent in accurately translating the Shakespearean text (24). In the English play the passage reads:

> Why look you now, how unworthy a thing you make of me! You would play upon me, you would know my stops, you would pluck out the heart of my mystery, you would sound me from my lowest note to the top of my compass; and there is much music, excellent voice, in this little organ, yet you cannot make it speak. 'Sblood, do you think I am easier to be play'd on than a pipe? Call me what instrument you will, though you fret me, yet you cannot play upon me [3.2.363–372].

France renders the Pasternak version as:

> See, what filth you have sullied me with. You are preparing to play on me. You ascribe yourselves knowledge of my stops. You are sure that you will wring from me the voice of my mystery. You imagine that all of my notes from bottom to top are open to you. And this little thing is fitted on purpose to be played, it has a wonderful tone, and yet you cannot force it to speak. Do you think that it is easier with me than with a flute? Declare me to be what instrument you will, you are able to upset[8] me, but not to play on me [25].

Kozintsev notes that in his stage production this speech was applauded (*STC* 226), and France states that Soviet critics writing after Stalin's death made frequent reference to this passage as well (25). In a later letter to Innokenti Smoktunovski (the actor who played Hamlet in the film), Kozintsev writes of Hamlet that "he is not a tender young man at all, but a heretic who attacks, burning with the intoxicating joy of struggle: power is against him and his only weapon is thought. But thought won, echoing through the centuries, and we repeat with enthusiasm: Man is not a pipe!" (*STC* 252) The whole Soviet experiment had been one of trying to force people to fall into line by playing and re-playing the same State-controlled messages over and over and insisting upon their regurgitation. People who failed to play the right tunes were either forced undergo even more violent forms of conditioning or were eliminated. These strategies failed. Kozintsev offers the actor a way of approaching the words he must speak in this speech: "fill them with energy [...] and with the inner strength of struggle, of opposition to evil. Fill them with hate. And with pain" (*STC* 252). These sentiments and instructions capture the brief flourishing of a collective catharsis and optimism following Stalin's death, when bitterness and grief could finally be expressed; when there was hope that the dark period of oppression was dead along with him.

CHAPTER THREE

Hamlet in the "Thaw" and Kozintsev's 1964 Film Adaptation

Kozintsev's filmed version of *Hamlet*, appearing in 1964, reflected the changes that had taken place between Stalin's death in 1953 and the early 1960s. His restoration of the Fortinbras ending (which he had removed from his earlier stage production feeling that it was too grim) reveals anxieties about the persistence of autocracy in the USSR. The film's emphasis on Norway's military preparations and the arrival of Fortinbras' soldiers evoke the violent suppression of dissent within the USSR and the international Cold War standoff—the Cuban missile crisis happened just before the film's release. Claudius continued to function as a Stalin-esque figure, as he had in Kozintsev's '53-54 production, but could just as easily have represented Khrushchev and those Party officials who remained mired in a Stalin-era mentality. The machinations of the State did not abate under Khrushchev, after all. In fact, as both First Secretary of the Party and Chairman of the Council of Ministers, Khrushchev consolidated power even more than had Stalin (Service 347). The infamous KGB was formed by Khrushchev, and Kozintsev's film accordingly dramatizes an Elsinore full of spying and secret plots where people like Hamlet have to guard themselves carefully. Many of Hamlet's monologues take place in voiceover because he cannot speak his thoughts aloud for fear he is being listened to. Khrushchev was not above retaliating against his detractors: after an attempted ouster in 1957, he sent those persons responsible to undesirable areas in less than glamorous positions. For instance, the Stalinist Molotov was sent to be the ambassador to Mongolia, and the interim Premier after Stalin's death, Malenkov, was put in charge of a Siberian power station (Hosking 532). These exiles recall Claudius' dispatching Hamlet off to England once his presence at Elsinore became inconvenient.

Most centrally, Kozintsev's 1964 *Hamlet* film deals allegorically with the plight of artists and intellectuals under the Soviet regime as they tried to produce works in a system dominated by the political and aesthetic dictates of the Party. The contradictory and increasingly conservative attitude to artistic expression of Khrushchev and Party officials throughout the Thaw is dramatized emphatically in Kozintsev's film. Themes and imagery in the film suggest the stifling of human expression and the limitation of people's physical movements. The spying and surveillance of the court under Claudius highlight the difficulties faced by Soviet citizens, especially artists, wishing to speak out against a corrupt regime intent upon keeping power through ideological hegemony and myopia. The play-within-the-play and Hamlet's relationship with the players offers an ideal motif for the theatrical or cinematic expression of the subversive potential of art. The Mousetrap, or Murder of Gonzago, episode represents the dangers of creating art that challenges powerful political leaders. The ultimate futility of creating protest art when an artist is continually pitted against a rigid and corrupt system is suggested by the senseless deaths at the play's close. It is this particular interpretive option, one that emphasizes politics and the relationship of the artist or intellectual to the state that Kozintsev seizes upon in his adaptations of *Hamlet*.

The period immediately following Stalin's death in 1953 was time of great promise and release for many Soviet citizens. It appeared that Stalin-era repression and censorship (as well as many other counterproductive internal and external political and economic policies) would be alleviated and the country could move forward more freely and fairly. Many persons who had been imprisoned or exiled under Stalin were "rehabilitated," and with their return came a greater awareness of what exactly had been going on in the Gulag and what officials and police really did behind closed doors. The wave of hopefulness also led to unrest as workers, prisoners, peasants and people living in satellite regions of the USSR rebelled, organizing strikes and demonstrations in the hopes that with Stalin removed, they need not fear drastic repercussions and might even effect positive outcomes. For a time, arts and public media were somewhat freer. Artists and intellectuals who had been blacklisted during the Stalin years were pardoned (including Shostakovich), and some works that had been banned were released. For instance, Kozintsev's 1945 film *Simple People*, his last collaboration with Leonid Trauberg, which was suppressed upon completion, was released in 1956 (albeit in a version Kozintsev disowned).

Publication of such incendiary and revelatory works as Ilya Ehrenburg's *The Thaw* (1954), from which the early Khrushchev era got its moniker, and later on of Solzhenitsyn's *One Day in the Life of Ivan Denisovich* (1962), were further hopeful signs that cultural discourse was being loosened from the state's vice-like grip.

The most significant cultural event of the early Thaw was Khrushchev's so-called "secret speech" at the Twentieth Party Congress of 1956 (Hosking 530–531; Service 338–342). In this speech, which went on for a mere four hours, Khrushchev exposed Stalin's crimes in no uncertain terms and denounced his "cult of personality." Much of this information was so disturbing to attendees that some of them actually fainted from shock (Service 341). Khrushchev was careful to exculpate himself and many other officials who had known of or been complicit in Stalin's offenses (Hosking 530–531; Service 339–340). Nonetheless, once the details of the speech and much of its actual text were publicly revealed at home and abroad, Soviet citizens had even more cause to feel that the government was aiming to make, and keep to, reversals from Stalinist practices and policies. Unfortunately, Khrushchev's power was uneasy and he constantly had to play off and play to his colleagues who supported Stalinism and were reluctant to allow reforms that might undermine their places of privilege and power (Hosking 531–532; Service 344–345). Strikes and demonstrations were met with violent suppression. In 1962, several cities saw mass protests of workers: for example in Novocherkassk, where the military was forced to intervene thereby killing twenty-three people and putting the city under "quarantine" in order to stop the unrest from spreading (Service 364). Similar attempted uprisings against Soviet hegemony in the post-war territories were squashed by decisive military action. As early as 1956, Khrushchev sent Soviet tanks into Hungary in order to suppress a rebellion against Soviet authority that was probably at least in part inspired by his own remarks on Stalin (Service 343). Kozintsev's cinematic depiction of Laertes' return to Elsinore with an army of supporters in tow might conjure such associations in the Soviet viewers' minds.

The aperture for public expression in arts and letters had also contracted by the late 1950s, as the *Doctor Zhivago* affair graphically illustrates. The novel was published abroad in 1957 and Pasternak received the Nobel Prize in 1958. He was forced to decline the award and was ousted from the Writers' Union, effectively rendering him a non-person who had to rely on the kindness of friends and admirers to survive. The ordeal cost him his health and he died in 1960. After this episode, Khrushchev became increasingly censorious of literary and artistic works, partly to avoid criticism and resistance from the more conservative leadership in the Party who felt that he was loosening the reins guiding cultural expression too much (Service 365–366). Emily Johnson's 2001 article discusses Khrushchev's betrayal of artists' and intellectuals' hopes in seeing a freer era of expression ushered in.

Khrushchev also ordered a massive crackdown on religion, from the Orthodox Church to Judaism to Islam, destroying places of worship, imprisoning clerics, and taking control of the clerics who remained, as well as severely curtailing the number of religious services that could be held (Service 368–370). The loosening of state control over religion that had come about during World War II had led to a gradual upsurge in religious life and participation across almost all demographics, but Khrushchev, and no doubt his detractors as well, clearly felt that this was a threat to the ideological uniformity desired by the officially atheist Party. Religious imagery pervades Kozintsev's *Hamlet* film, in which Hamlet and Ophelia are associated with Christianity. In addition, the images of the broken cross in the graveyard, and the somewhat feisty cleric at Ophelia's funeral, bring to mind Khrushchev's persecution of the Church and his appointment of clerics he could control. Herein also lies Kozintsev's paean to Pasternak, who imbued his Shakespeare translations with Christian symbolism. At the end of *Doctor Zhivago* Pasternak included a poem titled "Hamlet" that likens Hamlet to Christ. Furthermore, Ophelia's "maimed rites" bring to mind Pasternak's secular funeral, which went against his final wishes to have an Orthodox service. In short, Kozintsev had much to say about the Thaw era and its contradictions.

Kozintsev's 1957 Film *Don Quixote*

Before continuing with a more earnest analysis of his 1964 film version of *Hamlet*, it is important to give some attention to Kozintsev's 1957 film *Don Quixote*. This was the only other film Kozintsev made between Stalin's death and his two Shakespeare films; therefore it seems to warrant investigation in this study. Ivan Turgenev's influential essay, discussed here in chapter one, compared a Hamletist Hamlet with what, for Turgenev and other 19th century thinkers, was his fictional counterpoint, Don Quixote. Don Quixote represented the man of action who maintained an active commitment to his ideals, as opposed to the sort of resignation and inaction exhibited by Hamlet. That Kozintsev chose to grapple with Don Quixote after Stalin's death is significant.

The allegorical possibilities presented by Cervantes' tale are readily apparent given the realities of Soviet life in the 20th century. The film tells the story of a man who lives internally in a fantasy world of righteousness and moral integrity, yet who acts externally in a real world of injustice, social masking and cruelty. This old man goes out into the world to fight evils, some real, some imagined, and is, naturally, thought by almost everyone around him to be crazy. It is important that not everyone thinks so; he is defended and loved by Sancho Panza, Aldonza and the washerwoman at the inn, and is understood by the jester at the Duke's court. Don Quixote's commitment to virtuous action and to truth makes him a victim of ridicule, violence and repression. His actions are indeed insane, in as much as they go against the human instinct to self-preservation, but they are sane in as much as he cannot accept a lie for truth. The many dangers posed by the real-world Soviet apparatus to persons unwilling to submit to wearing its masks and accepting its propaganda, at least by their outward appearances, highlight the heroic side of Don Quixote's supposed madness. Certainly, the theme of madness is important in *Hamlet*, which sandwiches this film in Kozintsev's *oeuvre*.

Masking is an important image for Kozintsev as well: at several points in the film Don Quixote claims to see the human faces behind the masks his tormentors wear. If one views Don Quixote as an artist, he is analogous to those in the Soviet period who produce "fictions" that clearly contained enough truth to pose a threat. If fictions were inert politically and socially the Soviet government would not have needed to expend so much energy in controlling the arts. Don Quixote's books and the ideas and ideals they impart to him do not stay all in his head; rather, they prompt him to take action. Books, even fictions, *are* dangerous, not only to Don Quixote, but to the people who wish to control him. He becomes, in effect, a fictional character acting in a real world and therefore embodies the power that "fictions" have over actual people and events. Kozintsev reveals, as he does with his Shakespearean adaptations, the correspondences between art and life by dramatizing this relationship within the diegesis of the film, and outside of it, by inviting the audience to see the fictions created (by Cervantes, the authors Don Quixote reads, and Kozintsev's film) as having the potential to affect the worlds in which they are read or viewed. As in the case of *Hamlet*, words are weapons and a supposedly fictional play has a great deal of influence over political events.

The ability to transfer ideals and abstract moral concepts into concrete actions bridges the space between imagination or delusion and true effectuality. An artist or thinker such as Don Quixote could safely retreat from reality, using creativity and imagination to escape the contradictions and dangers of the world. Yet this retreat would make Don Quixote the sort of Hamletist Hamlet against whom Turgenev contrasted him in his essay, or it would make him truly insane, as many characters believe Hamlet to be in Shakespeare's play, which is to say, he could inhabit a world completely divorced from reality. Leaming, although her study's overall concerns are more aesthetic than political, suggests that in this way Kozintsev's *Don Quixote* confronts the fictions of Socialist realism. An artist could choose to accept the false positivity and logicality of Socialist realism and produce works which safely and falsely idealize the real world (Leaming 92). This is the sort of collective masking encouraged by propaganda that constructs an officially-sanctioned alternate reality, one which everyone knows to be untrue, but goes along with anyway in order to maintain material security and well-being. The alternatives — exile, imprisonment, death — certainly make this seem, superficially, the wisest choice. The Thaw period was one in which such guises and insincerities were being exposed and analyzed by many intellectuals and artistic cultural critics (von Geldern's essay provides a neat summation of such exposures in the Thaw). Kozintsev's decision to use color stock for the film instead of his favored black-and-white (as in *Hamlet* and *Lear*) is a nod towards the illegitimacy of the narratives of the State. As if painting reality in new colors, the propaganda machine and State pressures forced everyone to see (or at least pretend to see) a brightly-illumined, Technicolor world instead of the stark shapes and outlines created by the shadows of deception and suffering.

Kozintsev's treatment of *Don Quixote* engages the definitions of folly and insanity. He posits that to retreat from reality into a world of false truths is perhaps insanity or folly, yet to hold those truths as motives for actions and statements equals integrity, true wisdom and sanity (however dangerous it might be to take action or to speak out). Don Quixote refuses to change his notions of right and wrong to suit the debasement of the world around him. The fictions he reads espouse moral truths and he is uncompromising in applying them to the real world. The court jester at the Duke's court where Don Quixote is presented as an amusing fool remarks that Don Quixote is not the crazy one, rather it is the court that is full of fools because everyone there pretends to believe in untruths and accepts evil for good. Don Quixote is only insane in as much as he disregards his own safety. There is evil in his world. He fights actual injustices as often as he fights imaginary foes — on a symbolic level, *everything* he fights is real, since the objects and animals he mistakes for enemies metaphorically symbolize the real forces of evil around him. The masks that hide the faces of the people he meets are also real: the carnival excesses, sexual licentiousness and drunkenness of the people at the inn mask their poverty and oppression, while the stony, regal, beautiful faces of the Duke and his courtiers mask their desperation and uneasy consciences. The Duke claims that everything in the world is a farce, yet he never laughs or smiles. Only the jester and Don Quixote point this out, since they are both fearless. Writing of Hamlet, Kozintsev draws attention to the correspondence between truth-telling and insanity: "for Shakespeare, [...] madness always denotes the privileged of speaking the cruel and ugly truth about those who have come into power and the vileness of careerists and flatterers. Let our hero sit in the place prescribed by etiquette, and behave like a young Mayakovsky in fashionable drawing rooms" (*STC* 252[1]). The jester speaks boldly because he is permitted by the king to speak, as long as he softens his meanings with humor; Don Quixote speaks truth because he is too idealistic, or too naïve, to fear social rejection or punishment.

At the beginning of her chapter on this film, Leaming notes that in 1952, the year before Stalin's death, only five films were officially released in the USSR, indicating the extent to which creativity was stifled under the Party-controlled Unions (77). Socialist realism insisted upon a presentation of the world as already corrected: the Bolshevik Revolution had solved all the problems that existed and the new government could meet and solve any new ones because its logic was always sound. Socialist realism prescribed a belief in human progress and positivity that eliminated the truth of human nature and human failure: this is not serious realism, but rather comedic fictionalizing. Soviet criticism had to disregard the facts of reality all around in order to believe in this lie. For Kozintsev, such delusions meant to simply stop thinking altogether: "To consider that whatever exists is right is not to think" (*STC* 166). Don Quixote's imaginary world demands his active participation in justice and his commitment to fidelity and compassion because the world's problems have not been magically solved. He does not pretend that his values exist in a perfect world; instead he must go forth and fight in the name of those ideals to make the flawed world better. This is not insanity, it is heroism. Fictional ideals translate into real action because injustice and cruelty persist in degrading the human condition, just as surely as imagination, hope and creativity continue to elevate it.

Through casting the brilliant actor Nikolai Cherkasov, who had previously portrayed powerful heroes (Alexander Nevsky) and heroic villains (Ivan the Terrible), Kozintsev ensured that the audience took Quixote seriously and was prepared to admire him. Kozintsev also shot the film in order to make Quixote appear taller than everyone else in almost every scene. Moreover, Cherkasov's involvement in the Eisenstein *Ivan* films' debacle set him up as a person who maintained his artistic integrity under Stalin. Cherkasov was not afraid to collaborate with Eisenstein in his second *Ivan* film (completed in 1948, the year of Eisenstein's death, well before Stalin's death and the Thaw), which, in depicting Ivan as a demented demagogue, also implicated Stalin. Kozintsev's message was in keeping with the immediate post–Stalin mood as evidenced in his *Hamlet*, in particular his choice of changing its ending. The simultaneous pathos and hopefulness of the *Hamlet* ending finds an echo in the ending of *Don Quixote*. Despite being duped by his doctor and essentially imprisoned by his family, Don Quixote still dreams of his ideals, represented by his two loyal followers and sympathizers, Aldonza/Dulcinea and Sancho Panza, who appear as dream-visions or hallucinations and encourage Don Quixote not to give up. In the final image of the film, Don Quixote and Sancho Panza are traveling off again over the hills toward a brilliant sunset. The last shot is of the triumph of Don Quixote's version of reality, even though the audience understands that he is dead. Here, the earlier *Hamlet* production is echoed, since the final word in that play was not Fortinbras', but the hopeful voice of Sonnet 74 insisting on the immortality of art and its triumph over death. Both films spoke with hope to the Thaw audience, putting forth the notion that out of the death, darkness and silence of the Stalin period could emerge integrity and truth — the better part of humanity had not perished in those troubled times. Don Quixote represented all people who refused to accept the official version of reality.

Nikolai Cherkasov as Don Quixote in the film *Don Quixote* (1957) directed by Grigory Kozintsev.

1964: Kozintsev's Filmed Hamlet

Kozintsev, in an interview available on the special edition of the Ruscico DVD release of *Hamlet*, mentions that his *Hamlet* film was in planning for eight years, indicating that the idea to make it into a film was already developing during his theatrical production, which was produced in a time of great optimism. The intervening eight years were, however, as with most of the 20th century in the Soviet Bloc, eventful and contradictory. The more or less officially-tolerated expression of anti–Stalin sentiment led to a temporary and limited resurgence of freedom in the arts of which the many productions of *Hamlet* served as representatives. Yet the people's outpouring of feelings and information was not limited to Stalin-bashing and also included more general attacks upon a spectrum of abuses throughout the Soviet government both past and present. These sentiments were to be met with official censure just as they had been under Stalin. The State's organs of artistic control remained intact and were used to maintain a sense of cohesion and order when artists or critics went too far. Through the late '50s and early '60s Khrushchev came under pressure to subdue popular protests. He tried to pass the blame for the "excesses" of the early Thaw onto other officials (Conquest 27), and launched various crackdowns in the unquiet satellite regions of the USSR, suppressed prison revolts at home, etc., all in an attempt to rein in the exuberance of the post–Stalin period and to convince his detractors that he was firmly in control. It was all too late and too little. The deterioration of the relationship with China and the debacle of the Cuban missile crisis led to Khrushchev's ousting and the rise of Brezhnev, which ushered in a new era of strong repressions, effectively ending the already cooling Thaw — significantly, the nickname for the new era was the "Stagnation."

Kozintsev's book *Shakespeare: Time and Conscience* deals most directly with his work on *Hamlet*. It is important to bear in mind that this book was completed in 1965 and published in 1966, after the film's release and after Khrushchev's deposition. The sentiments expressed in the book and its omissions reflect more upon the pessimism of the end of the Thaw and the start of the Stagnation under Brezhnev than they do the early post–Stalin mood of optimism. Kozintsev never names Trauberg, his long-time collaborator and victim of Stalin's anti–Semitic campaigns of 1948–1953, an omission that could not have gone unnoticed by anyone who knew their theatrical collaborations and films, which were quite famous and influential. Kozintsev does, however, mention FEKS with great affection, and this might be his covert way of nodding to Trauberg, with whom he founded the experimental company. Still, it is puzzling why Kozintsev would omit referring directly to Trauberg, when he mentions Pasternak, Solomon Mikhoels and others quite freely. It is possible that Trauberg himself requested not to be mentioned directly in the book. Whatever the case, the silences in the text speak loudly.

The aftermath of the Bolshevik Revolution, Stalin's terrors, the post–Stalin Thaw, and the decline of Khrushchev, are all points at which Kozintsev and his like "suffered the loss of illusions" (*STC* 14). Kozintsev writes, "Hamlet could appear on the stage because he had already walked in the midst of life. It was not only the Danish prince who suffered the loss of his illusions, but also many of those who paid their penny for admission" (*STC* 14). Kozintsev's reading, in addition to complicating Socialist realist dogma, resists traditional Russian adaptations and critiques of *Hamlet*, which have seen Hamlet as something like a "superfluous man": hopelessly interior, morose, disenfranchised and politically inert. It is important that Kozintsev did not opt instead for a stereotypically "revolutionary" Hamlet. His Hamlet is not some sort of historical or mythical proto-Bolshevik hero fighting for the people against the monarchy, feudalism and capitalism. Nor is Laertes or Fortinbras for that matter, although they are also sometimes depicted as saviors of the people in Soviet Marxist Shakespeare criticism. Rather, Hamlet fights against the corruption and tyranny of Kozintsev's own *contemporary* situation. Kozintsev is keen to repeat in his writings his thesis that Shakespeare himself was employing distant times and places as plot material for the express purpose of critiquing his own times. This reiteration points to Kozintsev's own goal, which was to speak to his own time through Shakespeare. Therefore, Kozintsev was always topical — that he was writing about the most current political landscape should be remembered.

Kozintsev's restoration of the Fortinbras ending in his film reflected upon the post–Thaw despair of the late '50s and early '60s and seemed to anticipate the repressions to come under Brezhnev. Mark Sokolyansky quotes the critic Samarin, writing right around the same time as Kozintsev's film appeared: "had Shakespeare made the humanist Hamlet a prosperous king of Denmark, he would have abandoned truth to life. It is the real politician, Fortinbras, who will get the crown" (quoted 223). Indeed, in Shakespeare's play and Kozintsev's film, Fortinbras immediately takes control of the mode and manner of Hamlet's funeral and the venue in which his story will be told. Mark Burnett writes: "Fortinbras cleverly manages to make sure that the story will first be heard by a select, private gathering, thereby suppressing what might constitute threatening political secrets"

(39). Kozintsev's vision of the ending somewhat undercuts Horatio's desire to fulfill Hamlet's dying request in a much less politically-calculated manner than does Fortinbras. In 1954, Kozintsev could have hoped that someone might rise to power and set the "out of joint" time straight again, but after the events of the post–Stalin period, this could hardly have seemed anything but a futile, or, at best, deferred, wish. Therefore Fortinbras enters the scene and pushes Horatio aside much like Brezhnev did the beleaguered Khrushchev. Anthony Dawson quips: "The film remains uncertain whether he [Fortinbras] is Stalin or Khrushchev, but he is certainly not Hamlet" (188). The direction forward for the kingdom of the Danes and the nation of the Soviets is uncertain, but seems certainly not to belong yet to the discretion of the politically dissident.

Critical Background

Chapters and articles on Kozintsev's 1964 *Hamlet* film written by Western scholars began appearing in books and journals roughly six years after the film's making and four years after its first showings in the West. This delay is due to the fact that the film was still not widely shown or available abroad in the 1960s. It received more critical attention after Kozintsev's *King Lear* (1970) was screened with it at the 1971 World Shakespeare Conference in Canada. Earlier articles tend to avoid political readings of the film, and where they do offer any consideration at all generally call the Kozintsev approach "Marxist," mention that there is a critique of Stalin implied, and leave it at that. This group includes articles and chapters by Billingheimer, Brebach, Griffin, Hodgdon and Manvell, appearing from the late 1960s to the early 1980s. Interestingly, even Kozintsev's biographer Leaming (*Grigory Kozintsev*, 1980) gives only one paragraph in her chapter on *Hamlet* to speculation about the political meaning of the film, focusing instead on Soviet cinema practice and film theory.

This early group of articles reveals that Kozintsev's ethos was understood in the West to be uncritically Marxist, and that his critique or evocation of Stalin also followed the Party line in as much as Khrushchev himself denounced Stalin in 1956. Given the Cold War mentality and the relative lack of information about the reality of life for artists and intellectuals inside the USSR, it is understandable that many articles would not evidence culturally-, historically- or politically-sensitive readings. While it is true that Kozintsev probably remained a devoted Socialist and Marxist throughout his life, like many other artists and intellectuals of his generation, he saw the promise of the Bolshevik Revolution turn into an artistically and academically stifling and violently oppressive regime. Therefore, while one might recognize Socialist or Marxist ideals operating in the films, this does not suggest that Kozintsev avoided launching a critique of the vicissitudes of his era. Moreover, most of the early Western articles betray a limited understanding of the duration and nature of the "Thaw" period, assuming that it was a more peaceful, open and free time overall than it actually was. In fact, *Hamlet* was in production during the very trying times of the late Khrushchev era, the troublesome realities of which I have described above. Both of these assumptions — that Kozintsev was a Party-line Marxist, and that the Thaw was a much freer and safer time for artists than it really was — led to a certain lack of political engagement in readings of the film, especially before the 1980s.

Articles from the 1960s into the 1980s focus more on close reading of montage, imagery, etc., and discuss, often defending, the transposition of Shakespeare to film, using Kozintsev's textually pared-down version of *Hamlet* as an example of the characteristics and successes or failures of such projects. What was of greater concern to many critics were debates about the relative merits of Shakespearean translations and films. Some outstanding articles and chapters from this initial wave of criticism include work by Jack Jorgens in *Literature and Film Quarterly*, 1973; the more developed version of the same article in his book *Shakespeare on Film* of 1977; Bernice Kliman's article in *Hamlet Studies*, 1979; and her more developed version of this reading in *Hamlet*, 1988. Although these critics make scant or vague reference to the political contexts of the film, and therefore are not especially relevant to understanding it in its cultural, historical and political contexts, their works provide excellent close readings. Kliman's 1988 chapter marks the general time of the shift in the Western body of criticism towards greater interest in the political purposes of Kozintsev's film, as well as more attention to the influence of Pasternak's translations and other contextual information.

From the late 1980s through the most recent articles on Kozintsev's *Hamlet*, the criticism turned more towards politically-invested readings. Several factors probably account for this shift: such as the influence of new interpretive schools such as New Historicism, Feminism and Cultural Studies, which insist upon a greater attention to the contexts whence art arises. There was also greater access to information about the realities of Soviet life following the disintegration and fall of the USSR, which took place throughout the '80s and '90s as former republics and finally Russia proper broke away from Communist rule. Examples of the most recent work on the film, such as Sokolyansky's chapter in *The Cambridge Companion to Shakespeare on Film* (2000), Stribrny's book *Shakespeare in Eastern Europe* (2000), and Anthony Dawson's chapter from *Shakespeare in Performance: Hamlet* (1995), focus almost entirely on political contexts and implications in reading Kozintsev. Kozintsev's seeming duality of consciousness and Aesopian indirectness in his work might very well serve to complicate readings of the films (and the contributions of the similarly-situated Pasternak and Shostakovich), as John Collick explores in his chapter on Kozintsev's Shakespeare films in *Shakespeare, Cinema and Society* (1989, 128–148). Along with the recent work of Sokolyansky and Stribrny, Collick opens the door to a reading of Kozintsev's *Hamlet* as a work deeply connected to its time and place. Sokolyansky illuminates some of the details of his *Hamlet* production, such as casting choices, music and design, noting, among other things, that the use of black and white film was a politically motivated choice "determined by a desire to avoid bright coloration as a way of glossing over the truth — the tendency encouraged by official Soviet ideology and despised by Kozintsev" (201). Both Stribrny and Sokolyansky point out pertinent details, such as the fact that Innokenti Smoktunovski, who played Hamlet, was himself imprisoned under Stalin after World War II. They also offer a more nuanced view of Kozintsev's politics beyond what has been offered before (Stribrny 107). Stribrny writes, "He [Kozintsev] was a Marxist, convinced of the justice and humanity of Socialism, but, for that very reason, he became anti–Stalinist" (106). A seemingly simple point, but one that might have been easy to lose in the Cold War era when a great deal of Western propaganda might not have easily differentiated between a Marxist and a Stalinist, essentially equating Soviet Socialism with all manner of evils without a great deal of discernment. At any rate, better information about what life was really like inside the USSR has paved the way for new appraisals of Kozintsev's films and his collaborators' contributions. It is primarily from such recent works that I quote in this study.

Pasternak and *Doctor Zhivago*

If anything illustrates the contradictory nature of the late 1950s and early 1960s best in terms of artistic repression it is Pasternak's *Doctor Zhivago* episode. Kozintsev's use of Pasternak's translation of *Hamlet* in his film, released only a few years after his death, should be read against this background. Kozintsev was greatly influenced by Pasternak's translations and it appears that he was deeply affected by the author's troubles and untimely death. The journal *Novy Mir* rejected *Doctor Zhivago* in 1956, but it was published in Italy in 1957. The Nobel Award notification came in 1958, followed by a *Pravda* article condemning Pasternak and the novel and accusing the outside world of granting Pasternak the prize simply from anti–Soviet political sentiment. By the end of 1958, Pasternak had declined the award, but he was still expelled from the Writers Union and almost deported. Pasternak went so far as to write an open letter to Khrushchev asking not to be exiled. Despite this and other somewhat cowed public statements, Pasternak retained a great deal of integrity throughout this ordeal. In a 1958 interview with *The New York Times* he said, "I have borne witness as an artist; I have written about the times I have lived through" (quoted in Conquest). In 1959 Pasternak's close friend Olga Ivinskaya was implicated in a financial scandal over international royalties for *Doctor Zhivago*.[2] Not surprisingly, all of this stress caused Pasternak to become very ill and his death came less than two years after he declined the Nobel Prize (d.1960). Some 1500 persons attended his funeral, but no officials, since Pasternak had by this time become a non-person — he was officially unemployed and living in internal exile at the time of his death. In tribute to him, the "Hamlet" poem from the end of *Doctor Zhivago* was read at the service, an act of courage designed to conjure Pasternak's political problems. All of these events, including the fact that the "Hamlet" poem was read at the funeral, were widely known in artistic and political circles, even though they were not written about in the press. The novel itself was widely circulated in *samizdat* manuscript form as early as 1956. Several authors cite *Zhivago* as a work that caused a huge upsurge in *samizdat* publishing. The novel itself dramatizes the process as we find Zhivago's unpublished works ironically appearing in the hands of one of his employers. Pasternak had personally distributed parts of the book to his friends even before the piece was entirely completed (Conquest 80).

In the Soviet Union, under Stalin and afterwards, the popularity of artists and their works abroad, especially if they were not approved by the Party and Unions at home, was considered highly embarrassing to the Soviet state and put the artists concerned in a great deal of danger, especially if they still resided inside the USSR. The award of the Nobel Prize, added to the fact that the novel was published abroad, not to mention its content, infuriated the Party. This eventuality allowed the Party to use Pasternak as a scapegoat and deterrent for those artists who were getting a bit too outspoken, which was a problem Khrushchev was being pressured to address.

Pasternak was accused by the Party of evidencing a "bourgeois-anarchist, individualistic conception of the creative liberty of the artist, directed against the Party supervision of art" (Conquest 49). *Doctor Zhivago* was much more than an expression of anti–Stalinist sentiment or a catharsis of pent-up grief from World War II. It was a wholesale rejection of the very premises of the Bolshevik Revolution. Ironically, it was the novel's political ambivalence and the apolitical stance of its hero that was most infuriating to officials who were dedicated to promulgating Socialist realism and Party ideology. *Zhivago* did not so much take a stance against the Party as it declined to even enter into the political fray. Therefore it was branded as "mystical" and "reactionary." Robert Conquest offers a quote from Zaslavsky's Pasternak-lambasting article in *Pravda* 1958, suggesting that it was probably edited by Khrushchev himself: "He [Pasternak] seems to have succumbed to that putrid infection which for a very short time swept over some stagnant corners of Soviet literature and enlivened the hopes of the philistines embedded in its chinks" (169). This "infection" was anyone's dissatisfaction with the Soviet government, and could also refer to the renewal of interest in Orthodoxy and religion in the '60s and '70s (see Bourdeau). Khrushchev more-or-less turned against artists and intellectuals by the early '60s, who had, for a time, believed that he would continue to loosen State and Union oversight. One of the main purposes of the Party's very public condemnation of Pasternak and his novel was to curtail the "excesses" of the post–Stalin Thaw era's overly permissive stance towards criticism of Soviet culture and government.

Kozintsev was in pre-production for the *Hamlet* film during this time, therefore it is reasonable to see his characterization of Hamlet and his alteration of the ending of the film as taking on shades of the Pasternak affair. Lazar Fleishman, in his Pasternak biography, writes, "whether Pasternak was condemned to silence, or whether he was allowed to publish translations or sporadic selections of poetry, his very existence served as decisive proof of the tenacity of art, despite the stifling situation in the country and the demands imposed on artists by the regime" (69). Despite artistic crackdowns from the Party through its Unions, the seeds of new hopes and renewed boldness had already germinated. Parallels between the Pasternak affair and Hamlet's resistance to Claudius's reign and his use of the Mousetrap to expose the king's evil acts in Kozintsev's film are readily apparent. Fleishman's sentiments converge with the positive aspects of Kozintsev's endings in his theatrical and film versions of *Hamlet*, both of which contain nods to Pasternak. Timothy Sergay writes of the poem "Hamlet" that it is "frequently interpreted, with good grounds, as primarily emblematic of its author's struggle with Soviet literary and governmental officialdom, his self-sacrificial determination to publish *Doctor Zhivago* whatever may come" (402). Golub mentions that this poem was banned at the time of Pasternak's death and was read aloud illegally, as an act of open resistance to state authority, since it was from a banned work (181). The reading of the "Hamlet" poem at Pasternak's funeral further compounds an identification of Pasternak with Hamlet, and therefore of Hamlet's fate with the fate of the artist under the Soviet regime.

Pasternak's "Hamlet," attributed to Yuri Zhivago, appears as the first of the cycle of poems at the end of *Doctor Zhivago*:

> The din is hushed. I've come out on the stage.
> [...]
> If only Thou wilt grant it, Abba, Father,
> I pray this cup may pass from me today.
> I love Thy purpose, steady and unbending,
> And I am quite content to play this role.
> But now a different drama is impending:
> I beg of Thee, this time release my soul.
> Life's script of acts and scenes, however, bounds me.
> No turning back: my destiny is sealed.
> I'm all alone; hypocrisy surrounds me...
> To live a life is not to cross a field.³

The central images in this poem make its speaker both Christ-figure and a general evocation of Christ's prayers in Gethsemane before his Crucifixion: an actor in a play scripted entirely beyond his own will. Rowe references *The Blind Beauty*, one of Pasternak's unfinished plays, in which the character Agafon, a serf and an actor, says "*Hamlet* is a play written by an actor for an actor" (quoted in Rowe 160). It is the situation the speaker finds himself in that dictates his actions, not his own desires or interests; his only choice is to respond to external contingencies. This should not, however, be taken as the passivity of Hamletism, and certainly the Christ analogy makes the speaker's sacrifice seem even more heroic: his is a productive martyrdom precipitated by an unwavering commitment to truth, conscience and service to humanity.

Golub remarks upon Pasternak's concept of selfhood as radically communal and suggests that Pasternak saw the events if his own life in this way: "[Pasternak's] prototype in this regard was the actor, and he clearly recognized both Hamlet and himself as such" (181). He goes on to contextualize further, "The actor's brave act of self-nomination, [...] his search for the complete truth of being in selfhood and otherness, exploded the purposeful misrepresentations which produced moral failure in Soviet life"

(182). To see both actor and artist as seeking the "truth of being" raises interesting notions about Pasternak's and Kozintsev's portrayal of Hamlet in a way that emphasized his roles as artist and actor and insisted upon his political agency. In a world where people feared to speak the truth, and therefore acted roles not of their choosing, Hamlet's "self-nomination" as truth-teller, even as that required him to take on different roles himself, was indeed brave. In this characterization, Pasternak, like Kozintsev, moved away from the Hamletist interpretation, even as he acknowledged *Hamlet* as a "tragedy of the will" ("Translating Shakespeare" 130). It is not that Hamlet had no will, as in Hamletism, but rather that he decided to overcome his urge to self-preservation in service of greater truths and for the benefit of others.

Hamlet, says Pasternak, as heir to the throne and "darling of an ancient court" is not neurotic or without will, "rather the opposite is true: the audience, impressed by his brilliant prospects, is left to judge of the greatness of his sacrifice in giving them up for a higher aim" (130). In line with his view of Hamlet as a Christ-figure, he writes of Hamlet's sense of "duty" and self-denial": "chance has allotted Hamlet the role of judge of his own time and servant of the future" (130). Kozintsev's productions and writings on *Hamlet* demonstrate his sympathy with Pasternak's worldview, including his religiosity. Kozintsev writes of Hamlet at several points in Christian terms that bring to mind the imagery of Pasternak's "Hamlet" poem. He writes of Hamlet's encounter with and mandate from Old Hamlet in clearly Biblical terms, "Only the son sees the father distinctly. [...] The father does not forsake his son again" (*STC* 242). To Pasternak *Hamlet* is the "drama of a high destiny, of a life devoted and preordained to a heroic task" (131). The urge to transform the past and the continuing struggles and losses of Soviet cultural battles into something positive and hopeful is the crux of Pasternak's *Hamlet*. This urge is manifest in Kozintsev's attitude to Shakespeare, and to art in general. Kozintsev writes in a very Pasternak-like tone, imagining the Soviet people as a collective Christ, to whom Hamlet's situation is painfully relevant: "Hamlet's words do not leave modern audiences cold. Our memories retain the fire and tears paid for by the numbing of the soul of human bonds, for power rooted in inhumanity. [...] A modern Elsinore would have no objection to closing the barbed wire of concentration camps around humanity like a crown of thorns" (*STC* 168). Christ's sacrifice elevates the martyrdom of far too many Soviet citizens, an elevation that might have done much to heal the wounds left by powerlessness.

Hamlet as Actor, Director and Voice of the *Narod*

Central to Kozintsev's conception of Hamlet in his film is Hamlet's affinity with the players (and by extension with the common folk, the *narod*) and his identity as director of the Murder of Gonzago play. Hamlet is not only Pasternak's Christ-like martyr, he is also an actor and artist. Hamlet's activity extends beyond Danish politics and the court of Elsinore; part of his *modus operandi* is to use theatrical arts as a way of exposing Claudius' crimes and revealing the truth behind Claudius' machinations to the court audience. Both the players and Hamlet act in relationship to the *narod* in as much as their performances are not dedicated to parroting or pandering to the sentiments and tastes of people in positions of power. Rather, as Kozintsev stresses in his books and his *mise-en-scène*, the purpose of their plays is to entertain the people and to reflect their unvarnished truths, not the veneers of truth preferred by the elite. The first time we see the players in Kozintsev's film they arrive outside the castle proper and occupy the courtyard space, which is where Kozintsev places representatives of the "masses," those people who are outside the political world of Elsinore, but clearly dependent upon it and influenced by it. There are peasants working at various tasks, farm animals running about, horses trotting through, giving the overall impression of the activities of everyday rural life. Kozintsev writes, "we must play tragic scenes in out-of-the-way places where there is rubbish scattered around, where hens are cackling and grooms unharnessing horses. Into this sort of place, which is natural in action, the van of the players arrives" (*STC* 249). The players arrive in their wagon with great deal of noise — this is actually the first time in the film anyone laughs — and are greeted enthusiastically by the people. These people, the players' true audience, understand the hollowness and corruption that hides behind the glamour of wealth and power. The art forms that they prefer often point out precisely the disparity between the higher and lower echelons of society, even if this is emphasized merely by the inherently earthy, primitive and unpretentious nature of folk art.

This is the audience Kozintsev envisions as Shakespeare's most important one, and they are the reason that Shakespeare's realism, which mixes the base and the bawdy with the elevated and refined, avoids the softened idealism of courtly arts and entertainments. Kozintsev imagines what the response of these audiences would be if the playwright or actors tried to place an over-rarefied character or overly-mannered situation on the stage: "I can distinctly hear a beautifully deafening whistle replete with the energy of life, and concert of catcalls, the shouts of London apprentices, impatient foot-stamping, and extravagant sixteenth-century abuse. And the whole house of cards crumbles, dashed by the guffaws of the Elizabethan audience" (*STC* 18). The peasants at the walls of Elsinore, and, by implication, Kozintsev's audience too, will not accept anything more or less than an unvarnished portrayal of reality.

Hamlet himself exits the inner realm of the castle into this liminal space to join the *narod* in greeting the players, thereby establishing the courtyard as a playing space in which distinctions of rank and power become blurred, much as Shakespeare's Globe and other public theaters would have been in the Renaissance period. In a later shot, Polonius remains above on the caste's courtyard wall above the plebian fray, decidedly not joining into the communality of the scene below. The players set about performing for this rustic, mixed audience in a spontaneous manner, creating a carnival, folk-art atmosphere reminiscent of FEKS and the inn scene in Kozintsev's *Don Quixote* (Leaming writes a great deal on the carnivalesque elements in Kozintsev's *oeuvre*). The players are dressed mostly as minstrels and jesters, play instruments and do acrobatics, emphasizing the carnival aspects of theater and the world of folk culture. Their accoutrements are minimal; they rely upon the folk audience's imaginative participation, as opposed to Polonius' complacent, aristocratic passivity.

As the troupe's lead actor gives the Hecuba speech, Hamlet's "O, what a rogue and peasant slave" monologue begins in a voiceover as he moves to sit inside the players' wagon. As his monologue continues, the screen frames Hamlet inside the wagon as if he were backstage, which, in a sense he is, surrounded by the players' masks, instruments, and, not accidentally, a crown that dangles from the roof's interior above his head. This is a clear homage to Akimov's stage production of the '30s, which featured a large, gaudy crown to conjure and denigrate the mystification of power under the tsars and Stalin. Writing of the crowns he saw at the Tower of London, and in Lawrence Olivier's film of *Richard the Third*, Kozintsev observes that "in spite of references to their gold content and the value of the precious stones set in them, these symbols of power invariably look like props. What is so special about these things? In order to grasp their significance, they must be perceived not as objects, but as symbols, the sinister associations of which were compounded from iron, fire, and blood by the history of a people" (*STC* 27). Hamlet sits below the cheap prop-crown in this shot, but has not previously nor later on evidenced the slightest interest in obtaining political power, or even the trappings of power. His cause therefore is pure. In a society in which the exercise of power has only led to corruption and repression, which has brought death and

Three. *Hamlet* in the "Thaw" and Kozintsev's 1964 Film Adaptation 93

Innokenti Smoktunovsky as Hamlet conversing with the players outside Elsinore in the film *Hamlet* (1964) directed by Grigory Kozintsev.

destruction upon the people, this is the only sort of hero who can be sympathetic to the audience, whether they be of 16th century England or 20th century Russia.

From the camera's view behind Hamlet and through the inside of the wagon, the players cease their activities and begin to watch Hamlet, effectively reversing the actor/audience relationship, making Hamlet the actor and they the spectators. (This reversal happens again several times in the Mousetrap/Gonzago sequence.) As if in a flash of inspiration, Hamlet asks for the Murder of Gonzago to be played. Brent Cohen, in his article on theatricality in the play, comments, "The Players arouse Hamlet's impulses for the heroic and forbidden, for action which it turns out, however, can be acted out only in the theatre" (231). This sequence emphasizes Hamlet's logical trajectory from feeling himself accused and shamed by the players, who can feign more emotion about strangers than he can muster real emotion for his own murdered father, to realizing that through theatrical art he can similarly accuse and shame Claudius.

Collick mentions several times the way Kozintsev allegorizes the position of the intellectual (and by logical extension I suggest the artist is allegorized here as well) in his Shakespeare films:

> Kozintsev perceived Hamlet's purpose as the destruction of a corrupt Machiavellian court and his tragedy as a "tragedy of conscience." That the conscience of an intellectual should be so important is, in itself, a revealing comment on Kozintsev's perception of himself and his work. Hamlet's indecision and final death proceed from his involvement in a historical process which has little room for intellectual honesty. The final sequence makes clear the overall significance of his motives and deeds: his killing of Claudius has merely cleared the way for the militaristic order of Fortinbras [Collick 141].

Collick sees Kozintsev's interpretation as resisting Socialist realism and seeing "history as a dynamic process," and certainly, a great portion of Kozintsev's writings on time and history bears this out despite his ultimately non–Kottian outlook. If we look at Hamlet as an artist in the mold of so many other Soviet artists, we could read him as someone who resists his isolation by the forces of oppression and censorship in order to speak the truth in a public manner — he is destroyed, but he is not silent. Art becomes the means by which he overcomes silence, by which he exposes the ruse of his supposed "antic disposition" or folly, holding up the crimes of the powerful to the view of all. The ending of the film still retains the quality of the Sonnet 74 version in as much as the truth, as expressed in art, is never really silenced, even though Hamlet's public criticism of Claudius led to his death.

Kozintsev places his emphasis on making Hamlet's play, and therefore theater and performance more generally (e.g., film), have real-world consequences, because for Kozintsev theater is inherently effectual (much as fictions are in *Don Quixote*). Earlier, Hamlet's screams upon seeing the ghost of his father were silent — "despair soundless, and anger choking in your throat" — but now Hamlet's excited yell is heard (*STC*). He has found his voice because he is now an actor in, and the director of, his own play, not merely an bit player in someone else's (Mendel 746). Kozintsev writes, "the screen must convey [...] the fate of a man determined to talk with his epoch on equal terms, and not to be an extra, with no speaking part, in one of its spectacular crowd scenes" (*STC* 232). Hamlet's voice is found in artistic expression, in the medium of the drama; he, like Kozintsev, will use a play written by someone else (i.e. *The Murder of Gonzago*) to "talk with his epoch." There is a moral imperative implied here, especially for the artist, who is "impotent when his inner discretion is replaced by the horror of silence" (*STC* 275). In the early portion of the film, Hamlet's speeches occur in voice-over to illustrate his hyper-awareness of the spies lurking about the castle and the success of Claudius' campaign to silence people through fear. Yet after this episode with the players, Hamlet becomes boisterously loud and talkative, confronting nearly every other person at the Court with his "verbal weapons" (*STC* 134).

The Murder of Gonzago or **The Mousetrap**

In Kozintsev's film Hamlet's play takes place outside the castle Elsinore, at the beach, upon a platform stage with the ocean and sky as backdrop. The film has already established this as Hamlet's space: the beach is his refuge as well as the location of his meeting with the ghost of his father (at the end of the film, he dies here and then is carried outside the walls of Elsinore). Torches are placed on the stage for illumination. Here, as elsewhere in the film, fire and flame represent truth: inside Elsinore, torches, candles and the fireplace, when lit, represent glimmerings of truth inside the castle's hyper-controlled world of falsity. As with the scene of the players' arrival, there is an inversion of the relationship between audience and players. The members of the court of Elsinore are seated on a stage-like platform somewhat higher than the Mousetrap stage in front of a more artificially theatrical backdrop than the open space of sea and sky behind the players' stage. Claudius and Gertrude are even further set apart on a platform of their own so that they are on display to everyone else as in theater in the round. While this placement would ordinarily enhance their power, making them the locus of attention, in this case it enables Hamlet, Horatio and everyone else to watch Claudius' reactions to the play: reactions which he might rather hide. The theatricality of political power is emphasized here, but is also reversed: Claudius' insistence on being seen also places him in a vulnerable position, since he cannot realistically always control the "action."

The processional entrance of the court is extremely stylized and full of grotesque theatricality: fake smiles, false deference, polite words and guarded displays of emotion. It is very like the court scene in *Don Quixote* that sets up the artifice of the court against the spontaneous, unmannered genuineness of Don Quixote. The false theatrics of the court are juxtaposed with Hamlet's reckless pursuit of truth and the emotionally sincere performances of the players. Hamlet alone circulates through this space with ease, moving from backstage conference with the players and Horatio, into the audience, onto the royal platform, upon the stage itself, and back and forth in the area between the two "stages." Hamlet, as in the players' arrival scene (and in many other shots and sequences in the film), is constantly in motion and seems to exist in his own liminal space literally, intellectually and emotionally. His spatial flexibility is linked to his function as director and artist. The crux of his art lies in its ability to occupy the space between power and art, politics and truth, and therefore to make them speak to each other. It is very dangerous for Hamlet to do this, and his play does lead to catastrophe.

The Mousetrap sequence unfolds with Claudius' increasing suspicion and discomfort. The line "is there no offense in it?" (3.2.234) is delivered with pointed seriousness. Several shots of Claudius are taken from a low angle, sometimes with Hamlet below him, adding to the visual and emotional tension of the scene. The climax, at which point Claudius stands, is powerfully rendered by Kozintsev: at first, Claudius seems to have lost his composure, he is shocked, irate, and then, seeming to recall who he is and that the eyes of all are upon him, he applauds, covering up his first, unpremeditated, and therefore undesirable, response. Cohen's reading of this scene describes Claudius' reaction to the play as a "shrewdly improvised management of his audience's response" in the context of Claudius' understanding of the play as a direct threat to his life because Lucianus is introduced as "nephew to the king" (236). Alvin Kernan, writing on theater and politics, also mentions the duality of the message in Hamlet's theatrical (4). The context in the film is different, and elides this ambiguity, but Kozintsev's staging makes Claudius' reaction pointedly designed to affect the people watching him. After this, he leaves abruptly, as do the rest of the court and the now very agitated players, who wisely sense that their welcome at the castle has come to an end.

The Mousetrap sequence represents the uneasy relationship between artist and ruler that obtained in the Stalin era. This sequence in Kozintsev's film also conjures Eisenstein's depiction of Stalin in his *Ivan* films. The first *Ivan* film, made during the "Great Patriotic War," (i.e., World War II), reflects the attitude of those years, during which many filmmakers readily (as opposed to those under duress) provided pro-Soviet propaganda films, including Kozintsev in his *Maxim* trilogy (which slightly predate the war, but were immensely popular for their patriotism long after their release). *Ivan* Part 1 portrays Ivan, and therefore Stalin, at whose behest these films were made, positively as heroic unifier of the people "against their external and internal enemies (Tartars and boyars, respectively)" (Gillespie 54). Part 2, finished in 1946, but unreleased due to censorship, was an entirely different film, which showed Ivan, and therefore Stalin, as vicious, paranoid, insane and without humanity. As David Gillespie writes, "for Eisenstein to hint that the despot may be mad was tantamount to a suicide note" (54).

Eisenstein was, after all, making these films for Stalin, knowing that he would see them and react, much as Hamlet's play for Claudius was not an accident, but a carefully contrived happening. Eisenstein and Cherkasov, who played Ivan (and Don Quixote in Kozintsev's film), were castigated in a private meeting with Stalin in 1947, soon after which Eisenstein became seriously ill, likely due to the stress he endured: he died of a heart attack in 1948. In a sense, the film ended his life, just as Hamlet's theatrical presentation led to a series of drastic reprisals and therefore signaled both a turning point in the plot and ushered him towards his death. What the Eisenstein comparison points to in a larger sense is the historical commitment of Russian and Soviet artists to use art as a way to explore and challenge social conditions and the operation of governments and monarchs. This commitment, according to critics such as Kernan, is perfectly in keeping with Shakespeare's ideas about the theater, which in turn reflect those of his Renaissance contemporaries. Kernan remarks, "Hamlet is the spokesman for a Renaissance ideal conception of the social effect of theater" (9). Kernan also points to Sidney's *Apology*, which states that tragedy "maketh Kings feare to be tyrants, and Tyrants manifest their tirranical humours" (quoted in Kernan 8). Eisenstein's *Ivan* certainly achieved both of Sidney's tragic effects for Stalin, just as Hamlet's *Mousetrap* did for Claudius.

Returning to the film, once Claudius re-enters Elsinore after viewing the Mousetrap, he goes off alone, visibly and violently angered. Hamlet and Horatio confer in a room with a huge fireplace and a raging fire. In a previous scene, this fireplace was dark and empty; the fire after Hamlet's play illustrates the hidden truths now brought to the surface, in keeping with Kozintsev's symbolic use of flame: he writes of "fire: anxiety, revolt, movement, the trembling flame of the candles at Claudius' celebrations; raging fiery tongues; the wind-blown lamps on the stage erected for 'The Mousetrap'" (*STC* 266). "Fiery tongues," incidentally, or not, is a provocative reference to Pentecost, which reveals Kozintsev's subtle and subversive use of positive religious imagery and allusion in his writings and his productions. Hamlet makes no secret of his satisfaction and delight with the play's effects, despite Rosencrantz and Guildensterns' warning that he should keep quiet and avoid any further trouble. Their concern, Polonius' frantic bustling about, the court minions' agitation, and the players' hasty preparations for departure indicate that everyone understands Hamlet's

Claudius' (Mikhail Nazvanov) self-examination with mirror, flame and cross in the film *Hamlet* (1964) directed by Grigory Kozintsev.

play has caused a major problem. At this point Hamlet gives the pipe speech, as rebuttal to Rosencrantz and Guildenstern, so central to Kozintsev and Pasternak's concept of the play in the 1950s. The pipe speech rides the emotional crest of the Mousetrap sequence, therefore emphasizing the connections among art and truth-telling, public political resistance and personal risk.

The next scene finds Claudius sending Rosencrantz and Guildenstern off with their instructions for removing Hamlet to England — a version of Soviet exile and an attempt at a Terror-esque summary execution. Claudius is left alone for the prayer scene. He looks into a mirror framed by two candles in a candlestick with a cross adornment; alone, he must face the truth of his crimes. The mirror is a clear sign of self-examination in cinema; flame, as elsewhere in the film, represents truth. The cross functions on several levels, as it does throughout the film: inside of Elsinore it is a mere decoration devoid of any correspondence to the nature of the government; outside Elsinore, or in relation to a character such as Ophelia, the cross become a symbol of moral authenticity. Claudius' lines about being judged after his death and having to give evidence before God are emphasized in Kozintsev's abridgement of the scene. In a world in which the grossest injustices are meted out unpunished, the idea of justice in the afterlife is sometimes the only possible consolation. The artist must die and hope his truth is heard after him, and the tyrant must be punished after his death. Kozintsev makes this scene the climax of the first part of the film. The dramatic turning point then has very little to do with Hamlet, nothing at all to do with Fortinbras, but everything to do with the exposure of the crimes of the tyrant. It is the apotheosis of Kozintsev's condemnation of Stalin and the continuation of Stalinism under Khrushchev on behalf of his audience.

The opening of the following scene, which is the opening of part two of the film, shows Hamlet active and determined as he strides down one of the dark hallways of Elsinore to his mother's room to confront her with the truths he has discovered. Claudius is the focus of part one; Hamlet's ability to undermine him is the focus of part two. Kozintsev's emphasis is not merely upon exposing crime and evil, but in depicting someone actually doing something about it. As in *Don Quixote*, art is not merely designed to illustrate and inform, but to spur people to take action — acting is not only for the stage. Herein we find art's power and its danger, which the tyrant fears with good reason. Kozintsev's commitment to this view of art is dramatized here and will become even more explicit at the end of *King Lear* in which Edgar, in the final shot of the film, looks directly into the camera and at the audience as if to command them to act.

The Graveyard

Despite Claudius' attempt to exterminate him, Hamlet manages to return from the dead to continue his fight at Elsinore. This is much like the life of Smoktunovski, the actor who played him, who returned from the Gulag after his post–World War II imprisonment, by most accounts, a feat akin to overcoming death. Kozintsev's treatment of the graveyard scene emphasizes the question of how to live, in all its religious and philosophical importance, in the face of an inevitable death. For the Soviets, the specter of a premature death was as ubiquitous as it was for Shakespeare's audience living under the threat of the Plague. Death is treated here in its fullest sense as frightening, mysterious and liberating, but also pathetic, grotesque, rendering all human endeavor essentially futile. For

Pasternak, the absurdity and grotesqueness of the gravedigger's attitude to death and the convergence of death and comedy in the scene point to a particularly Shakespearean brand of realism. Pasternak writes of Shakespeare's blurring the lines between tragedy and comedy: "his style is between the two and made up of both; it is thus closer to the true face of life than either, for in life, too, horrors and delights are mixed" (148). Realism in this case, and for Kozintsev as well, who, like Pasternak was part of the experimental carnival of arts and letters in the early 20th century, was not a capitulation to Socialist realism and the aesthetic dictates of the Party overlords of culture. Realism emerged as the new radicalism if one saw the world of official propaganda and dictated versions of history and aesthetics for what they were, which was anything but a real, factual, honest depiction of Soviet life.

Socialist realism was in a generic sense comedic: its purpose was to show life as better than it was, history always progressing, and people always more than able to overcome adversity and evil. This left very little room for pessimism, doubt, despair, failure and tragedy. Kozintsev and Pasternak's tragic realism, following Shakespeare's presentation of tragedy, as they saw it, was an inherently political statement. Pasternak, in an interview near the end of his life, maintained his dignity by claiming "I have not become a Socialist realist [...] but I have become a realist, and for that I am grateful" (quoted in Conquest 48). Even something as simple as the choice of shooting in black and white fed into this message, since Kozintsev chose the documentary style for *Hamlet* over the comic book colors of his *Don Quixote*, which used color stock to lampoon the dictates of Socialist realism. In Soviet life loss and death constituted the stuff of reality. The 20th century Soviet experience contained horrible, unthinkably catastrophic events visited upon the peoples and nations of the USSR. As Pasternak quips in his comments on *Hamlet*: "in Denmark they are used to everything" (219). Realism could hardly claim to be real for the Soviet audience without including tragedy, suffering and death.

The visual presentation of Kozintsev's graveyard scene, with the broken cross and Hamlet wearing what looks like a friar's or monk's robe, manifests Pasternak's translation's emphasis on Christian symbolism in cinematic imagery.[4] The image of the cross appears at several points in part two of the film and appears to serve different purposes. Ophelia wears a large cross when she is dressed in mourning after her father's funeral. Additionally, there is chanting, in Latin, for Polonius' wake — providing a contrast to Ophelia's "maimed rites" in the graveyard scene. There is also a large plain cross on the wall above Claudius and Gertrude's chairs in the council room, which lends an extra element of perversion to Claudius' ability to act against his conscience and against the rules of human decency at many points in the film (the main visual metaphor for this is the mirror and candles at the end of part one). Most importantly, the cross appears in the graveyard scene with the left side of the lateral beam broken off. This stone cross is the dominant feature in the landscape of the graveyard.

Hamlet is dressed as friar, in a robe resembling that of a Franciscan or Jesuit, and Horatio is dressed as a classic Wittenberg scholar, looking very like the famous picture of Erasmus, and as such he stands for philosophy as Hamlet represents Christianity. This is a brilliant visualization of the two characters, illustrating Hamlet's line "there are more things in heaven and earth, Horatio, than are dreamt of in your philosophy" (1.5.165–166). Kozintsev writes of Hamlet, "he knew of what Horatio's philosophy had dreamt, and of what it had not" (*STC* 160). Hamlet and Horatio collectively represent the freedom and flowering of thought at Wittenberg, where they have been at school, versus the stifling, repressive culture of Elsinore (Kozintsev embellishes this comparison in *STC* 157–168 in the chapter "Wittenberg and Elsinore"). The humanism of Wittenberg, which Hamlet and Horatio struggle to uphold, is unwelcome in Elsinore. For Kozintsev "there is probably not even another Shakespeare play in which the preachings of Humanism, and the negation of it, are pronounced with such passion" (*STC* 162). Humanism was a common "buzzword" in Soviet Marxist criticism: Kozintsev's underlying critique of Stalinism and its continuation into the Khrushchev years is fairly transparent here and serves as an example of critical, linguistic double-voicing. The Soviet State is the Elsinore that crushed the early aspirations of Socialism and Communism. The humanism that the Marxist critics saw as operative in *Hamlet* and its suppression by Claudius and Fortinbras allegorically represent the thwarted aspirations of Kozintsev and many other Soviet people.

In his costuming, Hamlet's fatalistic, metaphysical and moral sensibilities are visually opposed to Horatio's more sober, logical and objective worldview. As with most of the imagery of life outside the walls of Elsinore, the landscape of the graveyard reflects reality. Therefore the whole cross adorns Claudius' council room and Ophelia's chest, but the reality of hopelessness, poverty and death find expression in the broken cross of the graveyard. Additionally, the persecution of religion, which was especially harsh under Khrushchev, is undoubtedly conjured in this sequence as well (Service 368–370). Some commentators try to push parallels between the imagery here and Russian Orthodoxy (e.g. Rothwell claims that Ophelia

Horatio (Vladimir Erenberg) and Hamlet (Innokenti Smoktunovsky) in the graveyard in the film *Hamlet* (1964) directed by Grigory Kozintsev.

wears an Orthodox cross, but this is really not the case). The evocation is probably intended, but Kozintsev does try to make the imagery of Christianity more generic and more historically accurate (Denmark would not have been Orthodox, but Catholic, and, after the Reformation, also Protestant), which could certainly be seen as a screen intended to elide censorship during times of great difficulty for the Orthodox Church. Given the problems facing the Russian Orthodox Church, its hierarchy, and its believers, in the Soviet period (see the Ellis article in *Russian Cultural Studies*) any evocation of Christianity would have likely piqued the interest of Kozintsev's audience who were bombarded with anti-religious propaganda (there was even a Union of Militant Atheists). To depict the Orthodox Church obviously and sympathetically might have been too dangerous a move given the official Soviet position on religion and Khrushchev's renewal of persecutions, better to imply the Western Church and let the audience fill in the rest.[5]

Ophelia's *ad hoc* funeral, similar to the inappropriateness of Gertrude and Claudius' wedding following Old Hamlet's murder, bring to mind the efforts of the State under Khrushchev to "supplant religious practice" with "Soviet patriotism and secular ceremony" (Service 368). Hamlet's death pose, which mirrors the broken cross, adds him finally to this list of those who are victims of the rotten state and groups all such victims together as martyrs. With a nod to Pasternak's decidedly Christian interpretation of the play, Hamlet's dying pose echoes the broken cross prominently featured on the horizon of the gravedigger scene (Jorgens, 1977, 233; Kliman, 1988, 94; and others all cite this correspondence). The Christian symbolism of the ending functions here in much the same way as Sonnet 74 in the 1950s theatrical production. Christ, although he died for upsetting the existing religious and political order, was, for believers, resurrected. His soul and his message outlived his sacrifice, much as art outlives age and death in the Sonnet chosen for the play's ending. Pasternak and Kozintsev recognized, in keeping with the observations of historian Robert Service, that "the persistence of belief in God was displeasing to the atheistic state and was also regarded as a potential instrument for covert political opposition" (368–69). Hamlet's association with religion in the imagery of the film reinforces his identity as enemy of the State — both Elsinore and the USSR. Pasternak's religious, or rather "mystical," sensibilities were anathema to the State and were a large part of official censure of *Zhivago*. The replacement of religious ritual with rituals of state repeats in the treatment of Hamlet's death when Fortinbras takes over and decides the manner of Hamlet's funeral, giving him military rites, thereby co-opting his identification with spirituality and religion much as Claudius sought to silence Hamlet's oppositional voice.

Kozintsev's depiction of Hamlet and Horatio in the graveyard further suggests the image and ethos of the fool and folly. By his costume, Hamlet, as cleric and Christian, evokes the Russian Holy Fool with his close connection to the Christian Fool for Christ as described in 1 Corinthians.[6] Horatio, in his scholar's robe and hat, recalls Erasmus, who wrote *The*

Praise of Folly, a philosophical treatise on the wisdom of folly; the work also makes use of the *theatrum mundi* metaphor so prominent in *Hamlet*. Yorick, the court jester, is the significant absence in the scene and Hamlet both laments his death and takes on his role. In the absence of a jester or fool using his seemingly benign antics, riddles and jokes to point out the follies of the court and the king, Hamlet assumes this task. Hamlet, like Don Quixote, is only foolish in as much as his commitment to truth puts him in danger — he is not truly insane, he only seems so because of the foolish commitment to untruth of everyone else around him.

Hamlet's counterpoint in this regard is Ophelia, whose madness is real and without fruit, while Hamlet's feigned insanity reveals reality and leads to change. This is symbolized in Kozintsev's staging by her removing sticks from an empty fireplace to distribute as flowers: the lack of a fire symbolizes the absence of truth, the barren flowers her ineffectuality. Hamlet and Ophelia will both die victims of Claudius' regime, but Ophelia's death is useless and leaves no legacy (except for Laertes' desire for revenge, but he too will die without a trace). Hamlet's death, on the other hand, is productive and will have continuing effects. Kozintsev's envisioning Horatio as the Erasmian humanist figure departs from the Soviet scholars' habit of seeing Hamlet as a "humanist on a horse." Instead, Horatio represents humanism and Hamlet becomes a clerical figure. For instance, Akimov, in his controversial 1932 production, evidently depicted Hamlet as an Erasmian scholar type and even had an extra character named Erasmus make remarks during the play (Gibian 1952). It is likely that Kozintsev was familiar with this production. His costuming is perfectly in keeping with the religious themes in the play, Pasternak's development of them in his translation, and was perhaps inspired by previous interpretations, such as the Michael Chekhov *Hamlet*, which was unpopular with official critics because of its use of Christian imagery and themes.

Kozintsev's vision of *Hamlet* was actively engaged in dialogue with, and deliberately extended the relevance of Russian and Soviet interpretations of Shakespeare's *Hamlet*. Overall, Kozintsev's film version of 1964 is hopeful and positive, despite the severe disappointments and setbacks of the Khrushchev era. The film is realistic in its references to the difficulties and traumas suffered by the Soviet people under a stifling, autocratic regime, but the ultimate message is that individuals can — and must — make a difference, and that, no matter how cruel the censorship, art still can serve as a tool against tyranny. Hamlet's commitment to truth and his self-sacrificing bravery were perhaps even more relevant to the end of the Thaw period than they were immediately after Stalin's death. There was a sense of desperate urgency, the need to act decisively and persistently against the forces that aimed to return life to the manner of the Stalin era. The final deposition of Khrushchev and the appointment of Brezhnev in 1964 was demoralizing for the majority of Soviet citizens, who saw their hopes for lasting governmental reform crushed. For all his flaws and compromises with the conservatives, Khrushchev had stood for change and effected some positive changes in Soviet society. Essentially, the times had indeed changed; although the fruit of the aspirations of the post–Stalin period would not ripen until the 1980s, the groundwork was laid. Khrushchev quipped about his ouster that "perhaps the most important thing I did was just this — that they were able to get rid of me simply by voting. Stalin would have had them all arrested" (Hosking 540). Nonetheless, Brezhnev's "Stagnation" period would frustrate Soviets in all spheres and levels of society to the point that many of them would turn into Hamlets, ready to fight, however they could and at whatever cost, for the changes so desperately needed and desired.

Kozintsev did not release another motion picture after *Hamlet* until his *King Lear* of 1970, almost a full six years later. In such a prolific career, this lull is remarkable, but it speaks to the frustration and repression of cultural expression ushered in by the Brezhnev regime. Kozintsev's last extended period of low-production was during the Stalin era: his 1945 film *Simple People* was denounced and suppressed, after which he made one film, released in 1947, and another, his biography of Belinsky, released six years later, in 1953. In the meantime, much like Pasternak had turned to Shakespeare translation, or critics such as Lunacharsky had turned to Shakespeare studies under Stalin's repressions, Kozintsev seemed focused entirely on Shakespeare during the Brezhnev period, turning out his book *Shakespeare: Time and Conscience* in 1966, then entering production for the *Lear* film (released in 1971) while writing *King Lear: the Space of Tragedy* between 1968 and 1972, which was published in 1973, the year of his death.

CHAPTER FOUR

Kozintsev's Contexts 3: Russian and Soviet *King Lears* from the 18th Century through World War II

Shakespeare's plays were adapted to suit both ends of the political spectrum throughout the history of their appearance in Russia. Sometimes, the plays were translated, performed and written about in the service of the status quo. Conservative, pro-government artists and intellectuals used them to express their allegiance to and support of the tsarist system. Later on in the Soviet period, this sort of allegiance was expressed in criticism and performances that adhered to Party-derived Marxist ideology, reflecting the views of Marx, Engels and Lenin on history, and furthering the dictates of Socialist realism. In the 18th and 19th centuries the plays were claimed or disowned by conservatives and radical progressives, as well as Francophiles and Slavophiles. Shakespeare's plays were used to confront and critique the government and became a vehicle for expression of views about cultural and political problems that did not reflect the points of view endorsed by tsar or Party. *King Lear* provided especially useful fodder for this cultural warfare since the play features a powerful monarch whose errors have led to war, civil strife and the disruption of traditional familial and moral values. In the 19th century, especially for Pushkin, King Lear became a stand-in for Nicholas I and therefore the play was used as a screen for voicing objections to his policies. In the Soviet era, the king resembled Stalin, Khrushchev and/or Brezhnev, and the play was viewed as a profile of Soviet tyranny.

The representation in *King Lear* of the attempted destruction of the old order, as embodied by Lear, Kent and Gloucester, and the inception of a new one, as embodied by Edmund, Oswald, Cornwall, Goneril and Regan, spoke directly to the post–Revolutionary Soviet audience. In the end, the best of the older generation (and perhaps the best of the new one as well) prevails against the evils of the new order in the persons of Edgar, Cordelia and Albany. The virtuous of the new epoch are contemporaries of the new order's purveyors of evil, but do not subscribe to their ethos or methods (although they do use violence, but only under duress). All of these correspondences reverberated with the post–Revolutionary situation for Soviet citizens. In them the audience found the clash of ideologies, Civil War, generational conflict, the presence of "clientism," fawning and craven subservience to power, and moral compromise in the service of self-interest and self-preservation. The play also found particular poignancy during wartime, during the Civil War, World War II and the Cold War. For example, *King Lear* was performed frequently during the Second World War and through it artists and audiences found both a means to express their grief and trauma over the tumultuous events of the post–Bolshevik Revolutionary period, obliquely critiquing Stalin and Stalinism. In addition, the play served as a locus for solidarity and patriotism against the common external foes, the Nazis.

King Lear from the 1700s to the 20th Century

King Lear was translated and performed in Russia from just prior to the turn of the 19th century. Historian and writer Nikolai Karamzin (1766–1826) began translating Shakespeare at the same time that Catherine II (ruled 1762–1796) was adapting some of Shakespeare's plays, which brought Shakespearean characters and themes great popularity on the stage. Catherine's loose adaptations were marked by their use of Russian vernacular and their mockery of Russian Francophilism. Unlike Alexander Sumarokov (1717–1777), whose translation of *Hamlet* in 1748 relied upon a French neo-classical version, Karamzin used the English text as the basis for his translation of *Julius Caesar* in 1787. Karamzin's translation marked the start of a gradual movement away from classicism and free translations towards greater textual fidelity — as the use of the English sources indicates — and a more vernacular, Russian idiom.

As the Russians turned away from the cultural influences of France and Western Europe, focusing instead upon creating their own works and reconnecting with their own cultural and linguistic legacies, more Shakespeare translations were made from English sources. Shakespeare's dramatic style was adopted directly and not digested via revisionist French neoclassical versions. The Petrine taste for all things French waned by the turn of the 19th century, while affection for England and Germany grew. Karamzin's defense of Shakespeare's breaking of the classical "unities" coincided with the reassertion of Russian artistic and linguistic heritage, launched by Catherine the Great, which was finally fully effected in the mid–19th century by Alexander Pushkin, who was a great admirer of Shakespeare. Karamzin used the example of the storm in *Lear* to exhibit the English play's superior expression of emotion compared to the French-style plays that he felt were better suited to reading than acting: "they rend the soul; they thunder like the thunder described in them, capturing the reader's heart. [...] After that there is no need to ask: what is Lear's character, what is his soul?" (quoted in Stribrny 34) Translations of Shakespeare's plays proliferated in the period, although still mainly from the French, such as Nikolai Gnedich's *King Lear* of 1807, which Morozov claims was performed with success in the early 19th century (Morozov *SSS* 12). Karamzin is best known for his translation of *Julius Caesar*, in which, according to Stribrny, Brutus becomes the central hero, therefore setting into motion the alignment of Shakespeare with progressive politics in Russia. In fact, his *Julius* was burnt as "radical literature" under Catherine II in 1794, even though Karamzin was a conflicted, but fairly conservative monarchist (Stribrny 35). Pushkin, who was deeply influenced by Karamzin, continued this political use of Shakespeare in his Shakespearean commentaries and borrowings. There were also two other translations of *Lear* appearing around the same time, by Iakimov and Karatygin, which are described by Maurice Friedberg as "quite devoid of poetry," and "ponderous" (51).

In 1856 *Lear* was translated by the conservative writer and critic Alexander Druzhinin (1824–1864). Later Soviet critics, according to Friedberg, saw his choice of plays to translate as reactionary, especially his use of *Coriolanus*, asserting that Druzhinin chose themes promoting monarchy and class hierarchy in a deliberate counterpoint to Nikolai Chernyshevsky and other political progressives (51–52; 143). Both Druzhinin's and Gnedich's *King Lear* translations made Lear more sympathetic and highlighted the loyalty of his supporters, especially Kent, thereby making the play more about the restoration of the rightful king than about the flaws inherent in Lear's brand of monarchical feudalism (Friedberg 50–51; 143). Shakespeare then clearly served both ends of the political and cultural spectrum in the mid–19th century: the progressive, populist, Russophile or Slavophile groups as well as the conservative, monarchical, or Francophile camps. This is similar to the way Shakespeare was claimed earlier in the 19th century to be both representative of the oppressive French classicist influence and also a model for the new indigenous Russian literary movement.

Pushkin and Nicholas I

The influence of Alexander Pushkin (1799–1837), Russia's foremost and best-loved literary figure, brought Shakespeare fully onto the Russian cultural scene, and, at the same time, brought Russian language and literature into its own. Pushkin was among the first Russians to employ Shakespeare as mouthpiece for political and cultural dissent. Pushkin enthuses over Shakespeare, declaring "I feel that my soul has expanded suddenly, and I can create" (quoted in Stribrny 36). In keeping with Karamzin, he identifies the superiority of Shakespeare as a model for the Russian theater over the French: "the characters created by Shakespeare are not, as in Molière, types of this or that passion, this or that vice, but living beings, filled to overflowing with many passions and many vices; circumstances mold their varied and many-sided characters before the eyes of the audience" (quoted in Morozov, *SSU* 85). Instead of offering a one-dimensional, Tartuffe-like character, who behaves like a "hypocrite" in all situations, Pushkin argues that Shakespeare depicted Angelo in *Measure for Measure* as "the hypocrite [who] pronounces sentence with vainglorious severity; justifies his cruelty with the profound reasoning of a statesman; seduces innocence with powerful, attractive sophistries" (quoted in Bethea 80). Pushkin's embrace of Shakespeare's style of characterization and plot construction, along with his rejection of the neo-classical and French influences on arts and letters, led to Russia's emergence as a literary and artistic nation on its own terms and in its own language. The critic Vissaron Belinsky was also part of the early 19th-century movement away from French and German influences, and like Pushkin, favored the use of Russian language and the use of Shakespeare as a model for the new Russian national drama. This brand of Russian patriotism and pride also ensured Pushkin's place as Russia's most beloved poet. The man who called Shakespeare "our father" later became the "our everything" ("*nashe vse*") of the Russian people (Bethea 78, 76). Later on, Kott and then Kozintsev would call Shakespeare "our contemporary," extending his adoption as honorary Russian into the Soviet period and into the satellite states of the USSR (Kott was Polish).

The most well-known of Pushkin's Shakespeare-influenced works is *Boris Godunov*, which was written and completed when Pushkin was in internal exile under Alexander I, just before Nicholas I came into power in 1825, around the time of the suppression of the revolt of the Decembrists, with whose cause Pushkin sympathized.[1] The play owes more perhaps to Shakespeare's histories than it does to *King Lear*, yet the scene of the confrontation between Godunov and the holy fool, Nikolka, owes a debt to Shakespeare's development of the relationship between the Fool and Lear (O'Neil 31).[2] In this brief scene, Nikolka waits, begging for alms outside the cathedral, for Godunov to emerge. Nikolka twice alludes to the Tsar's guilt in killing the rightful heir to the throne, Dmitri. Although the Tsar's advisers take exception to the fool's treasonous insubordination, Godunov insists the fool be left unharmed — he even asks the fool to pray for him, which could be read as an oblique acknowledgment of his guilt. The scene is reminiscent of Lear's Fool's berating Lear about his mistakes and weak character, but doing so without drawing calamity upon himself, as did Cordelia and Kent who lack the license of the Fool.

Pushkin referred to himself and his position under the patronage and sometime protection of Nicholas I in just these terms, calling himself *yurodivy* (a fool) to the tsar, with his writing as the medium of his dissent. Pushkin wrote tellingly in a letter penned after he finished *Godunov*: "Zhukovsky says that the Tsar will pardon me because of my tragedy — hardly, my dear fellow. Although it is written in a well-meaning spirit, I couldn't hide my ears completely beneath the holy fool's pointed cap. They stick out!" (quoted in Fomichev 140; Blustain 190). Pushkin's play was highly controversial; although it was completed in 1825 (the end of Alexander I's reign and the start of Nicholas I's), it was not passed by the censors until 1830. Among other things, his depiction of the outspoken dissatisfaction of the people, the characterization of the pretender as a renegade monk who was not the true son of Ivan IV, along with the portrayal of clergy and tsar onstage did not sit well with the censors in a time when Church and State were synonymous; moreover, it was forbidden to portray clergy or monarchs on the stage during the reign of Nicholas. Although the play was published in 1831, it was not performed until after Pushkin's death in 1870 (Blustain 186–187). Some of Pushkin's self-authored changes, done to placate the censors, however minimally, seem to have brought his version of events into line with the preferred Romanov history, even while other alterations actually added further ambiguity. Most famously, the change from the people's shouts of support for the crowned pretender to their silence at the end of the play is an example of Pushkin's eloquent ambivalence. Reading *Boris Godunov*, scholar Chester Dunning enlarges the new ending along these lines: "the silence of the *narod* is Pushkin's own stilled voice — now tamed, now safe for the likes of Nicholas and the censors but still (obscurely) speaking to his audience and saying: This is not right, and we should not be silent" (122).³ In addition to Pushkin's resentment of censorship, *Boris* raised other controversial political themes. As discussed previously in the context of the banned translations of *Hamlet* from the early 19th century, Alexander I probably owed his throne to the murder of Paul I, his father. This is just one example of the many potentially "uncomfortable truths" uttered by the fool in Pushkin's play, submitted against the official history of the Romanovs (Emerson xvi).

Turgenev's *King Lear of the Steppes*

Writer Ivan Turgenev (1818–1883) was an admirer of Shakespeare, and several of his works contain themes from the plays, such as *Hamlet of the Shchigrov District*. Turgenev, like Pushkin, lived under the oppressive censorship of Nicholas I and he too used Shakespeare as a means to subvert tsarist dominance and to critique Russian culture. Turgenev's most direct adaptation from Shakespeare is his story *King Lear of the Steppes,* published in 1870. This tale is told in a frame story by a man who grew up in the same town as the protagonist Harlov, a provincial landowner and beloved friend of the narrator's mother. Harlov, of impressive size and stature ("every inch a king"), decides to retire and pass on his property to his two undeserving daughters, one of whom is married to an obsequious, craven husband, who appears to be a hybrid of both Cornwall and Oswald. There is no Cordelia figure, which adds to the deliberate moral bleakness of the tale. As in the source play, Harlov is treated very badly by these daughters upon his divestiture. The once submissive son-in-law becomes a dominant figure and, Edmund-like, begins an affair with his wife's sister, who is unmarried. There is a quasi-Fool figure in the person of Souvenir, who comes across as a foppish freeloader and mercilessly taunts Harlov, eventually driving him to seek revenge upon his daughters for neglecting him. Harlov literally starts tearing down his house from the rooftop, dying grotesquely and pathetically in the effort when he is crushed beneath a falling beam.

Turgenev's story is an entertainingly dramatic critique of the moral hypocrisy and bankruptcy of Russian provincial life. Although the serfs had been officially freed in 1861, Turgenev was still concerned with the iniquities and injustices suffered by Russian peasants and farmers. He bemoaned the intellectual and ethical corruption of the privileged classes, as is shown in his depiction of the people's suffering under the selfish stewardship of Harlov, his daughters and his son-in-law. The depiction of the majority of the non-peasant characters in the story is similarly negative, showing them motivated by greed and self-interest, such as the avaricious would-be suitor to Harlov's unmarried daughter and Harlov's crooked lawyer. To underscore the general lack of care for the impoverished majority in the midst of the upper class's greed and materialism, the local priest is shown dressed in a ragged old robe and suffering from extreme hunger (as are the malnourished "small boys with their shirts open to reveal large stomachs"): "all bore witness to a joyless and hard-working life, for his parish was extremely poor" (Turgenev 223). Turgenev's thematic focus anticipates later Marxist interpretations of *King Lear*, which emphasize those passages and lines in which Lear laments his neglect of "poor naked wretches" (3.4.28) and points out the moral hypocrisy of people in power (e.g., the storm scene and his conversation with Gloucester in act four). The crucial difference is that Turgenev's Lear figure never comes to similar realizations, though it is suggested that his surviving daughter chooses a severe penitential practice after Harlov's death in a somewhat perverse effort to make atonement.

After enduring prison and internal exile under Nicholas I, Turgenev moved abroad, and continued adding to a string of works critical of Russia and the Russians. His exile explains his extremely pessimistic reworking of the source play in his story — he had in a sense given up on his homeland. As with his borrowings from *Hamlet*, Turgenev's use of *Lear* served his critique of the political and moral landscape of his times. Nina Diakonova writes that Harlov's "revenge stands as an embodiment of the hideous cruelty of Russian life" (105). Although Harlov himself never realizes that he had "taken too little care" of the people in his community and in his employ, Turgenev made sure that his readers understood the poverty and desperation experienced by the under-privileged and recognized whom to blame for it. Harlov's inability to see the error of his ways, to forgive, or to feel compassion for the poor departs from Shakespeare's development of Lear's character in the service of Turgenev's larger purpose: Diakonova notes that Harlov remains "disfigured by ignorance and absolute power" (107). Turgenev's story reveals that the freeing of the serfs, although this was a great boon to the progressive cause, did not necessarily erase the backwards mentality and skewed power relationships entrenched by years of abuse and inequality. Hence his story lacks even the glimmers of hope at the end of Shakespeare's bleak drama.

Anton Chekhov

Writer Anton Chekhov (1860–1904) often used Shakespearean themes and borrowings in his works, including direct quotation from Russian translations of the plays. (Chekhov could not read English and relied upon Russian translations.) Chekhov's plays are much less overtly politically subversive than the works of Pushkin or Turgenev, yet his negative critique of late 19th century Russians' character and culture is palpable. The play that contains the clearest debt to *Lear* is *The Three Sisters* (which also contains themes from *Macbeth*), although glancing reference has been made to *Lear*'s influence on *Uncle Vanya* and some other of Chekhov's major and minor works (such as in analyses by Rzepka and Winner). In his article on Chekhov and *The Three Sisters*, Charles Rzepka notes correspondences between the Lear-Cordelia relationship and the characters Tchebutykin and Irina. Tchebutykin dotes upon Irina as a favorite and expresses a wish to retire and live near her, much like Lear dreams of living out the end of his life with Cordelia in prison (Rzepka 20). Rzepka also points to the relationship between Solyoni and Tusenbach as parallel to that of the Fool and King Lear. Solyoni jests and uses wordplay with other characters, making himself into a type of the Shakespearean fool similar to Lear's Fool and Feste of *Twelfth Night* (Rzepka 19).

Leo (Lev) Tolstoy

Unlike his friends and colleagues Turgenev and Chekhov, Lev (Leo) Tolstoy (1828–1910) was decidedly not an admirer of Shakespeare and was a very famous and vocal member of a minority of Russian artists and critics who disliked (or at least admitted to disliking) Shakespeare. Unlike Russian nationalists such as Pushkin, or Slavophiles such as Dostoevsky, Tolstoy envisioned a Russian national and cultural identity without Shakespeare as a model. On the contrary, Tolstoy's political and cultural worldview eschewed all things foreign, even the Bard. In 1906, Tolstoy's essay "Shakespeare and the Drama" appeared, containing a lengthy disparaging of Shakespeare's plays, with special derision set aside for *King Lear*. Tolstoy accused Shakespeare of despising the common people and being in favor of the monarchial status-quo, being irreligious and anti-humanitarian, and creating characters that are unnatural, insincere and undifferentiated. As for poetry and thematic content, Shakespeare "is not in earnest but is playing with words" (364). Shakespeare is, in his final estimation, "not only non-moral, but plainly immoral" (382). Tolstoy's summary and criticism of *King Lear* illustrate how the play manifested all of Tolstoy's grievances against Shakespeare. Tolstoy claims to separate his critique into two parts, the first an impartial recapitulation of the plot, the second his interpretation of it. Yet Tolstoy definitely failed to render anything like the impartial recap of the play's events that he promises to deliver before moving into his critique in part two; rather, his "objective" retelling of the plot quickly succumbs to brutal editorializing.

Kozintsev observes in his 1941 essay on *King Lear* that Tolstoy wrote "in the language of inventory, he enumerated metaphor and hyperbole, maintaining the unruffled intonation of protocol" (55). For Kozintsev this was "particularly inappropriate language for the dynamism of Shakespeare. Setting forth the external action in detail, he omitted everything that gave any sense to the scene, as though he had neither noticed its inner development nor cared to hear its poetic subtext" (55). Tolstoy disregarded the fact that plays depend upon staging to be truly effective, especially on the level of characterization, a concession he acknowledges only briefly in mentioning *Hamlet* on the stage (352). Tolstoy was unwilling to account for linguistic and cultural differences in his exasperation over the failure of humor on the part of Lear's Fool (316 and elsewhere). Tolstoy's bias against Shakespeare appears willful at many points. For example, he repeatedly calls characters and situations "unnatural" and "inappropriate" without stopping to consider that these problems in human relationships are, in fact, major thematic elements of the play, which are likely meant to be more illustrative than prescriptive. Nor does Tolstoy consider that the impression given by the play of a world without justice or values might also have been part of a cautionary message and not somehow a vision of what could or should be.

Tolstoy bemoaned the intractable Russian worship of Shakespeare, blaming the Germans for its existence and suggesting that, despite over one hundred years of Shakespeare's popularity in Russia — which at the turn of the century showed no signs of abating — it was a craze or a fad that would inevitably pass. Tolstoy was correct in seeing a pattern of foreign influence on Russian arts and letters that was demoralizing and marginalizing. Yet it is also true that Tolstoy followed foreign forms in his own novels — inevitably, since the novel form itself was a European export to Russia. Shakespeare is actually to be credited for helping Russians eschew the constraints of foreign influence and develop their own literary culture and therefore does not deserve Tolstoy's wholesale rejection of him as useless to a genuinely Russian cultural revival.

There are several theories as to what led Tolstoy to such an extreme position against Shakespeare and, by extension, against the prevailing opinion of his fellow countrymen. Tolstoy's hostility to Germany precluded his interpreting Russian admiration for Shakespeare as not just another version of foreign influence, as it had been with French neo-classicism. Despite the fact that it was indeed German Romanticism that inspired Russians to return to Shakespeare as a model, this led to the development of Russian language and forms in literature, not a slavish imitation of all things German. Zdenek Stribrny illustrates that Tolstoy, as a novelist and aristocrat who came of age and developed as a writer during the influence of French neo-classicism in 19th century Russia, would have had lingering difficulties with Shakespeare's style for precisely the reasons that Russians who had rejected neo-classicism loved and imitated him (50–53). Shakespeare's departure from the artificial norms of neo-classicist aesthetics appealed to Russians who were tired of the Petrine subservience to Western culture. For Tolstoy, however, the identification of Shakespeare with France and Germany was simply too difficult to shake off.

Taking a more psychoanalytic turn, George Orwell, in his 1947 essay "Lear, Tolstoy and the Fool," speculates that Tolstoy's vehement attack upon *King Lear*, selected from the entire Shakespearean *oeuvre* for special abuse, might have been due to his ironically analogous situation to the aging King. Orwell notes that Tolstoy had undergone his own failed renunciation of title and worldly goods when he decided to try to adopt peasant life (296–7). Tolstoy endured ridicule for this decision and, like Lear, had his offspring turn against him (Orwell 297). Stribrny writes that Tolstoy had, towards the end of his life when this essay was written, become pietistic following his religious conversion, and therefore had little patience with anything that smacked of moral ambiguity (50–53). Whatever the consciously political, religious and aesthetic objections, or the unconsciously personal factors at play in Tolstoy's anti–Shakespeareanism, it still fits into the general trend of Russians discussing political and national issues through Shakespeare.

Kozintsev, unlike Orwell and many other critics of Tolstoy's position, remained generous and reverential towards Tolstoy, positing that his critique of Shakespeare might have even been embellished or even faked in order to make his point clear. Kozintsev writes "Tolstoy, who well understood music, feigned deafness only to demonstrate that art deprived of an ethicoreligious idea is not necessary to people" (55). In other words, in the service of his sense of duty to his fellow man, Tolstoy was rigorous and unbending in his insistence that art speak to common people and provide them with moral and spiritual instruction. Kozintsev continues, "at this time, [i.e., circa 1906, just after the failed revolt of 1905] poetry struck the novelist as no more than unprincipled mischief-making" (55). In this light, Tolstoy is easily understood as a sympathetic figure to an idealistic Marxist such as Kozintsev. Tolstoy's position, quite ironically, anticipated the dictates of Socialist realism. Kozintsev was likely not a supporter of enforced Socialist realism or of the sort of myopia evidenced in Tolstoy's later opinions, in the sense that they both unduly constrained the freedom of artistic expression. Yet it is clear from Kozintsev's writings that he was, like Tolstoy, in favor of art that offered a moral point of view and that was comprehensible and relevant to regular people, not just an artistic elite.

The Progressives

Other anti–Shakespeareans of the late 19th century include some of the progressives, such as Chernyshevsky, who saw Shakespeare as an aristocrat with monarchist sympathies that ran against the cause of the common people. This position unexpectedly allied Chernyshevsky with conservative translators such as Druzhinin, who chose to translate Shakespeare precisely in order to rebut the liberal cause. Just as Tolstoy's objections ran counter to prevailing literary preferences, so too did some progressives, such as Chernyshevsky, work against the predominant view of the Communists and Bolsheviks, who, following Marx and Engels, saw Shakespeare as exposing the corruption of the monarchy and taking the side of the common people.

Soviet-era critic Yuri Levin, writing about Shakespeare in the 19th century, notes that some of the most politically-progressive artists and thinkers of the later century rejected Shakespeare, even though his works were still largely venerated and praised. Levin cites revolutionary democrat Chernyshevsky disparaging Russian Bardolatry as well as suggesting that Shakespeare's works were not sufficiently politically engaged (92–93). In a foreshadowing of Soviet Socialist realism, art was, according to most radical and progressive intellectuals of the late 19th century, supposed to be created in the service of solving social problems. Some therefore branded Shakespeare as writing "art for art's sake" (Levin 93). Levin, himself a product of the Soviet era and therefore more pro-Shakespeare than his pre–Revolutionary counterparts, is quick to defend: "Shakespeare's objective art is not an explicitly engaged art and the implicit democratic passion that pervades his every line was unrecognized by most Russian men of letters active in the [eighteen-]sixties" (93). This distinction between the implicit and the explicit in characterizing Shakespearean adaptations that seem politically disengaged is not just an historical reassessment, but also a cue for readers to look more deeply and find the submerged currents of dissent. Levin's description utilizes Aesopian code for readers and viewers searching, as ever, for the under-the-radar critiques of the government. Shakespeare, because he was associated with the French neo-classical and German Romantic literary and aesthetic movements, was rejected by some progressives as Russian political and cultural life moved closer to revolution. In their quest to foster national pride by returning to an emphasis on Russian cultural heritage and the Russian language they had little use for Shakespeare. This anti–Shakespeare sentiment would not last long and was not pervasive. Shakespeare's adoption as an honorary Russian was never disowned by a majority in any faction. The large number of new translations of Shakespeare appearing around the turn of the 20th century attests to this. Moreover, the influence of Marx and Engels, who found in Shakespeare a chronicler of the problems inherent to the rise of capitalism, ensured Shakespeare's survival into the Soviet era.

Alexander Blok

After the Revolution of 1917 Shakespeare once again served the purposes of both ends of the political spectrum. Shakespeare's works were read in light of Party-line Marxist theory, yet they were also interpreted in ways that highlighted their more subversive themes, ones that could be used to question the validity of the Bolshevik cause. Alexander Blok (1880–1921) was a prominent Symbolist poet. He, like Maxim Gorky, Boris Pasternak, and many other writers, was committed to revolutionizing art during the experimental early 20th century. His focus turned to Shakespeare towards the end of his life. Blok served briefly on the Bolshoi Drama Theater's board of directors and lectured on Shakespeare for the actors, as well as for soldiers of the Red Army who attended a production of *Much Ado About Nothing*. The three wartime plays Blok spoke about in his brief tenure on the Bolshoi board all had martial themes and military characters: *Much Ado*, *Othello* and *Lear*. Between 1918 and 1922 the Bolshoi also produced *Macbeth*, *Hamlet*, and *Julius Caesar*, each of which is highly political and contains themes or scenes of battle (Gibian 25). Evidently, Blok insisted on producing *Macbeth*, a play about war, murder and corruption, even if it were to be performed "before an empty house" (quoted in Gibian

25). His lecture on *King Lear* was written and published in 1920, and therefore appeared during the Civil War. It is impossible to read this essay without making connections between Blok's reading of the play and the country's terrible condition. The action that impels the chaos of the play's unfolding is the division of the kingdom, from which it is not difficult to extrapolate that an audience whose country was in the midst of a civil war might find its own plight reflected.[4] In fact this correspondence seems precisely the reason for Blok's interest in Shakespeare's tragedies: they spoke to his "insane years and days" (quoted in Gibian 25). Many Russian people were fleeing into voluntary exile or were forcibly expatriated, thereby adding to the resonance and pathos of the flight of Kent, whom King Lear condemned to internal exile. Further correspondences to the contemporary situation could be found in Cordelia's banishment to external exile and Edgar's internal exile from his father's home. Blok's breakdown of *King Lear's* characters allegorizes the state of human attitudes and relationships in the Civil War period by dividing the characters into four generations engaged in a bitter conflict. Blok repeats three words over and over again in his description of *Lear*: "adult," "dry" and "bitter." He claims, perhaps in a solipsistic projection, that at the time of Shakespeare's composition of the play, the early 17th century, there was a "dark stretch" (18). By this he implies the period of transfer of power from Elizabeth I to James I, again, evoking the uncertainty of a nation awaiting the outcome of its own transition of power. Kozintsev, in a discussion of the influence of Goya on the designer Tyshler's sketches for Solomon Mikhoels' 1935 staged *Lear*, cites the Inquisition, another period in which the clash of ideas descended into violence. He writes, "every century knows its own inhumanity, and the grotesque thereof. In every century, people sometimes feel that they dream a walking nightmare" (*STC* 43). Like Blok, Kozintsev identifies the unhappy recognition and brotherhood of all peoples who have endured war.

Blok's final assessment of the ending of *Lear* injects into it the horror experienced in the post–Revolutionary "dark stretch" for a great number of Russians, whether those on the side of the Bolsheviks, against them, or merely victimized bystanders. Of Lear's storm, taken metaphorically, he says, "the darkness will not triumph, but the light comes too late" (23). This is an allusion to the Gospel of St John 1:5: "And the light shines in the darkness, and the darkness did not overcome it," which underscores the Biblically apocalyptic themes in *King Lear* pointing to "the promised end." Knowledge and understanding are born of suffering, even irrational, disproportionate suffering in which it seems that the side of light and good cannot win. Those people who fight darkness suffer unjustly and are destroyed before they can see the fruits of their labors — if their actions bear fruit at all. Blok concludes:

> Why was all this written? In order to open our eyes on those bottomless pits which do exist in life and which it is not within our own volition to avoid. But, if there are such frightful abysses in this life, if it really does happen that there are times when, although vice does not conquer and does not triumph, virtue does not triumph either, for she has come too late — must we not then look for another and more perfect life?
>
> Not one word of this crosses the lips of that cruel, sad, bitter artist Shakespeare. Courageously, he ends on a full stop, on the exhortation:
> *The weight of this sad time we must obey.*
> After all, he is an artist, not a priest, and he seems to repeat the ancient words "learn in suffering" [24].

Blok tellingly omits the rest of the ending lines: "Speak what we feel and not what we ought to say. The oldest hath borne most: we that are young shall never see so much, nor live so long" (5.5.324–327). It is unclear which translation(s) Blok knew, but both Q and F contain these final lines, even though in Q they are attributed to Albany and not Edgar. Given the advanced state of Shakespearean scholarship and performance in Russia, it is highly unlikely that Blok was unaware of the rest of the speech, so his omission is significant. Blok was dying when he gave this speech. He had also withdrawn from writing original verse and taken refuge, as was the pattern among so many Soviet critics and artists, in the world of Shakespeare. It was safer to use Shakespeare's plays as a screen behind which to confront the truth than it was to create original works. "Another and more perfect life" represents Blok's capitulation to death, literally and creatively, and also his despair over the fate of his country. Blok's fraught career as a writer came to a close with his position at the Bolshoi Drama Theater, studying Shakespeare during wartime as his health rapidly declined. His Lear lecture betrays a great deal about his weariness with war, both that of the artist against oppression and that of the Reds versus Whites.

Blok's dystopian vision, expressed through *King Lear*, is a pointed rebuttal to the promised utopia of the Bolsheviks. Other writers and thinkers of this period were quick to anticipate the failure of the Bolshevik utopia. Given the fact that the institution of the Socialist new world order was established through violence, suppression and enforceable (and often violently enforced) ideological and aesthetic uniformity, there was ample evidence to support the dystopian point of view taken by many writers and artists. Yevgeny Zamyatin's *We* appeared around the same time as

Blok's essay on *King Lear*. The novel presents a rigidly organized, totalitarian state, highly technological and urban, in which people are reduced to numbers and wear identical outfits, as if the whole empire were a penal colony or army barracks. The ruler, the "Benefactor," was bald, no doubt an evocation of Lenin. The government's solution to the problem of those people who did not welcome the new regime at its inception was the creation of an enormous, impenetrable wall separating "One State" from the rest of the world. For those remaining within who come to question the system, the government finally discovers how to surgically alter their brains, rendering them obedient automatons.

Naturally, this work of fiction was banned by the Soviet authorities under the newly formed *Glavlit*, whose function was to censor works unacceptable to the Leninist regime (Service 137). It was published abroad in English 1924, but was not published in Russia until 1988. Zamyatin eventually was allowed to emigrate in 1931. Many artists and other citizens were surprised and dismayed at the State's crackdown on freedom of expression after the promising freedoms of the pre–Revolutionary period. Artists and intellectuals initially supported the Bolsheviks in large numbers, thinking that the Party would foster and encourage artistic and intellectual development much as it did other innovations, both social and technological. Creative people, like many peasants and workers, anticipated a utopia, as a continuation of the zeitgeist of the 1910s. These utopian visions quickly dissolved, however. Historian Robert Service writes, "the October Revolution and the Civil War were awesome experiences from which most intellectuals recoiled in shock. Many entered a mental black hole where they tried to rethink their notions about the world" (139). Soviet writers found a vehicle in the events of *King Lear* and the experiences of its characters, especially Lear himself, to engage this sense of shock and disorientation. Lear's world crumbles. People enter into voluntary and involuntary internal and external exile. Civil war ensues and enables a military invasion from France. A new worldview emerges with Edmund and his followers, and its establishment is (almost) effected through violence and the radical dissolution of traditional values such as loyalty to family. Edmund seeks to create his own utopia based upon self-interest and ultimate power. Lear enters "a mental black hole" during this time of disintegration and chaos only to emerge into understanding too late: his own utopian vision of his and Cordelia's happy retreat into their prison cell is cut short by her death. For many Soviet citizens, there was no escape from the walking nightmare except in death; too many people either died because of the regime or died before they could see it overcome.

From Civil War to Bolshevik State

At several points in his 1941 essay on *King Lear*, Kozintsev engages themes relating to dystopia in *King Lear*.[5] His emphasis on the ravages of war, both civil and foreign, the disintegration of the social order, and the fracturing of social and familial relationships point to an anti-utopian sensibility analogous to that evidenced by Blok, Zamyatin, and others, who came to the realization that the finest aspirations of the Bolshevik Revolution had been co-opted by tyranny, war, famine, repression and imprisonment. Of Kozintsev's book *Shakespeare: Time and Conscience*, in which his 1941 essay is reprinted, Stribrny writes: "ostensibly condemning the Nazi terror, he was equally concerned about the immediate Stalin past. He was a Marxist, convinced of the justice and humanity of Socialism but, for that very reason, he became an anti–Stalinist" (106). Perhaps more than any other Shakespeare play, *King Lear* lends itself to a dystopian reading. The play presents a world in which traditional values and relationships are overturned with nothing but death, betrayal, conflict and chaos to fill the void. The survival of Albany and Edgar and the heroism of the servant who defends Gloucester, serve as glimmers of hope, despite the fact that the play ends with the deaths of Cordelia, Lear (and possibly the Fool and Kent), all of whom display courage and virtue, but are only victorious in a moral sense. The direction for the future is uncertain: there are no guarantees that the "gored state" will be healed.

Several of the Soviet critics mentioned in this study abandoned the dangers of trying to create original works, instead turning to studying, adapting and translating Shakespeare, much as Blok did comparatively early in the post–1917 period. Boris Pasternak's shift from writing poetry to translating Shakespeare occurred as a response first to Lenin's and then Stalin's crackdowns on freedom in artistic expression. A similar pattern appears in the careers of Soviet critics Smirnov and Morozov, indicating that intellectuals were also constrained by the new government's tastes and agendas. It is apparent from the trajectory of Kozintsev's career that he too was compelled to move away from the experimentation and novelty of his early work in the '20s. As a result, he devoted more energy to Shakespearean adaptation and scholarship, especially after World War II. Shakespeare served as a shield, like Hamlet's guise of insanity or Lear's Fool's imbecility and jesting, masking or excusing the presence of criticism of the "Tsar." The violence and chaos that accompanied the Revolution shocked many, even among the supporters of the new State. Trauma and fear quickly supplanted zeal and optimism and it seems like retreat was forced upon people from above, yet also a result of their willing retreat.

Anatoly Lunacharsky

Anatoly Lunacharsky's (1875–1933) essay, "Bacon and the Characters of Shakespeare's Play" (published posthumously in 1934), is a wide-ranging work that considers a series of Shakespeare's characters as manifestations of "the emancipated individual": man acting from reason, freed from the constraints of "religious and moral nonsense, all preconceived opinions, all false values" (25, 26). Lunacharsky was a prominent figure from the earliest days of the Revolution, an early member of the Bolsheviks and Lenin's first Commissar of Enlightenment (which later became the Ministry of Education) and therefore was instrumental in spreading literacy and art all over the territory of the Soviet Union. After 1929, however, Lunacharsky lost his important public offices, no doubt due to Stalin's revised program for artistic oversight and aesthetics. Like many of the figures studied here, Lunacharsky supported the artistic avant-garde of the pre–Stalin period, which had, by the time of his essay's release, been removed under the banner of Socialist realism. In his essay, his first examples are characters representative of the drawbacks of the Renaissance ethos whom he labels the "cynics": Richard III, Edmund and Iago. Lunacharsky's analysis is historicized and based upon close reading of the plays these three figures inhabit. The political players and situations of the 1930s are clearly evoked in his selection of these particular characters. He ascribes to each of them a degree of "Machiavellianism," thereby directing his readers to envision their relationships to the world of politics and power. The emancipated individuals Lunacharsky describes seem to embody the opportunists of the Stalin era: those men, like Edmund, who would happily take advantage of the moral vacuum created by a violent shift in political and cultural values.

Historian Oleg Khlevniuk, in his study of the Stalin-era Gulag, writes: "as was typical in an age of terror, both mean and mediocre people, as well as scoundrels, had a better chance of survival, even promotion, than ordinary, decent people" (170). These "mean people" operated from both the need to survive and a lack of scruples, the one being dependent upon the other at a time when integrity and honesty could lead to jail or death. Lunacharsky speculates that "Shakespeare ask[ed] himself: why has a type of man come into being who is prepared to put his reason at the service of careerism, of ambition, and who makes so dangerous a servant of this reason, so sharp, a poisoned dagger of his will?" (35) The question Lunacharsky puts into Shakespeare's mouth is appropriate to this early part of the Stalin era, as repression, corruption, famine and imprisonment became widespread and required complicity in and enforcement of injustice among the general population.

Lunacharsky consulted the most influential translation of *Lear* before Pasternak's, Alexander Druzhinin's, first published in 1856. He cites a lengthy passage from Druzhinin's preface commentary on Edmund, followed by the text of Edmund's "thou, Nature, art my goddess" speech. As with his treatment of Richard III and Iago in the same section of the essay, Lunacharsky's allusions to Stalin and the problematic values represented by his regime filter through his ostensible focus on Shakespeare's characters. He quotes Druzhinin: "Edmund is no mere narrow egoist, neither is he a blind villain capable of taking pleasure in his own ill-doing. Edmund is a richly gifted character, but a character who has been cankered at the root and who, because of this, can only use his exceptional talents to the detriment of his fellows. Edmund's genius is evident in his every step, in his every word, for not one step does he take and not one movement does he make which has not been carefully calculated" (quoted in Lunacharsky 35). It is interesting to note the differences in political motivation between the 20th-century Soviet Lunacharsky and the reactionary 19th-century Druzhinin, who was against the liberal, progressive political views of his time (Friedberg 51–52; 143). Lunacharsky's citation of Druzhinin's text and his assent to his commentary is perhaps an indicator of a subtly "reactionary" attitude on Lunacharsky's part. Certainly, one can also see here a sideways glance at Stalin and his legion of lackeys, from the highest to the lowest rungs of governance — Richards, Edmunds and Iagos who replicate themselves even as they become smaller, much like the Russian *Matryoshka* nesting dolls.

The larger purpose of Lunacharsky's essay was to describe a kind of moral movement from a collective mentality to an individualistic one during the Renaissance, personified, in his estimation, by Francis Bacon and dramatized by Shakespeare in his plays, specifically through development of certain character types. Bacon, for Lunacharsky, represented an amoral type of person who had thrown off all limitations of faith and morality, which Lunacharsky ascribed to a reaction against the Medieval hegemony of the Church. This "freedom" served only reason and self-interest, which Lunacharsky characterized as Machiavellian and saw most clearly embodied by Richard III, Edmund and Iago. Here, as elsewhere, Lunacharsky follows a common Materialist historical reading, but with an oddly disconcerting, reactionary sort of conservatism poking through. Kozintsev also discusses Richard III and Iago in his 1941 essay on *King Lear* in the same section as his meditation on the Machiavellian nature of Edmund's philosophy (*STC* 93). Of Richard Kozintsev writes "Machiavellianism is shown [...] in the scale of historical phenomena" (*STC* 93). Similarly, Iago "is an experimenter [...] testing a hypothesis concerning the immutability of man's animal nature" (*STC* 93–94). Kozintsev's discussion of Edmund resembles Lunacharsky's estimation of Bacon in seeing Edmund as revolting against religion and other traditional beliefs and structures merely to serve his own will. Edmund, according to Kozintsev, "despises superstition and religious belief. He laughs at astrology. He is amused by ideas of fidelity to sovereign and attachment to family" (*STC* 94). There are several ways these configurations could be analogized to the situation of post–Revolutionary, Stalinist Russia, but certainly a sense of pessimism and defeatism is bleeding through here, as it is in the example of Blok's essay. For all three writers *King Lear* provides a kind of post–Revolutionary double-sided mirror: reflecting on one side idealistic types who would retain their moral center in the aftermath of the destruction of the kingdom; on the other, depicting those who would fill the void with their desires for revenge, power and control.

Stage productions of Shakespeare's plays abounded in the Soviet era, much as they had in the 19th century. *King Lear* only grew in popularity in the theater after 1917. According to Soviet critic and performance historian Mikhail Morozov, the next significant *Lear* production after the 1920 Bolshoi presentation under Blok was in 1923 at the First Studio of the Moscow Art Theatre (*SSS* 34). This production was in keeping with the spirit of the times, as the trauma and tumult of the Civil War gave way to the chaos and upheaval inherent in the reformation of culture and society by the newly-situated Soviet government. In this interpretation the storm was taken as a central image and metaphor. Morozov quotes a critic who wrote of this production: "this storm is created not only by nature, but also by the violent passions of men. The purport of this scene is to reveal the inner essence of man by the pathos of chaos. The brutal scenes in this tragedy are merely the elements of the same storm" (quoted in *SSS* 35). As evidenced by the Blok commentary and the Bolshoi production, *Lear* was the ideal Shakespeare text for depicting the terrible, chaotic changes taking place between 1917 (the Revolution) and 1924 (Lenin's death), especially the violence of the revolt, the Civil War, and the consolidation of power that followed.

King Lear and the "Jewish Question"

Morozov notes that *King Lear* was not performed again until 1935, the year of the opening of what by all accounts was the first landmark production of *Lear* in the Soviet Union, that of the State Jewish Theatre (GOSET), directed by Sergei Radlov, starring Solomon Mikhoels, who, like Kozintsev, was a "People's Artist of the USSR" (*SSS* 35).[6] The play was translated into Yiddish — not from English, but from Russian — by Shmuel Halkin.[7] Towards the end of the 19th century and throughout the first half of the 20th, there were many adaptations and translations of Shakespeare and *King Lear* into Yiddish. The play's themes of displacement, exile, persecution, filiality and generational conflict, as well as images with parallels to Jewish folk culture (e.g., the Fool, Edgar in disguise, Lear's patriarchalism), resonated with Jews in Russia, and in other parts of Europe and the United States, especially New York City. Radlov's production was extremely popular, running for about another ten years, even after the company was relocated to Tashkent following the German invasion in 1939. Stribrny opines that this production "continued to offer wisdom and consolation throughout the horrible Stalinist trials and Gulag imprisonments as well as the whole of the Second World War during which the Nazis were operating their gas chambers in the concentration camps" (86). The Mikhoels *Lear* was also known in the outside world: it was extolled by Englishman Gordon Craig, a major international theater figure whose productions played in Russia in the early part of the century and remained a significant influence on Soviet theater practitioners, including Kozintsev, who cites him frequently in his books (see also Stribrny 85 and Ostrovsky 78). Kozintsev most admired Mikhoels' ability to capture the essence of Lear's character without being loud or overly dramatic, adding nuance and depth, emphasizing Lear's spiritual journey from delusion to wisdom (*STC* 44).

The main focus of the GOSET production was upon the character of Lear and his transition from illusion and solipsism to illumination and a true understanding of reality. The dominant Soviet critical estimation of *Lear* is evident in responses to this production. Similar to Lunacharsky's concept of the tragedy in its historical context, Soviet critic Abram Efros' response to the GOSET *Lear* was informed by the idea of the chaos of transition from one epoch to another. In this case, the transition is from the Middle Ages to the Renaissance, which Soviet critics saw as the advent of the chaos of individualism, born with emergent capitalism, after the collapse of the structures of family, religion and feudalism obtaining in the Medieval period.[8] Efros writes: "the stage of the State Jewish Theatre is full of the breath of a horrible age, the breath of legalized betrayals, legalized murders, legalized robberies, legalized brutalities, legalized war of everybody against everybody, where a son plots the murder of his father, where a brother poisons his brother, and a sister her sister" (quoted in Morozov *SSS* 36). Just as Blok's commentary on *Lear* for the Civil-War-era Bolshoi production reveals the correspondence between the play's themes and the audience's real-life situation, so too does this reading evoke analogies to the tumult of the 1930s. Following hard upon the famine of the early '30s — the human cost of bad government that one could well imagine might have befallen Lear's own subjects while he was distracted by other matters — was the wave of purges, imprisonments and executions of the mid– and late '30s. Stalin and his organs of state were busy rooting out dissent, whether real or conveniently imagined. Lear's perverse game of testing loyalties and his mock trial of Goneril and Regan could be seen writ large across Soviet society in which every institution, from government to university to family, seemed to be a place of danger where a citizen could be turned in by anyone at any moment and tried and convicted on the flimsiest of evidence and without the slightest regard for just legal procedure.

The other pertinent aspect of Radlov's production, which most of its contemporary critics appear to gloss over, is the very fact of its Jewishness: it was created by the State Jewish Theatre with a famous Jewish actor in the main role, and used a translation of Shakespeare that was not Russian, but Yiddish. There is a deep irony that this popular and influential production of *King Lear* was so well received in a country historically deeply hostile to Judaism, and on the eve of World War II and Stalin's anti–Semitic campaigns of the late '40s and early '50s. Solomon Mikhoels himself was murdered on Stalin's orders via a car crash in 1948, as one of the early victims of Stalin's anti–Semitic purges. Later, in 1951 a large number of Soviet Yiddish writers were arrested, tortured and killed at Stalin's behest. He nearly succeeded in doing the same to a group of Jewish physicians arrested the following year, but mercifully Stalin died before his plan could be carried out. Historians speculate that Stalin was on the verge of even more dramatic actions against the Soviet Jews before his death, and give evidence that the propaganda surrounding Stalin's actions in these years fueled a renewal of popular anti–Semitism in the country.[9] Like Mikhoels, Isa Goldberg was also killed during this time. Goldberg translated nine Shakespeare plays into Yiddish. Significantly, his last translation was *Macbeth*, completed in the late '30s at the height of the Terror (Prager

157). Mikhoels and Kozintsev evidently had plans to stage *Richard III*, which were thwarted by the actor's untimely demise (*STC* 43). For the Stalin era, the choice of these plays is timely, telling and incendiary: both feature a murderous, callous leader who values his own aggrandizement over human lives, even those of his family members.[10] Playing scenes from *Richard* for Kozintsev in private, Mikhoels "gained stature, some kind of diabolical arrogance caught fire in his eyes. ... An awesome and tragic myth sprang suddenly to life in a small Moscow room" (*STC* 43). In keeping with the many grotesque ironies of the era, Mikhoels was embodying Stalin, the man who would have him killed just a short time after these meetings.

Popular anti–Semitism had existed in Russia before and after the Revolution. Rights for Jews before the Revolution were limited: there was a ban on Jews living in urban centers and a designated area called the "Pale of Settlement" in which Jews still were often denied property rights. The identification of tsarist Russia with the Orthodox Church, coupled with the Church's, the tsar's and the wider culture's anti–Semitic attitudes, caused the situation to be essentially intractable (Service 12–13). Interestingly, the Progressives, Marxists, Communists and Bolsheviks contained their own strains of anti–Semitism, even as many Jews in Russia and abroad joined their ranks in the hopes of better treatment under a system devoted to equality and against the Church-State apparatus. The official atheism of the Bolsheviks, though its main target was the Orthodox Church, was hostile to any religious practices or identifications. During the Civil War, the blatant anti–Semitism of the Whites allied the majority of Jews with the Reds, yet the Reds occasionally carried out attacks upon synagogues and Jews, in part due to the Bolshevik's atheist agenda, but no doubt also in part due to deeply ingrained anti–Semitic attitudes (Service 116). After the Bolshevik Revolution, Russia was reconfigured as a multi-ethnic republic with regions demarcated along ethnic lines, designed to preserve minority languages and cultures, including minority religions such as Islam. A Jewish Section of the Communist Party was created and Yiddish became the official language of Soviet Jews — as opposed to Hebrew, which was outlawed due to its Rabbinic and Zionist associations.

Oddly, still other policies and institutions were instated to benefit Jews and recognize their (secular) culture, such as Mikhoel's State Jewish Theater in Moscow (GOSET). There was often, however, a striking disconnect between the existence of Soviet institutions and the reality of life for most people. For one thing, all persons had to carry identification that definitively and unalterably stated one's nationality, ethnicity and religion (if any). Depending upon how the wind was blowing from above this requirement could be extremely problematic for Jews, especially those seeking higher education or jobs during times when anti–Semitism was stoked. Moreover, Stalin's multi-cultural vision of nationalism changed drastically after World War II in favor of a more narrowly-defined Russian nationalism, which led to a return to the sort of anti–Semitic (among other xenophobic policies) policies seen under Nicholas II, such as restricted access to higher education and professional employment (Service 317).

As with many of his policies and actions, Stalin was inconsistent and used ambiguity to his advantage. His establishment of the Jewish Autonomous Region, which predated the founding of the State of Israel, was a kind of recognition of Jews' right to identity and community, but this region was situated in the most remote and inhospitable part of Siberia bordering northwest China, an area even less desirable and more remote than the pre–Revolutionary Pale of Settlement. (After the war there was talk of moving the settlement to the lovely Crimea, but this never happened.) Various post-war policies put into effect officially limited Jewish access to education and employment. The reality and extent of Hitler's extermination campaign against the Jews was officially suppressed. This suppression of information pertaining to Hitler's "Final Solution" continued past the Stalin era and was especially evident in censorship surrounding the events at Babi Yar in Ukraine. Previously, Ukraine was the site of the worst anti–Jewish pogrom in Russian history, during the Civil War and perpetrated by the Whites, in which upwards of 100,000 people were killed (Hosking 410). That the Jewish population of Ukraine was then specifically targeted by the Germans was removed from accounts of the atrocities there. Works about these events were censored or banned altogether, such as Dmitri Shostakovich's symphony based upon the 1956 Yevtushenko poem *Babi Yar*. Among the many betrayals of the Soviet era was the betrayal of the many Jewish persons who initially supported the Communist cause in the late 19th and early 20th centuries.

King Lear and World War II

World War II became known in the Soviet Union as the "Great Patriotic War," partly due to the Party's desire to create a unified front and to foster a cohesive patriotism that trumped any ethnic, national or linguistic rifts, and partly due to a bottom-up surge in nationalism natural to any people facing occupation and war against an invader (Makaryk 121–122).

In her discussion of wartime *Hamlet* productions, Irena Makaryk suggests that Shakespeare's tragedies were not encouraged in performance during the war because of their pessimism and depiction of human capitulation to or victimization by evil: the Soviets preferred "optimistic tragedy" (123). Certainly, Shakespeareans can debate the ultimate meaning of the endings of the four major tragedies, but what is important here is that the Party itself, which controlled repertoire in theaters, discouraged tragic plays. Yet to conclude that therefore Shakespearean tragedies were not performed, or that wartime Shakespeare productions lacked the flavor of minority nationalism, is not entirely true. It would also be a mistake to suppose that the Party's, or Stalin's, tastes and the forced optimism of Socialist realism were entirely enforceable during the war. Many of the major theater groups were moved to outlying regions and many also ended up in occupied territory or abroad and therefore were far away from administrative centers, which gave them freedom from official scrutiny. Moreover, location notwithstanding, the priority of the higher echelons of government was fighting the war; although Stalin was keen to see new patriotic fiction films and plays written and produced as well as films documenting the war his time for such matters was limited. Because of attention to war effort and the money allocated to it, as well as the need to foster as much morale as possible, censorship was fairly lax in this period and it is known as something of an expressive oasis in the midst of the Stalin era. Film production was more scant than other arts, however, since films are expensive to make and the state controlled funding. Therefore, most of the small number of wartime films were devoted to war propaganda. As ever, there was a balance to be struck between the federation's multiculturalism and the desire to rally patriotically against the common foe under the pan-Soviet banner.

The tragedies were indeed being performed in theaters during the war with full acknowledgment of their more apocalyptic, pessimistic themes. The choice of *King Lear* as wartime Shakespeare points to willingness on the part of audiences and producers to depict and work through the terrifying destruction of the war without softening he message in the name of patriotic optimism. Of all the tragedies, *Lear* is arguably the most bleak and brutal, and therefore most near the Soviet situation in the war, much as it was for Blok in the Civil War period. Kenneth Rowe writes of the relevance of *King Lear* (as well as *Hamlet*, *Othello* and *The Tempest*) to college students in 1944. He remarks that the war experience actually made *Lear* more interesting to his students, which is an interesting parallel to these numerous productions during World War II. The Soviet Union was physically divided within its borders; many people were forced into exile both internally and externally, much like Kent and Cordelia. Others were imprisoned as POWs, as are Lear and Cordelia. Additionally, there was an invading, occupying army, like France's army under Cordelia in the midst of the civil war between the Edmund and Albany camps. There was a great deal of suffering and death on top of what had already been endured since the Revolution. That Stalin himself, Lear-like in his blithe overconfidence, had more or less opened the door to Germany in the failed secret Hitler-Stalin pact would not have been widely known until many years later, but it is certain that people noticed Stalin's slow reaction to the invasion. He mistakenly assumed that his relationship with Germany was strong and that the USSR's defensive capacity would not be tested by an attack from without (see Conquest's chapter on Stalin and World War II 236–268, as well as Service 259–266 on Stalin's early hubris and blunders). Wartime deprivation, while it no doubt brought out the best in the vast majority of citizens, also encouraged animalistic selfishness, exploitation and opportunism, making Edmund, Oswald, Goneril and Regan seem all too real for the Soviet audience. Morozov provides an anecdote of the audience response to a production of *Lear* during which an audience member heckled Goneril and Regan, crying out: "Fascists!" (71) The negative characters in *Lear* represented both the German invaders from without and the corrupt or inept citizens within.

Morozov cites five productions of *King Lear* in 1941 alone, in addition to the Mikhoels production that had been relocated from Moscow to Tashkent. In the outlying provinces *Lear* was being translated into other languages, such as Azerbaijani, Kirghiz and Georgian, and was performed in the more remote territories with great success. The ambiguity of *Lear*'s ending makes it an especially poignant choice for wartime, since the question of the human ability to rise above evil is questioned no matter how positive a light is shone upon heroic Edgar's closing lines, loyal Kent's final exit, or moral Albany's aptness as a leader. *Lear* is a play that presents an unflinchingly unsentimental portrayal of the power and cost of human evil and error. Villains are overcome, but the virtuous die in the fight too. Morozov quotes an Azerbaijani professor who tries to see beyond the devastation in describing the 1941 production in Baku: "single-handed, the Shakespearean heroes are carrying on an unequal struggle against the brutalities of their age. In this struggle they suffer defeat, but their thoughts and their dreams, fixed on a brighter future, survive the individual deaths of the heroes" (quoted in Morozov *SSS* 38). From the '30s, through World War II, and beyond, Shakespeare came to serve several new purposes for intellectuals and artists. Because his works were seldom directly banned or censored, they provided a refuge for those in need of a blind from behind which to express themselves in ways not always in line with Party dictates. Hence, in wartime, when official theatrical repertoire, films and public discourse had to serve the patriotic optimism of the national war effort, Shakespeare's tragedies provided a depiction of the grimness, despair and hopefulness of people enduring unspeakable devastation.

The ultimately positive conclusion drawn by Morozov fits in well with the Party's insistence upon a particular emphasis in staging tragedy, yet the selection of this particular play still spoke to a firm commitment to making challenging and topical art: art that respected the audience's life experience, while at the same time encouraging hope. As Blok's commentary says, *Lear* is an "adult" play; it cannot be made childish or simplistic, it acknowledges evil and death even while it maintains a sober belief in the survival of love and goodness. Smirnov, a Soviet literary critic and professor, who was part of the wave of scholars and artists who turned Shakespearean in the 1930s, wrote about Shakespeare's tragic sensibility in an essay published in 1946, finding a middle way between the delusional insistence on optimism and progress in Socialist realism and the real, tragic experiences and knowledge of the people. He linked the humanist and the tragic by way of reference to *King Lear*:

> Shakespeare's tragedies emanate a bracing vigor, a courageous call to the struggle, even though this struggle may not always promise success. [...] At base it is still the same humanism [...] a *tragic* and *heroic* humanism, which is far from signifying any renunciation of the joy and fullness of life, but which brings to those feelings important corrections and delimitations. Of course, the carefree exultation of the Renaissance is no longer there, and that "superflux" which Shakespeare always demands is no longer an abundance of kindliness and pleasure but an abundance of mental effort and, most of all, heroic action and great deed [82].

Smirnov's "corrections and delimitations" spoke to a truthful representation of the human experience that moderated the stories of official wartime and post-war propaganda. He points to the post–Revolutionary period's obvious failure to deliver a radically improved life — a "Renaissance" that never came and a "superflux" (using Lear's terminology) whose distribution was still awaited. Here is another evocation of the themes of utopia and dystopia: the humanist paradise, the Bolshevik "Renaissance," is usurped by an authoritarian regime under which people's needs remained unmet and their freedoms were undercut. Even worse, the new regime not only failed to deliver a utopia, it unleashed the very worst of conditions upon its citizens, enacting policies that led to starvation, imprisonment, torture and murder, as well as essentially opening the door to a foreign invasion the battling of which cost millions of lives. Smirnov's writing attests to the supremacy of the positive Marxist interpretation of Shakespeare that won out in the critical battle that had begun in earnest in the late 19th century between those who saw Shakespeare as simply a reactionary mouthpiece of the aristocracy and those who saw him as a lover of the people and a "humanist" (Gibian 26–31). Despite the underlying pessimism of his reading, which flows against Socialist realism, for Smirnov, Shakespeare's tragedy was appealingly Marxist, on the side of the common people, reflecting their suffering with honesty. The play also encouraged the battered Soviet citizenry to ally themselves imaginatively with Cordelia, Kent, Edgar, and other positive characters who maintained their fight against evil to the bitter end. No matter what one's political leanings, such imaginary allies were crucial during the war for keeping despair at bay and soldiering on.

Shakespeare's body of work provided a script for patriotism and became part of Soviet national identity for Russians as well as citizens of the republics or minority groups, therefore uniting everyone in the multi-ethnic, multi-national federation through a common adopted artistic heritage. Shakespeare was both Russo-Soviet and transnational, a presence in the Russian national cultural heritage, as well as a means of bringing into community the various minority nationalities and ethnic and religious groups of the USSR — a unity that Stalin wanted and that the country needed in the face of the common enemy. The examples of the various productions of *King Lear* attest to this phenomenon. Morozov's writings also reveal other uses for Shakespeare in wartime (Morozov *SSS* 70–71). Shakespeare's histories provided patriotic speeches for soldiers to recite, and plays with martial themes were performed at the front, such as *Othello*. Kozintsev himself produced a stage production of *Othello* in 1943. Morozov's own versions of *Henry V*'s "Once more unto the breach" and "If we are marked to die" speeches were read for a radio broadcast (71). Morozov concludes his book's war chapter by emphasizing the kinship of England and the USSR through Shakespeare and the war experience. The introduction to Morozov's 1947 book is by J. Dover Wilson, a well-known British Shakespearean, further testament to the rapport created by the war and the two nations' mutual love of Shakespeare. Indeed, the emphasis during the war was on fostering friendship with Western allies by foregrounding common cultural heritage in Shakespeare (Gibian 33). Yet this friendliness changed as post-war relations with the West quickly deteriorated, as reflected in critical debates among the nations, for instance in

Morozov's 1949 essays, attacking Western Shakespeare critics and theatrical workers (Gibian 33–34). Kozintsev's later recollections of his visits to England in the 1950s and 1960s, however, continued to express this spirit of unity into the post-war, Cold-War era. He writes of his experience seeing Peter Hall's *Midsummer Night's Dream* at Stratford-upon-Avon in 1959:

> I went out onto the balcony during intermission. Under the roof hung a spotlit yellow pennant emblazoned with a lance and raven. This was Shakespeare's coat of arms, and is now the symbol of the Memorial Theatre. Not long ago, this flag had hung at the entrances of Moscow and Leningrad theatres. It was also not long ago that the curtain with the seagull rose in London. Happily there can be a rapprochement of peoples under the banner of art, a banner that bears both Shakespeare's raven and Chekhov's seagull [*STC* 34; the seagull flag is the symbol of the Moscow Art Theater].

This nostalgic, idealistic passage is quite striking and outspoken for its era, written in the 1960s during a time of great mistrust and conflict between Brezhnev's Soviet Union and the West. Kozintsev was allowed to travel to England throughout this period and he clearly saw past ideology and propaganda, preferring instead an attitude of openness and understanding.

Morozov points to the annual Shakespeare conference that was held every year of the war in Moscow after its first meeting in April 1939 (only in 1944 was it relocated to Erevan, Armenia to avoid danger), with panels and performances that went on despite the fact that they sometimes had to be moved into bomb shelters and that many of the city's theatrical companies and academic departments had been evacuated. The conference itself became, like the many performances and events that went on during the siege of Leningrad, a protest against the Germans, boldly illustrating the fortitude of the Soviet people, whose cultural life would not be interrupted by the invasion. Morozov calls Shakespeare "a true friend" during the war and extols the actors killed at the front who "waged war against a cruel foe with the weapons of art" (70). That theater was one of the country's most valued weapons speaks volumes about the Russo-Soviet people's passion for art.

Kozintsev's 1941 Stage Production of *King Lear*

Kozintsev's *King Lear* was staged in 1941 in Leningrad during World War II at the Bolshoi Dramatic Theater. The city was under siege, surrounded by German forces in what was called the Leningrad Blockade (officially dated from September 1941 to January 1944, but evacuations and bombardments had begun by June 1941). The Leningrad theater was soon evacuated and Kozintsev staged *Othello* in Novosibirsk 1943-4, another play in which themes of war and betrayal made it particularly appealing to Soviet audiences in wartime. Shostakovich was also in Leningrad during the blockade and he provided music for Kozintsev's *Lear*. At this time he also composed his 7th symphony, the "Leningrad," which was outwardly a denunciation of Fascism and the German invasion, but its subtext can be seen as referring to Stalin's regime and his terrorization and victimization of the people. Very little information is available about Kozintsev's theatrical production, but he published an essay on *King Lear* in the same year that the stage play opened.[11]

Kozintsev's 1941 essay on *Lear* evidences a similar duality to Shostakovich's symphony: on the surface Kozintsev's references to the "storm" throughout the play, the backdrop of war and the landscape of battlefields, the depiction of Lear's delusion and tyranny, as well as the depravity of Edmund, Cornwall, Goneril and Regan versus the moral tenacity of Kent, the Fool, Edgar and the warrior-queen Cordelia, could all easily be read as descriptions of the German invasion, Hitler, German atrocities, and the patriotism and heroism of the Soviet people, who ultimately repelled the Germans despite a multitude of tactical disadvantages and incredible loss of life. On the other hand, beneath these (sincere) screens Kozintsev's thematic emphases also point to the devastation and chaos that obtained in the Soviet Union before the Nazis ever arrived: the country had already suffered a civil war, and had seen death, internal displacement and mass imprisonment on a scale similar to that of wartime, but due almost entirely to the misguided internal policies of Stalinism. The disruption of moral, societal and familial order and the resultant rise of persons such as Edmund, Goneril, Regan and Oswald can be easily equated to Soviet propaganda and policy that sought to place the State and Party in the place of faith, friendship and family. Clientism and corruption, after all, were well-established in Soviet life before 1939. Kozintsev's patriotism and his desire to encourage his compatriots is palpable in the essay (just as it is in Shostakovich's wartime works), yet the reader senses that he is not only rallying his readers against the invading Germans, but also against the destructive forces at work within Soviet culture.

The post-war period plunged the Soviet people even more deeply into repression and despair. Soldiers returning from German imprisonment, or who had fought abroad, were not greeted with a hero's welcome, but rather were sent to the Gulag because Stalin feared that they might carry home with them ideas and experiences that undermined the preferred State-engineered reality. The temporary distraction of the war effort over, Stalin also redoubled his efforts to rein in artistic expression. Both Kozintsev-Trauberg's *Simple People* and Eisenstein's second part of *Ivan the Terrible* were denounced in a 1946 Central Committee resolution designed to reinforce Party control of the film industry following the war. (Much other such public and specific castigations occurred in the years following the war.) This censure ended Kozintsev's collaborations with Leonid Trauberg, who had been his professional partner since the FEKS days of the 1920s. Stalin's rejection of the second *Ivan* film led to the decline of Eisenstein's health and his death in 1948. (There was a third *Ivan* film in production, but Stalin prevented its completion and destroyed nearly all the film that had been shot for it.) Kozintsev made only two more films between the end of the war and Stalin's death — one of these was called *Pirogov* (1947, a biography of a 19th century physician), the other an eponymous biography of Belinsky (released in 1953) — after which he made his *Don Quixote* of 1957, then his two Shakespeare films. The immediate postwar period was for Kozintsev a time of retreat from the difficulties of creating original art under Stalin and a period to regroup after parting ways with his longtime collaborator. Kozintsev's creative resurrection would be effected by Stalin's death, beginning with his theatrical production of *Hamlet* (1953-4) and ending with his film version of *King Lear* (1970). Shakespeare, and his Renaissance peer Cervantes, were the material through which Kozintsev loosened the noose of State authority and publicly manifested his personal assessments of Soviet reality.

CHAPTER FIVE

King Lear Revisited in the Brezhnev Era: Kozintsev's 1970 Film Adaptation

After his *Hamlet* film of 1963, Kozintsev did not complete and release another film until *King Lear* in 1970. The research, notes and letters pertaining to the film became the contents of his last book, *King Lear: The Space of Tragedy*, published in the USSR in 1973, the year of his death.[1] Kozintsev had other projects planned before he died (such as a film adaptation of *The Tempest*), but the film and the book remain as his final works, fittingly containing the themes of age and succession in *King Lear*. Kozintsev was in his late 60s when *Lear* was released, after a career that had already spanned five decades. Those decades were among the most tumultuous in all of Russian history, not only in governmental, political and ideological terms, but also in light of major changes in artistic technology and aesthetics. Kozintsev came of age as a theater practitioner and a filmmaker in the 1920s. The technology of film and the sophistication of montage, thanks to Russians such as Sergei Eisenstein, made this an exciting time for the very young Kozintsev (he was born in 1905), whose work with FEKS included experimental film and theater productions. He also participated in the spread of Bolshevik Revolutionary ideology through the traveling cinema groups of the 1910s and '20s, who were Lenin's emissaries to distant reaches of the Russian empire sent to instruct the masses using film, since the majority was still illiterate.

The work of FEKS came to a premature close with the institution of Socialist realism in 1935, and this, coupled with the formation of new artistic unions and ministries for ideology and censorship, ushered in tremendous changes for artists. Kozintsev continued to work in the theater and the cinema, but his works had to eschew the carnival, avant-garde abandon of the FEKS days. His *Maxim* trilogy films, which won the Stalin Prize in 1941, were a capitulation to Socialist realism, as well as marking Kozintsev's contribution to the war effort, which demanded films that celebrated patriotism, unity and heroism. After the war, and the banning of his 1945 film *Simple People,* Kozintsev's cinematic output slowed significantly as he was forced to negotiate his survival in Stalin's post-war renewal of repression: he made only two films between 1945 and 1953. After Stalin's death, Kozintsev embraced the Khrushchev Thaw, and released *Don Quixote* (1957) and *Hamlet* (1963) before this era of a somewhat freer atmosphere too came to an abrupt end and Brezhnev's Stagnation began. This was the period in which Kozintsev revisited *King Lear,* which he had produced theatrically in 1941, during World War II, as a direct commentary upon the war, Stalin's flaws, and the moral and social problems that had arisen since the Bolshevik Revolution.

It is not surprising that Kozintsev would return to *Lear* in the Brezhnev era. It must have seemed to him and many others that there was a return to Stalin-esque government as well as the renewal of wartime fears as military actions took place throughout the USSR and the threat of the Cold War conjured up the imagery of the horrors of Hiroshima and Nagasaki. The depiction of war and ravaged, burning homes and landscapes in Kozintsev's *Lear* film reflect the persistence of governmental bellicosity and violence against the masses, against popular uprisings in regions not formerly part of Russia (e.g., Poland and Czechoslovakia) and inside traditionally Russian territory as well. The ubiquity of clientism and corruption at all levels of government and in many institutions finds its manifestation in Kozintsev's characterization of, and writings about, figures such as Oswald, Edmund, Goneril, Regan and Cornwall, whom he describes as odious beasts who have succumbed to the worst in human nature in the interest of self-promotion and self-preservation. The renewals of Stalinesque religious persecution and artistic stifling are referenced in the film's subtly positive portrayal of Christianity and in its treatment of the Fool, who is both an artist struggling to be heard and an emblematic victim of Soviet anti–Semitism.

Growth in resistance and dissent also characterized the Brezhnev era. Despite the betrayals under Khrushchev and the return of repression under Brezhnev, artists and intellectuals had become emboldened, galvanized by the need to resist by whatever means possible any further attempts to silence them. There was expansion of *samizdat* and *tamizdat* publishing, through which exiles and émigrés of the '60s and '70s were not afraid to expose what they had lived through to the rest of the world. Moreover, there was a new, bolder generation coming up, one that had not lived through the worst of the Stalin years and perhaps as a result lacked the same fears as their elders.

Generational conflict is a central theme in *King Lear*. Lear's and Gloucester's time of effectual power has passed by the time of the play's opening scene, and the direction of the country will be determined by their offspring. In that generation too, there is division: Cordelia versus her sisters, Edgar versus his brother. Cordelia and Edgar represent a path that preserves (or perhaps reinstates) personal integrity, compassion, family and justice against the rapacious self-aggrandizement and moral turpitude of Edmund, Goneril, Regan and their co-conspirators. Although Cordelia dies and Edgar remains a reluctant inheritor of the state, their ethos is victorious, especially in Kozintsev's interpretation. His film passes on their hopes and aspirations to the audience, encouraging the younger generation to continue to fight and to believe in the possibility of a society and government based upon goodness and truth, even though their reality might make it appear that the dissemblers have won the upper hand forever. Kozintsev's steadfastly hopeful and positive outlook, his faith in art and the human spirit, are qualities that pervade his final book and are evident even in this very bleak and violent film.

This dark period, during which many Shakespeare productions evidenced a Kottian bleakness and resignation, was also a time of renewed interest and urgency in wielding the weapons of art and literature against the regime. In the midst of political upheaval and oppression, artists and intellectuals were emboldened "to agitate for real freedom in every sphere of Soviet life" (Ellis 283). Despite setbacks and continuing pressure from above, the movements that would eventually precipitate the downfall of the regime were in place: "thus was born the human rights movement, including the campaign for religious freedom, as well as self-sacrificing efforts by writers, artists and film-makers to break free of the confining ideological bonds of Socialist realism" (Ellis 283). It was as if, despite all efforts to the contrary, Stalin's death had opened a Pandora's Box that simply could not be shut.

Kozintsev's *Lear* deals with a broad range of dismal topics, fully reflecting the problems of 1960s: the nuclear threat, repercussions of war, suppression of truthful expression, global isolation, the return of despotism, and the persecution of religious believers. The ending of the film silently challenges the audience to do something in response, not to acquiesce in fear. Shakespeare had come to serve the cause of the next revolution, in the Russian territory and the USSR more broadly, providing a means to express dissent and therefore inspiring and encouraging resistance to Communist dictatorship. Alexander Shurbanov writes that "Shakespeare had been irremediably politicized," and used to challenge Communist dogma: "Shakespearean discourse helped to erode the doctrine's central postulates, those of historical optimism, heroic humanism, revolutionary violence and beneficent dictatorship" (143). Kozintsev's *King Lear* appears at the birth of the final phase of Soviet Shakespeare adaptation, the one that finally wrested the plays from the Party-liners and placed them in the service of Party-decriers.

Critical Background

There are more articles on Kozintsev's *Lear* than on his *Hamlet*; most likely, this is because of the film's showing at the 1971 World Shakespeare Conference, where Kozintsev himself was allowed to attend and to present a lecture (*Proceedings*). Judging by the dates of most of the *Hamlet* criticism, Kozintsev's appearance and the audience's positive reaction to *King Lear* led to a great deal of interest in both of his Shakespearean films, bringing his *Hamlet* of six years prior to many Western scholars' attention for the first time. The films were well-received, at least by those not averse to seeing Shakespeare interpreted for cinema and translated into Russian. Most of the critical articles on the *Lear* film are formal close-readings concerned with the ways in which the Shakespearean text is rendered into cinematic language. A great many of these also compare Kozintsev's *Lear* to Peter Brook's *Lear* of 1970, yet such comparisons often attribute more existential negativity to Kozintsev than is warranted. The temporal proximity of these films, and the evidence of communication between Brook and Kozintsev, makes comparisons inevitable and compelling (see Leaming's discussion of the two filmmakers, 123–131). The differences between their interpretations and directorial styles illustrate much about interpretive debates over *King Lear,* as well as the different responses to Soviet and Soviet-style rule in diverse areas of Asia and Eastern Europe. Simply stated, Brook's vision is more existential and bleak, and envisions a Kottian cycle of tyranny that the individual is helpless to overcome. Kozintsev's vision takes this sort of despair into account, but insists that the individual does have agency and can, and must, alter his external reality.

The group of articles falling into the category of formal and largely non-political, non-historical ones includes those by Carnovsky, McNeir, Willson, Welsh, Hodgdon, Schmalz, Rothwell, Andrews, Jorgens, Brode and Buchman. Most of these articles are concerned with a close reading of the film's imagery in order to consider its relationship to the play's text. Many of them also compare the Kozintsev *Lear* with Peter Brook's cinematic adaptation of *Lear*, but, as with Leaming's analysis of the same relationship, they tend to focus on aesthetic choices without any particular historical context. Some mention Jan Kott's work, but too often fail to see the ways in which Kozintsev departs from Kott's bleak, circular reading in the same way that some fail to see how Kozintsev's interpretive choices depart from the more existential vision of Brook's film. Welsh explains the distinction this way: "Kozintsev does not attempt to Kotterize *Lear*. [...] His Lear is placed in a cruel and questioning universe, but it is not necessarily an absurd one" (154). Much the same could be said of any attempt to "Brook-ize" Kozintsev's film.

The next group includes articles by Western critics who attempt a more developed incorporation of cultural, political and biographical information into their interpretations of Kozintsev's *Lear*. These include examinations by Womack, Radcliff-Ulmstead, Griggs and Collick, as well as the chapter on *Lear* in Leaming's book on Kozintsev, published in 1980. Leaming's chapter on Kozintsev's *Lear* offers an historical context by way of other contemporary artistic works. Leaming primarily considers the film and its aesthetic influences and qualities. Her first section considers the film in the context of Kozintsev's other films, theatrical productions and his writings, giving a sense of the intertextuality of his artistic approach and ethos, especially his tendency to read Renaissance works through the lens of the present. The second part compares Kozintsev's approach and style with Brook's, paying special attention to evidence from Kozintsev's writings of his convergences and departures from Brook's interpretation of the play and on film aesthetics. Kozintsev's assertion that Brook's *Lear* makes a hero of art itself, which Leaming highlights, informs her reading of the film. Leaming's third section describes the place of nature and landscape in the film, again in an attempt to flesh out Kozintsev's general approach to cinematic space and his ideas about the limitations of filmic mimesis. Carnivalistic elements of the film, especially the Fool and the *narod*, are presented in the fourth section, aligning Kozintsev's use of the Fool as a "subversive, carnivalistic voice" with FEKS (133). The Leaming chapter plants many seeds that can be germinated by greater attention to historical contexts instead of her largely formal, aesthetic concerns, which are understandable and desirable in light of her book's purpose in presenting Kozintsev as *auteur* and proving an overall sense of his *oeuvre*.

John Collick's 1989 chapter on Kozintsev's *Hamlet* and *King Lear* grapples more directly with historical, political, critical and biographical contexts. In this treatment, he seems, like Leaming, especially concerned with artistic movements and influences, citing Kozintsev's early experimental work with FEKS, Constructivism, the Bakhtinian carnivalesque, and the influence of the Noh, which Kozintsev writes about in *Space of Tragedy*. Collick's aim is to see "whether the result is truly revolutionary or whether Kozintsev's experience of alienation under Stalin ultimately counteracts the radical elements in the films" (129; Collick's answer is that it does, mine is that it does not). Kenneth Womack's 1993 article on *King Lear* focuses on the play's text and its variations in different Soviet translations: specifically, two different versions of Pasternak's translation, Kozintsev's adaptation of Pasternak's work, and the film's subtitles, which are from an English Shakespeare text rather than translations of Pasternak's text. Womack's goal is to offer historical context for Kozintsev's *Lear* by way of textual history. In particular, Womack considers Pasternak's problematic career, his relationship to Stalin, and how these manifest in his roles as writer and translator. Womack also makes mention of film composer Shostakovich's problems with Stalin and the censors (154–155). The article acknowledges Kozintsev's own career trajectory and brands him a "dissident" along with Pasternak whom he implicitly posits as the same. Womack explores problems of creating art under the Soviet regime, briefly discussing publishing and its subservience to the State as well as Pasternak's editors, Morozov and Anikst, who had different attitudes to translation and different degrees of resistance to the dominant ideology. Morozov was the more conservative figure, and he favored more literal translations, while Anikst, editing the plays after Pasternak's death, was an admirer of Pasternak's translations and his looser style, as well as evidencing more resistance to the Party line in his criticism than Morozov (Womack 151–153). Womack ends, in the vein of W. B. Worthen, whom he also cites in the opening paragraph, by saying "performance is not the product of a static representation of the text, but instead, an historical reconfiguration of that text" (157). Bringing Shakespeare and his afterlives down from the abstract realm of the universal and into the realms of the particular is a useful critical choice.

This brings the discussion to a third grouping of the critical works, those that take a strikingly more comprehensive approach to reading Kozintsev's films; these are readings that spring forth from an understanding of the inherently social and political aspects of Soviet art and acknowledge the Aesopian nature of this engagement. These writers bring to bear a full range of historical materials upon their studies. The representative works in this group are those by Stribrny, Sokolyansky and Gillespie. Sokolyansky's chapter on Kozintsev's films appears in 2000 in *The Cambridge Companion to Shakespeare on Film*. This treatment draws largely from biography, but shows an engagement with politics and history not found in the majority of the Western criticism. Sokolyansky reads the films as more resistant and subversive, not merely saying Kozintsev is a "Marxist" and leaving it at that. He acknowledges Kozintsev's "moral idealism" and "historical optimism." The crucial difference between Kozintsev and Kott, or Kozintsev and Brook and their other Western counterparts, is that Kozintsev can at once be a realist *and* believe entirely in the power of art to effect change in individuals and social systems. Sokolyansky further elaborates Kozintsev's artistic and cultural optimism: "his deep historical optimism had an ethical basis. In the film the director and his team made a protest against the cynical, Edmundian view of life and stated that there are real moral values in this world — and that every epoch begets defenders of those values" (209). Sokolyansky argues that for the Soviet filmmaker and his audience there could be no resignation in the face of tragedy and evil. Rather, there was an insistence upon fighting and transcending that is perhaps lost on people who have enjoyed the freedoms of the West, where there is much less to be lost by "checking out" of engagement with the world and its problems (or indeed where checking out is possible to an extent the average Soviet citizen could not have done). An overly negating concept of *Lear*, such as Brook's or Kott's, would not be ethical in the Soviet context, according to Kozintsev's values and faith in art. Kott and Brook somewhat divorce the play from history, both its original context and their own cultural experiences, but Kozintsev cannot do this. Sokolyansky expresses the distance between Kott and Kozintsev (and by implication Brook as well): "Kott analyzed the British tragedy as a kind of absurd drama, an *Endgame* for the Shakespearean epoch. [...] Kozintsev saw the deep meaning of *King Lear* in its presentation of the greatest human and social collisions — in themselves altogether topical for modern audiences. To screen this tragedy he needed more concrete reality, more closeness to the audience's social and historical experience" (208). Kozintsev's artistic and social optimism and his insistence upon historical grounding are dependent upon each other — oddly this is the characteristic that makes him most clearly a Marxist and yet also most emphatically against the Soviet regime, in as much as the Party strove to rewrite history, evade reality and enforce the myths of Socialist realism.

Dmitri Shostakovich, Soviet Public Enemy Number One

Shostakovich provided musical scores for Kozintsev's *Hamlet* and *King Lear* films. Kozintsev writes, "Shostakovich's music is another matter. There is no point in my thinking about it. I would not be able to make a Shakespearean film without it just as I would not be able to do without Pasternak's translation" (*KLST* 254). Although in his comments it is clear that Shostakovich did not generally enjoy film scoring, it seems that his love for Shakespeare and relationship with Kozintsev made him an interested and willing participant in these projects (see *Testimony* 83–89 for Shostakovich on Shakespeare). Like many other composers, Shostakovich wearied of the pressure to take on film work and bemoaned the fact that at various points in his career, especially during the Stalin-era artistic crackdowns of the late '30s and '40s, he was compelled to take on such projects for the lack of other gainful employment (similar to the way that Pasternak turned to translation). Thus cinematic composing conjured up memories of his early days supporting his family by playing piano at the movie house for silent films as well as being as a reminder of his occasional status as "enemy of the people" and servant of Stalin's whims. The young Shostakovich worked with Kozintsev and his partner Leonid Trauberg as early as 1928, for their film *The New Babylon*, and worked on six other films with the Kozintsev-Trauberg team and Kozintsev alone between their first collaborations and the later Shakespeare films (Volkov 2004, 132). Shostakovich provided music for Kozintsev's 1941 Bolshoi Dramatic Theater production of *King Lear*, composing the "Ten Songs of the Fool" as incidental music (Fay 122). As with *Hamlet*, Shostakovich did not recycle any of the music for the stage production of *Lear* into the film score, but rather decided to start over fresh, another indication of his eagerness to work with Kozintsev again.

The relationship between the film director and composer was close and full of mutual admiration. Here is Kozintsev on Shostakovich, a passage indicating his love for the composer and the motivation behind collaborating with him:

> Music, for Shostakovich, is the necessity to speak out and convey what lies behind the lives of people. To depict our age and our country. Nature has endowed him with a particular sensibility of hearing — he hears people weep, he hears their low murmur of anger, a tearing of hearts, the trembling groans of despair. He has hearkened to the rumbling of the earth, the crowds marching for justice, the strikers' whistles, the angry songs erupting in the city's outskirts, the penny harmonium screeching out trite melodies and the wind that carries them to every corner of the earth. At times, ideas

and thought were muzzled and yoked, whips were cracked and art was made to dance, to beg favors in front of petty despots. Throughout it all, Dmitri Dmitrievich labored on. His inner life runs like an incessantly running motor, an ever-open wound. He is the conscience of our time [quoted in Greenberg].

Kozintsev's emphasis is on Shostakovich's connections to his place and time above all other considerations. Shostakovich both understood the people's troubles and experienced them personally. Unlike some of his musical contemporaries, Shostakovich stayed in the Soviet Union throughout his entire life. Quite famously, he remained in Leningrad during the siege, composing and performing his 7th Symphony, which is both homage to the bravery and tenacity of the Soviet people and protest against Stalin's mismanagement of the country, in a sense blaming him for placing the nation in danger. To stay in the besieged city by choice shows Shostakovich's commitment to suffering along with his fellows in order to be better able to express their feelings and offer appropriate healing through his music.

Shostakovich's works often carried personal and political importance for him throughout his troubled life and career. Many of his works resonated with audiences far beyond the impact of mere entertainment, and audiences grew to expect to listen into Shostakovich's compositions to hear the expressions of pain and dissent, which they often shared with him, and to partake in the palpable spirit of integrity and fortitude undermining the obvious forces working against him, forces that also worked against his audience in their own lives. Occasionally, Shostakovich's works were suppressed, sometimes even by Shostakovich himself, who learned from bitter experience to tread carefully through the Soviet cultural authorities' minefields. He was well-known for keeping some of his music "in the drawer," sharing and performing many pieces only for a small circle of close friends.

Shostakovich's musical relationship with Shakespeare predates his cinematic collaborations with Kozintsev. In 1932, Shostakovich composed music for an *avant-garde*, farcical, entirely cynical and satirical version of *Hamlet* by Nikolai Akimov (see chapter two). The play displeased the critics as it was certainly not within the aesthetic mandates of Socialist realism and clearly satirized Soviet power and rhetoric. In Hamlet's scene with Rosencrantz and Guildenstern, as per Akimov's interpretation, when Hamlet remarks that his friends cannot play upon him as a pipe, he places a recorder at his posterior and "farts" out a parody of a familiar revolutionary melody. The intended message need hardly be explained: the enforced repetition of revolutionary songs is exposed as absurd, even obscene. Akimov and Shostakovich (like Kozintsev and Pasternak), had started their careers in the new experimental, *avant-garde* theater and film movement of the '20s only to have to eschew such "anti-people" forms upon Stalin's institution of Socialist realism. Akimov's *Hamlet* was something of a throwback to the days of experimental and highly political theater, very similar to the productions by Kozintsev-Trauberg's FEKS, and was therefore doomed to a short run.

Shostakovich's opera *Lady Macbeth of Mtsensk District* was the first highly-publicized victim of Stalin's cultural-cleansing campaign of the 1930s. The opera is an adaptation of an adaptation of *Macbeth* in short-story form by Nikolai Leskov (this is the same story was used as the basis for Polish director Andrzej Wajda's 1968 film *Siberian Lady Macbeth*—set in the Yugoslav region before it was Yugoslavia). The story transposes a loose version of *Macbeth* to a rural village in Russia. Katerina Izmailova, for whom the opera was later renamed in its post–Stalin re-release, the revised Lady Macbeth, is a bored housewife who falls for a roguish farmhand, Sergei. Her obsession with him leads to her killing her father-in-law, husband and nephew (on a high Orthodox holy day no less) without expressing any feelings of remorse. She feels that because of her lot in life she is entitled to exact revenge and to stand above conventional morality. Katerina and Sergei are caught by nosey neighbors and sent to a Siberian labor camp where Sergei turns on Katerina, entering into liaisons with two other women, even stealing Katerina's woolen stockings to give as a present to the vapid, cruel Sonyetka. In a jealous fit, Katerina drowns herself, taking Sergei's love-interest with her, again, without remorse. Indeed, she is quite unlike Shakespeare's Lady Macbeth in as much as she never seems affected by guilt or insanity. The third-person narration of the story is dispassionate, leaving the reader feeling hopelessness in the face of the world's purposeless evil, which is perhaps its strongest connection to Shakespeare's play. Purportedly, Shostakovich's intention was to write a trilogy of operas on the topic of women pre- and post–Revolution. Shostakovich's opera (dedicated to his wife Nina upon its completion) simplifies the Leskov story and creates a much more sympathetic Katerina. The obvious point is to give an illustration of women's pre–Soviet lives. Katerina is a victim of the injustices of her age. Her only outlets and escape from her role as housewife in a loveless marriage are sex and violence; her immorality and criminal acts are simply a reflection of the hypocrisy and depravity all around her. Shostakovich fleshes out her characterization with a wistful, plaintive aria sung just before she drowns herself, murdering Sergei's lover in the process.

Perhaps most interesting, and potentially inflammatory, is the opera's depiction of the structures of authority: the police and the prison guards are depicted as hopelessly stupid and corrupt buffoons, and thus Katerina's punishment lacks any moral force. Caryl Emerson writes of the depiction of the police that "Shostakovich casts his scene more in the spirit of Gogol: crime is exposed randomly, farcically; the law-abiding world appears more ludicrous and self-serving than the two criminals" (63). Although on the surface about pre–Revolutionary times, in the 1930s this opera could hardly fail to conjure up associations with the current state of affairs in Soviet life. Capricious arrest and exile were already facts of life for many of Shostakovich's colleagues and audience members. Katerina's moral transgressions are a natural outcome of living in a world seemingly stripped of any rational standards of honesty or personal privacy and safety — a circumstance obtaining both before and after the Bolsheviks' rise to power. Nina Diakonova writes of Katerina's actions as born "of the inhuman conditions she had to live in": "general and particular circumstances have brought her to a state where she is not entirely responsible for what she does. In unnatural conditions her natural feelings bring her to unnatural actions: she is both victim and executioner" (109, 108). By implication, Shostakovich's opera suggests that in a world of "inhuman" and "unnatural" values and social relations, in which survival and success are contingent upon constantly shifting positions according to the prevailing dogma, one can hardly bemoan the moral bankruptcy of such a culture's "offspring." Nor, for that matter, can one take seriously the enforcers of the law, since that law is not based upon honest, stable values. Katerina acts desperately and without scruples, as is demanded by her times. Parallels with Soviet life in the '20s and '30s, during which many of the social and moral structures of society were being destroyed and overturned, only to be replaced by corruption and absurdity, explain the relevance of such an anti-hero for Shostakovich and his audience.

The opera premiered in 1934, with great success both in the USSR and abroad. Unfortunately, the artistic repressions of the "anti-formalist" movement caught up with Shostakovich when Stalin's anonymous "Muddle Instead of Music" article lambasting the work appeared in *Pravda* in January 1936, ushering in waves of new attacks on art and artists during the first of Stalin's major purges, the Terror (Volkov 2004, 103–109). Apparently, Stalin had gone to see the opera and left after the first act. There are several different hypotheses in circulation about what it was that made Stalin dislike the opera so much and decide to use Shostakovich as the first musical victim of his latest cultural-cleansing campaign. It is within the realm of possibility that Stalin already knew quite a bit about the work; it was, after all, widely liked and performed for almost two full years, and he probably merely went to see it to confirm his pre-formed ideas. Part of the problem must certainly have involved the popularity of the piece abroad: the very fact of an artist's popularity in the West had proved a major irritant to Stalin in the case of artists whose productions did not adhere to Party dictates. Moreover, Stalin, and this era of Soviet cultural history in general, was noted for a high degree of prudery and sexual conservatism. Emerson notes that the "prim" Stalinist press called the opera overly "physiological," meaning, in the parlance of the times, too sexual (65). The music and blocking for the scene of Katerina and Sergei's first assignation is charged and explicit. The music here and elsewhere is full of tension and discord as well as heavy irony, frequent satire and black humor, all of which could be used to launch accusations of anti–Soviet "formalism," meaning it was too *avant-garde*, complex or ambiguous. For any or all of these reasons, Stalin decided to react to the opera in a very public fashion. The *Pravda* article, although anonymous, left little doubt that it was Stalin's own displeasure being voiced and that rough times were ahead for Shostakovich and for musicians in general.

This was only the start of Shostakovich's troubles with Stalin and the Soviet cultural authorities. He would be repeatedly vilified and exalted throughout his career, even after the death of the "Great Leader." Yet he continued to write subversive and oppositional music even while he often publicly appeared to be a puppet of the regime. As with many artists, this guise of complicity was necessary to stay alive. By all accounts Shostakovich loved Russia and cared deeply about trying to support and protect his family and friends. It is remarkable that he managed to do so while others who received similarly harsh public censure either were eliminated, exiled, committed suicide or died from diseases related to the stresses and deprivations of Soviet life and Party persecution (for instance Pasternak and Eisenstein). Like many other artists, Shostakovich shared his more controversial works with friends and family during the times when he felt most threatened. As with the *samizdat* tradition in journalism and literature, musicians and composers kept many works private, circulating and performing them outside of official media and venues instead of risking official interventions in their lives. Shostakovich's popularity in the West was probably both blessing and curse, as it was not only the thing that singled him out as threat to Stalin, but also the fact that kept Stalin from being able to punish him too severely. It seems that his survival was partly due to Western admiration of, and Stalin's interest in, his work, or at least

Stalin's interest in using Shostakovich as alternately a scapegoat and posterboy. Other artists known and well-regarded in the West suffered worse treatment, but trying to figure out the logic of Stalin's behavior remains a puzzle for most historians and scholars.

Shostakovich appears to have been very good at playing this public-versus-private identity game, as dangerous as it was for him. This game-playing has added to some of the controversy surrounding his real attitudes towards the political structures and leaders of the Soviet Union: he was so good at it that many people still believe he wasn't playing at all. Some scholars have taken his public platitudes to the Party and to the Soviet government at face value and see him in quite a different light from that presented by Volkov and others who privilege the attitudes that can be gleaned from Shostakovich's private discussions and musical works. The majority of the evidence from unofficial statements and those of his close friends and family members indicate that Shostakovich was in no way a fawning Party adherent. Rather, one finds him constrained in making his official speeches, inserting irony wherever possible, much like Pasternak in his "anti-apology" written to the government during the *Zhivago* debacle. An artist in the USSR could expect that his artistic works (musical, cinematic, etc.) as well as public statements, especially those given by command performance, were known to contain multiple meanings and would be received and read as a sort of code. In an era in which legal rights protecting freedom of speech, expression and conscience were effectively non-existent, almost all communication contained levels of allegory, metaphor and irony. In fact, even officially-sanctioned or officially-produced pronouncements were encoded with double meanings, usually in the form of veiled threats. Shostakovich himself recalled whispered conversations with his wife in the middle of the night. If frank conversations with one's own family had to be conducted thus, how much more covert must have been public exchanges? It would seem that Shostakovich was deliberately both patriotic and pandering, the one serving the other. His loyalty to his country and his family meant that he had to stay in the Soviet Union and do whatever was necessary to keep composing and to tell the truth as he saw it.

Shostakovich chose to produce works whose implicit meanings undercut, contradicted or layered the explicit ones. Jennifer Gerstel writes of Soviet double-voicing in art and asserts Shostakovich's use of this technique to communicate to audiences messages directed against the Party and its tastes and dictates. She expands on double-voicedness and dissent: "to lie and tell the truth at the same time was the supreme act of subversion during Stalin's tyranny. And no one did it better, or with more wit, humor, sarcasm and irony, than Shostakovich" (37). Shostakovich's apologetic article, published before the 1937 Moscow premiere of his 5th Symphony, said that the piece was optimistic and positive, it was even subtitled "a constructive creative answer of a Soviet artist to just criticism," that criticism being Stalin's to his *Lady Macbeth* opera (Volkov 2004, 153). Yet, the work itself, because musical language, especially ironic or satiric music, is often subjective, connotative and impressionistic — in Volkov's words, "encrypted"— told an entirely different story. In one section, Shostakovich quotes Mussorgsky's *Boris Godunov* from the scene in which the monk Pimen's manuscript serves to show "the descendants of the true believers […] the past history of their native land" (quoted in McBurney 122). Gerard McBurney explains that during the days of reform under Gorbachev, Shostakovich was called "the Pimen of our time" (122). This comparison was certainly common before the '80s, as when Kozintsev called Shostakovich "the conscience of our time." The response to the 5th Symphony at its Leningrad premiere in 1937 (during the Terror) proved that audiences were attuned to the layering of meanings in artistic works. That they were so sensitive to the layering of the obscure language of music is testament to their training in interpreting Soviet art in its multiplicity of voices. McBurney writes that music had in the Soviet period "a large welleducated, and expectant audience, by no means confined to Leningrad and Moscow, and, for political reasons, likely to be highly responsive to music offering so obvious a possibility of subversive interpretation" (123). Personal accounts of the premiere of the 5th Symphony tell of people weeping during the final movement and that the ovation lasted for nearly an hour (Gerstel 48). It was, by some accounts, almost on the verge of becoming a demonstration or riot; such reactions became commonplace in response to its performances.

The outpouring of pent-up emotions during the era of "mass arrests, disappearances and executions" was threatening to the Party watchdogs (quoted in Gerstel 48). Shostakovich might have been the Party's sometime "enemy of the people," but the people themselves clearly did not view him as such. Episodes such as these illustrate the ways in which artists circumvented the heavy-handed censorship of the party and its cultural police and the ways in which audiences were fully aware of the different strategies of circumvention and were listening, watching and looking for the unofficial voices speaking in works of art. Pasternak, evidently, was himself envious of Shostakovich's ability to encode truth and yet to survive artistically: "just think, he went and said everything [in the 5th] and no one did anything to him for it" (quoted in Volkov 2004, 156). Interestingly, his boldness clearly inspired boldness on the part of audiences who were not afraid to respond to so evidently subversive a piece with what amounted to very public demonstrations of their approval.

Kozintsev chose Shostakovich to compose the music for *King Lear* because of his ability to write music that expressed to the people and for the people their true emotions in a time when truth in public forums, and even private ones, was scarce. Kozintsev refers to the music that Shostakovich gave to Cordelia's scenes as "the voice of truth" (*KLST* 246–247). Shostakovich's works expressed people's grief over the trauma of war and loss, and this too was part of Kozintsev's vision for *Lear* and another key reason for his collaboration with the composer: "the cry of grief, bursting through the dumbness of the ages, through the deafness of time, must be heard. We made the film with the very purpose that it should be heard" (*KLST* 251). This quality of Shostakovich's work set it apart for Kozintsev, not least of all because of the power and bravery necessary to continually stand up against the force of the regime. Shostakovich was perpetually fearful of repercussions against himself and his family, yet for all his cozening speeches, his music remained "fierce" (*lyuty*): "in Russian art goodness does not exist without a fierce hatred of everything which destroys a man. In Shostakovich's music I can hear a ferocious hatred of cruelty, the cult of power and the oppression of justice. This is a special goodness: a fearless goodness which has a threatening quality" (*KLST* 254). As with Hamlet's use of the theater as a weapon against Claudius' secrecy and treachery, music, seemingly inert and abstract to some, for others becomes a tool to effect an almost violent expression of truth. In the context of the assertion of Party-driven aesthetics against Western artistic "decadence" McBurney cites the use of "musical material as weapon in the continuing confrontation with the enemy" (132).[2] Music serves just such a purpose in Kozintsev's films, and the very choice of Shostakovich as collaborator would have signaled to his audiences that there were subversive meanings to be discovered if they listened and watched carefully enough.

The contradictory nature of the relationship of the musically outspoken Shostakovich and the tyrant leader led some of his contemporaries (and even Shostakovich himself, albeit indirectly) to compare him to the *yurodivy* or holy fool of Russian tradition. Indeed, Shostakovich reports that he was well aware of other people casting him as such, for example the conductor Mravinsky (*Testimony* 22[3]). Shostakovich was a self-styled *yurodivy* whose relationship with Stalin was tenuous, alternating between censure and punishment, coercion and protection (much like Pushkin and

Nicholas I). He describes his awareness of his relationship with Stalin obliquely: "Stalin was a morbidly superstitious man. All the unforgiven fathers of their countries and saviors of humanity suffer from it, it's an inevitable trait, and that's why they have a certain respect for a fear of the *yurodivye*. Some people think that the *yurodivye* who dared to tell the whole truth to Tsars are a thing of the past. [...] But the *yurodivye* aren't gone, and tyrants fear them as before" (*Testimony* 192). Shostakovich's awareness of the *yurodivye*'s history is clear from his reworking of Mussorgsky's operatic version of *Boris Godunov* during the Stalin era (Shostakovich also calls Mussorgsky a *yurodivy*). In one scene the holy fool Nikolka accuses the tsar of murder, which would have meant death for anyone else who said it, but Godunov left the fool alone.

Due to the inevitable parallels with Stalin and the Stalinist regime, Shostakovich voluntarily withheld his *Boris* opera from production, possibly to protect himself. Shostakovich muses over Stalin's dislike of the *Boris Godunov* story: "what bothered Stalin in *Boris*? That the blood of the innocent will sooner or later rise from the soil. [...] You will have to answer for your crimes someday" (*Testimony* 232). Indeed, Stalin objected to the composer Samosud on just this point, and his words reveal much about his ethos of violence and political expedience: Stalin claims "there is no need to produce the opera *Boris Godunov*. Pushkin and Mussorgsky perverted the image of the outstanding state figure. [...] Because he killed some kid, he suffered torments of conscience, even though he, [...] as a leading figure, knew perfectly well that this act was necessary in order to bring Russia onto the path of progress and true humanism" (quoted in Volkov 2004, 26). This statement provides an interesting parallel to Stalin's views on Ivan IV and his displeasure over Eisenstein's negative portrayal of the tsar in *Ivan the Terrible Part 2*. Ivan was also publicly chastised by a holy fool against whom, like Boris, he took no punitive measures. The figure of the fool and his challenge to the tsar were therefore a natural part of the inherent controversy in *Boris*, which Shostakovich would have found both attractive and, due to his experiences, something to treat with caution. Shostakovich composed music for the Fool in Kozintsev's film: in it the Fool carries a small flute-like pipe, which he plays throughout and in the film's important closing sequence. Kozintsev kept the Fool present throughout the film, and with Shostakovich's music, made sure to punctuate his presence. Shostakovich and Kozintsev spoke to the present through highlighting the Fool's role: in Shostakovich's words "tyrants and *yurodivye* are the same in all eras. Read Shakespeare and Pushkin, read Gogol and Chekhov. Listen to Mussorgsky" (*Testimony* 194). Shostakovich was aware of and welcomed his role as a yurodivy, a role which linked him to many great truth-tellers of the past.

Shostakovich, Kozintsev and Jewish Culture in the Soviet Union

Kozintsev's Fool is a complex figure, representing an unusual variety of historical and cultural themes. He is Lear's Fool, an evocation of the Russian holy fool (as in *Boris Godunov*), a victim of German and Russian anti–Semitism, and, much like Hamlet in the 1964 film, the voice of the artist or intellectual in opposition to tyranny. The connections among the Fool, the *narod*, the *yurodivye*, folk music, Soviet Jewish culture, visual homage to Mikhoels, allusions to war, exile and exodus, the Holocaust and Shostakovich's interest in Jewish and folk music, are especially intriguing in the way they manifest in Kozintsev's *Lear*. These aspects of the production have not been considered elsewhere in the critical literature, yet it seems that allusions to the Jewish experience are palpable and find expression in Kozintsev's treatment of the Fool, his depiction of the *narod*, and in Lear's appearance. The Fool and his tenuous position in society and ambivalent relationship to the King allude precisely to Shostakovich's own experience as one of Stalin's "fools" and to the relationship of artists to the government more broadly. Moreover, the film calls to mind the many victims of war, famine and the capricious tyranny of the Soviet era. The Fool expresses uncomfortable truths; indeed, this is demanded of him not only by his own integrity, but also by way of his connection to the people, and by the mandate of the king himself, even though his master is often punishing and censorious. Stalin, like Lenin before him, Khrushchev, and, to a lesser extent perhaps, Brezhnev after him, used the arts to disseminate ideology and to illustrate Soviet superiority to the West. International musical competitions were often dominated by Soviet composers and performers. Shostakovich was sent all over the world and given many honors for his works. At the same time, at home, his works were often banned and he was many times publicly criticized and his career at home jeopardized mainly because he composed with integrity, trying to avoid sacrificing truth for honors or absolute safety. Like the Fool he was dependent, exploited and yet also needed and valued.

Here also is the first among many intersections of Kozintsev's vision of *Lear* with Jewish life in the Soviet Union. The marginalization of the Jews that had obtained in the pre–Revolutionary period continued in the

USSR, inspired by Lenin's view that "the idea of a distinct Jewish people is scientifically untenable, and from a political point of view — reactionary" (quoted in Braun 1985, 69). Although official and unofficial anti–Semitism was rampant in the USSR, Jews held Party membership and offices, attended universities, and so on. Jewish musicians were often sent to perform at major competitions, which they very often won, and music was an important way for Jews to express themselves in a culture that barred and silenced them in many other forums. Folk music, and by extension, Jewish music, was very popular in the USSR and its study was encouraged by the authorities, though not without important limitations (see Braun's *Jews* for more on Jewish music and musical life through the 1960s). Under the guise of transcribing or studying "folk music," which the authorities encouraged, a great deal of Jewish music was preserved and its themes and sensibilities influenced and were absorbed by many Soviet composers. Shostakovich composed works with Jewish themes, including folk songs, although many of them were withheld from performance and publication. Most of the Jewish-themed compositions he wrote during the Stalin years were not performed or published until after 1953 (see table in Braun 1985, 70–71).

Among these works the most famous is the *Babi Yar* movement of Shostakovich's highly controversial 13th Symphony (premiered in 1962), which eulogizes the massacre of Jews in the Ukraine during World War II, an event that was a forbidden topic in the Soviet Union. This was a bold move for Shostakovich, one that was likely motivated not only by his love for Jewish music, but also his marriage to a Jewish woman, his sympathy with the Jewish musicians of his acquaintance, and his sense of outrage over the secrecy and hypocrisy of the Soviet state. Braun comments: "Shostakovich belongs to that section of the Soviet Russian intelligentsia whose views are often controversial, which sees in the Soviet Jewish situation a human tragedy and which, in its sympathy towards the Jews, expresses a kind of protest against the regime" (*Jews* 93). The entire symphony contains references to anti–Semitism and is highly critical of the State, with a special movement, titled "Fears" (based, as the rest of the symphony's vocal text, on poems by Yevtushenko) that makes nearly direct reference to Stalin and Stalinism (Volkov 274). Earlier, Shostakovich's Piano Trio contained Jewish musical themes in its finale and was also a direct musical reference to the Holocaust. Volkov mentions that Shostakovich's "From Jewish Folk Music" was composed in the midst of tremendous scrutiny and persecution of artists in the late '40s. Shostakovich made it to the top of the list of anti–Party "formalist" composers in 1948. The Jewish song cycle operated as both a paean to the suffering of Jews — labeled "cosmopolitan" and, hence, anti–Party, along with the formalists — and also an expression of Shostakovich's fellow-feeling for the Jews. He paralleled his own personal suffering with the suffering described in the poems that formed the vocal text of the piece (Volkov 246–250). The aesthetic of Jewish music worked on many levels for Shostakovich: it served as both a sincere and a mocking expression of "optimistic tragedy," that ability to "laugh through tears and weep through laughter" (Volkov 1985, 188). Jewish music itself embodies the sort of double-voicing used in Soviet art. It is the mode of the Fool who uses music and humor in an ironic fashion, joking and dancing when he is being deadly, dangerously serious.

Kozintsev's writings on the Fool and his characterization in the *Lear* film allude to Jewish persecutions. The liminal position of the Fool is very like the relationship of the Jews to the dominant culture in the USSR — and that of many artists and intellectuals as well. Braun's comment on the Jews in the Soviet state could just as easily describe the Fool: he is "permitted but undesired, forbidden but not unlawful" (1985, 69). The imagery in the film of the constant wanderings of the people, the war and fire, conjure the continuing problems facing Soviet Jews. The text used for Shostakovich's 13th Symphony was censored and had to be revised to remove direct references to the massacre as well as to the Jews' flight from Egypt. Despite the allowances made for criticism during the Thaw, the Babi Yar massacre, and Jewish problems in general, were not approved subjects; both Khrushchev and Brezhnev employed anti–Semitic rhetoric and policies. Indeed, by the time of the release of *King Lear*, a mass migration of Jews from the Soviet Union was well underway (see Ettinger 18–19). The film also depicts people in constant motion from place to place: the people, Lear, Gloucester, Edgar, Cordelia, Kent and the Fool are always on the move through a landscape of war, desolation, poverty and fire. Yvonne Griggs, in an interesting article comparing Kozintsev's *Lear* to the genre of the road-trip film, writes of the numerous scenes of traveling peasants that "we return to such sequences throughout the film, bearing witness to the ways in which Lear's actions impact upon the masses, forcing them back on the road as exiles in a war-torn country" (101). Under the tsars, the Jews moved to settlement areas, then after the Bolshevik Revolution they moved back into the cities, fled the Revolution and the Civil War, then suffered in the Second World War, moving again in and out of safety, all the while, like so many Soviets, being sent to prison, ejected from schools and jobs, entering internal exile or seeking to flee to other countries. In the post-war era and through the '60s and '70s, many Soviet Jews left the USSR for Israel and the West (Ettinger 18–19). The constant movement of people in Kozintsev's film evokes contemporary migrations and Old Testament peregrinations, the Jews' movements in and out of Egypt: a reference the censors cut from Yevtushenko's *Babi Yar* and that Kozintsev took up again for his film's *mise-en-scène*.

Solomon Mikhoels as King Lear in the Yiddish production of King Lear (circa late 1920s to early 1930s) at the State Jewish Theater in Moscow (GOSET).

Striking as well in terms of the Jewish themes that inform Kozintsev's film is the association between Kozintsev's visual presentation of Lear and that of the actor Solomon Mikhoels, who was killed on Stalin's orders in 1948. This was during the time of Stalin's "anti-cosmopolitan" (meaning anti–Jewish) campaign, which included the dissolution of the Jewish Anti-Fascist Committee, of which Mikhoels was chair; the end of Jewish cultural institutions, such as GOSET, the State Jewish Theater, also headed by Mikhoels; and the prohibition of publications in Yiddish. Mikhoels' *Lear* was one of the most famous productions of Shakespeare in Russo-Soviet history, which is even more remarkable because the work was a Yiddish translation that likely very few people who saw it even understood. Kozintsev's and Mikhoel's Lears are both conceived against the "type" of the powerful, kingly, old man with a beard and crown. In both cases, Lear is instead shown as physically weak; with unkempt hair and no facial hair or crown (Mikhoel's Lear enters with crown, but quickly loses it). The trappings of power and stateliness are deliberately stripped from Lear in order to anticipate and punctuate that his fall from power is more of a return to an original reality than a transformation. Moreover, in both productions, the relationship between the ruler and the Fool is made central, even from the beginning: in Kozintsev's production Lear and the Fool enter together, while in Mikhoel's the King's first interaction in the play is with the Fool. In both cases this is a directorial decision: in the play the Fool does not appear until the first scene is over.

Yuri Yarvet as King Lear (center), flanked by Regan (Galina Volchek, far left), Cornwall (Aleksandr Vokach, second from left), an attendant, and Goneril (Elza Radzina, far right) in the film *King Lear* (1970) directed by Grigory Kozintsev.

Collick also notes the sympathy between Kozintsev's and Mikhoel's Lears not only in appearance, but also in ethos: "Mikhoels saw the situation of Lear as a conflict between subjective and objective perceptions of reality" (146). This dichotomy runs as strain throughout all three of Kozintsev's post–Stalin films: *Don Quixote*, using Bakhtinian, FEKS-like gruesome and carnivalistic imagery, presents the tragedy of a man whose ideals and knowledge are crushed by a world immersed in lies and hypocrisy. *Hamlet* depicts its hero's struggle to assert his values and the actions prompted by his conscience against Claudius' structures of obfuscation and oppression. Lear similarly confronts his interior illusions as well as the ways in which his errors have (mis-)shaped the lives of his children and his citizens. Kozintsev frequently mentions Mikhoels and extols his *Lear* interpretation in both of his books.

Shostakovich remarks of *King Lear* and Shakespeare as subject matter: "everyone knows that our best Lear was Mikhoels in the Jewish Theater and everyone knows his fate. A terrible fate. And what about the fate of our best translator of Shakespeare — Pasternak? Almost every name bears a tragedy, more tragic than anything in Shakespeare. No, it's better not to become too involved with Shakespeare. Only careless people would take on such a losing proposition. That Shakespeare is highly explosive" (*Testimony* 87). Kozintsev's insertion of themes, sounds and imagery that evoked comparisons with Jewish culture and history, past and present, were part of the larger movement in arts and letters through the '60s and '70s to break free from State control. Being interested in and on the side of the Jewish cause aligned one with the forces of freedom and progress against the state's persistent anti–Semitism. Braun writes:

> Just as anti–Semitism was combined with political dictatorship and artistic conformity, so the Jewish resistance of this period was linked with the Russian democratic (civil rights) movement and progressive tendencies in art. Both the act of self-expression in art by Jews and the act of solidarity by non–Jewish musicians [and other artists] became, in Soviet conditions, a symbol of humanism and resistance [1984, 94].

The post-war period, from the late '40s into the '70s, saw both an increase in official anti–Semitism, but also a much greater, more powerful, counter-movement from "below" that saw the fate of the Jews as emblem of the fate of all the Soviet victims of tyranny and oppression.

War

In a similar fashion to the way the use of Jewish themes illustrated a connection to the dissident movement, the use of imagery and themes of war was also a method of subterfuge. Kozintsev's first *King Lear* was produced in 1941, and there were many productions of it in wartime (see chapter four). Kozintsev's 1973 book takes up this theme much more explicitly than his 1941 essay on *King Lear*, no doubt due to the somewhat freer climate, or at least, his decreased sense of fear from repercussions, which seems to be a trend well-established in the arts and letters by the late '60s and early '70s. During the war, films had to be positive and patriotic, lifting morale and deflecting engagement with the true horrors of life. After the war, while Stalin was still alive, many soldiers returning from the front or from abroad were sent to prison camps in an effort to avoid letting their stories sully the Party's favored version of the war experience and myths about life outside the USSR. Once Stalin died, and especially after Khrushchev's denunciation, these prisoners were released, and their true experiences became a less avoidable part of the national story.

The imagery of war is very important symbolically for Kozintsev for other reasons as well. He emphasizes the destruction and chaos of war throughout the film, a strategy that serves various purposes at once. Although matters such as Jewish persecution would have to have been avoided until after the fall of Communism, there was a general allowance for artists to depict and grapple honestly with the Second World War in their works. In Stalin's time this could still draw criticism for exhibiting "excessive pessimism," but after 1953, the war was generally fair game as subject matter. Catriona Kelly explains that "war mythology was [...] a supremely efficient basis of national identity in the post–Stalin era. Unlike the history of the Communist Party or even revolutionary history, it invoked what was universally perceived as a just cause: the righteousness of the war was never questioned, even in private" (265). The war experience provided a common referent for all the Soviet people, not merely for patriotism or national feeling, but also as a sort of sub-culture of unity outside of the Party and dominant public discourse. Kozintsev's writings, especially his *King Lear* book, constantly recycle themes of war, chaos, destruction and human evil as well as human suffering, grief, hope and love. Kelly notes that "representing the Second World War was one of the few ways in which writers, painters, film-makers, and musicians could give voice to the tragic aspects of Soviet history and Soviet reality" (264). Kozintsev's cinematic war in *King Lear* takes place in a landscape calculated to transcend any specific historical moment and, as such, it could reference any past, present or future wars. Kozintsev mentions Hiroshima in his book, and constantly uses fire in the film's *mise-en-scène* as sideways glances at the nuclear fears of the Cold War, topics too politically dangerous to handle directly. He writes of looking at war documentaries from World War II as research for the film: "burned houses, scorched ovens in a landscape covered in snow, bodies of the executed dug out of pits; the inhabitants had returned to their village (or what used to be a village) which had been laid waste by our army (a large number of old people were with them); they wandered among the bodies in the snow, recognized members of their families, wept, and could not tear themselves away from the bodies of the dead" (*KLST* 39–40). Throughout the second half of his *Lear* film, images of this sort of sorrow and destruction abound. As Shostakovich did in his war-themed compositions, Kozintsev attempted to effect healing by not shying away from illustrating the grim realities of war. For both artists, confronting reality was a deliberate challenge to the official chronicles of the State.

The Fool

One of Pasternak's observations fits Kozintsev's film quite well: he says, "the positive heroes [in *King* Lear] are the fools, the madmen, the dying, and the vanquished" (*Translating Shakespeare*, 147). The Fool conjures many associations for the Russian audience that are part of Kozintsev's thematic approach to Lear. Some of these associations are the Fool's connection to folk culture, the carnivalesque and the life of the *narod* as it manifests beyond the oversight of Church and State, and the Fool's relationship to power, in particular to Tsars and Soviet autocracy. Kozintsev's Fool also finds his counterpart in the Russian minstrel or *skomorokh*, similar to the one found in Tarkovsky's *Andrei Rublev* (1966), who is censured by the clergy, but loved by the peasants. Bernice Otto, citing Heinrick Birnbaum, writes, "in Russia, the skomorokhi, a term that [...] covers a wide range of entertainers including the court jester, also performed as magicians, animal trainers, and puppeteers and 'were certainly part of the counterculture that existed beneath the surface of officialdom'"; "They were loved for their uninhibited mockery of the church and other institutions" (11). They are further associated with Kievan bards—*gusliari*—who were itinerant poets and chroniclers (Otto 13). Due to their outspokenness, there was even a ban imposed on the *skomorokhi* in 1648 by Tsar Alexis I (Otto 11; 257). In *Rublev*, the jester is just such a figure, and one cannot help but see this film's influence upon Kozintsev's concept for Lear's Fool, especially in his provocative relationship to powerful individuals and institutions. Kozintsev writes, "the wandering comedians, the lawless defenders of freedom summoned their audience from all four corners of the earth to their stage on the market squares; the power of the emotional message has to be such that echoes of the alarum bell could be heard in the sound of the fool's bells. [...] In all history the priest and the comedian have never stood side by side, they have always been enemies" (*KLST* 220). The allegorical depiction of the Church and clergy in *Rublev* divides the Church into two separate currents: one that seeks to censor any and all opposition to it, as in the clerics who try to silence the jester; the other one, embodied by Rublev, the other iconographers and the bell-maker, represent faith as it is experienced by individuals not seeking to achieve or hold on to power. This duality parallels Kozintsev's own two minds: on the one side, he clearly retains his faith in the promises of the early Socialist movement, but on the other, he decries the tactics and failures of the Soviet regime. Moreover, it is clear that Tarkovsky intends a subversive parallel between the Church's power structure in his 14th-century story and the contemporary Soviet state, much as did Kozintsev is his linkage of Claudius' Elsinore with the image of the Cross.

Peter the Great issued further edicts against the *skomorokhi* and their like, which demonstrated that the prior edicts of the 17th century had little effect (Heller & Volkova 155). In the 1880s, for example, an article appeared in a Russian publication calling for a censorship of "clowns," similar to that imposed upon the theater, specifically bemoaning the sort of grassroots authority they assume: "who has given them the right to speak like this? There is only one answer: they have given it to themselves" (quoted in Otto 177). However, in keeping with European tradition, Peter himself kept fools and evidently encouraged them to mock the Russian nobles for the supposedly "backward" native habits that Peter strove to correct (Otto 116). Therefore, the State's varying hostility or acceptance of fools and minstrels depended upon matters of control and utility. The Russian Church did not canonize any fools after the 17th century. John Saward attributes this to their inherently extra-institutional status: "not even the cultus of the yurodivye was sufficient for the Church to admit another subversive to the ranks of the blessed. However, the literary motif, and the living reality, of the fool for Christ's sake was not eradicated from the Russian tradition" (23). The upper echelons of the Church could not abide any further official protection of such unruly dissenters, but the people held on to them.

In the Soviet era artists and intellectuals were useful and promoted when they toed the Party line, but were censored and punished when their voices subverted the State's ideology and edicts. People laugh at the Fool, sometimes mocking him, like the courtiers do to Don Quixote in the earlier film, but this is because the whole society's sense of truth has been distorted. Kozintsev writes, "for these people nothing is funnier than the truth. They roar with laughter at the truth, kick it like a dog, hold it on a leash and make a laughing stock of it — *like art under a tyrannical regime*" (*Proceedings* 1972, 198, emphasis mine). Kozintsev illustrates this in his film by showing the Fool led by a rope around his neck, like an animal, a pet or puppet (which further evokes the tethering of artist to ruler similar to Pushkin to Nicholas or Shostakovich to Stalin). He wears a scragglylooking fur vest for much of the first part of the film, which makes him akin to one of Lear's many dogs and horses. Kozintsev writes, he is "a tortured boy, taken from among the servants, clever, talented — the voice of truth, the voice of the poor; art driven into a dog's kennel with a dog's collar round its neck" (238; this echoes the Fool's line "truth's a dog must to kennel"— making the Fool a dog makes him, therefore, a direct embodiment of truth). At the very end of the film, he is even kicked aside like a homeless cur as he plays his pipe amongst the burning rubble.

Kozintsev's concept for the Fool eschewed most previous interpretations and signs of his role, especially Western imagery of the jester or clown figure, with which Kozintsev was entirely familiar, but which he felt was unsuitable for the film's depiction (*KLST* 71–72). This represents a departure from his earlier concept for the Fool in the 1941 production, about which he writes of the fool's cap and bauble, his motley and coxcomb. Kozintsev intends his film's Fool as more of a blank canvas upon which he and the audience can paint new associations, ones that are closer to the contemporary audience's lives, cultural heritage and milieu. The one traditional marker of the Western jester or clown Kozintsev kept are the bells. We never see them in the film, we only hear them when the Fool moves about — they are tied to his leg. Instead of a leitmotif (which he asked Shostakovich to write and then rejected) the Fool has only this very simple marker of his traditional garb. In keeping with Kozintsev's interest in Japanese arts and culture, these bells are like those at the Buddhist monastery, bringing the faithful back to attention in the present moment. Kozintsev writes, "the difference is not so much visible as audible. He is distinguished by sound. Before his entrance there is a soft jingle. Something like a call sign: the listener knows that the broadcast is about to begin and the he must tune in on the exact wave. [...] All I needed were bells and nothing else. A barely audible sound, soft but persistent, stubborn and continuous. [...] The Fool's toy rings out in the storm, resounds over the earth ... the tocsin of the Fool's bells. This is the call sign of conscience" (*KLST* 72). Note here how Kozintsev says that the audience is being primed to expect a message when the bells sound; a message that expresses conscience, a term that in Kozintsev's verbal economy signifies the realm of unofficial truth. The Fool's physical appearance is also strikingly like that of a concentration camp inmate: his gaunt appearance, shaved head and distressed uniform-like costume evokes both the Soviet Gulag and the Holocaust. Kozintsev explicitly points to this visual allusion and ties it to the Fool's musicality: "he is the boy from Auschwitz whom they forced to play the violin in an orchestra of dead men; and beat him so that he should play merrier tunes" (*KLST* 72, see also *Proceedings* 1972, 198). One also finds here an allusion to the enforcement of Socialist realism, which is certainly akin to beating artists into telling merry stories in their works.

Revisiting the themes of *Hamlet* and *Shakespeare: Time and Conscience*, Kozintsev places the Fool as stand-in for the artist or intellectual and for art itself, which persistently repeats the truth. In a further explanation of the Fool's bells, Kozintsev writes that this was his subtle homage to FEKS and to the experimentalism of his early years: "fortunately (or unfortunately?) my time for daring experiments was over. [...] I wanted the Fool's bells to ring out and peal as a salute to FEKS (The Factory of the Eccentric

Actor)!" (*KLST* 119). Not only is the connection between the Fool and the artist or intellectual suggested here, but there is also the acknowledgment, however oblique, of the demise of the freely experimental period of the early 20th century that was squashed by Stalin and the imposition of Socialist realism. The inclusion of the parenthetical phrase "or unfortunately?" is a marker of the subtle changes taking place in public discourse in the Soviet Union in the 60s. In the 20s and 30s, artists had to disown their previous "formalist" works and pay homage to the wisdom of Socialist realism. Under Stalin, Kozintsev's cinematic production slowed enormously compared to the FEKS years, and his most famous works were the officially acclaimed, patriotic *Maxim* trilogy films. Later, in *King Lear: The Space of Tragedy*, Kozintsev revisits the theme of changes in the artistic landscape. He discusses the early theories of montage, Eisenstein, the experimental film *The New Babylon* (1929), and then says of the present:

> What we did then helped me now in making a Shakespearean film. But I could not work in the same way now. The reason was not that the cinema of the twenties was silent, and that the technology of editing changed when the sound film came. A lot of water had flowed under the bridge since then and even more blood. [...] This is why I was studying Shakespeare. Why I was writing this book. The years (marvelous, priceless years) of pure cinema, of straight cinema, were past [173].

This passage reveals a great deal. Like many of his fellow artists and intellectuals Kozintsev picked up Shakespeare as a response to the limitations upon expression enforced by the state (see also *KLST* 190). It was also a response to violence, to the "blood" that "had flowed under the bridge." Since he could not create "pure" or "straight" cinema, he used Shakespeare (and Cervantes) to get his points across. Like the Fool used jests, Kozintsev used Shakespeare. Kozintsev went along with the times when necessary, as his 1930s *Maxim* films attest, but his later writings and his post–Stalin films reveal much more of his true attitudes towards the State and its imposed aesthetic program.

Two very famous fools in Russian history, and one from the Soviet era, provide further context for Kozintsev's depiction of the relationship between Lear and the Fool. One of these 16th century *yurodivye* was St. Basil the Blessed who famously stood up to Ivan IV (the Terrible) and was, instead of being punished, actually protected by the tsar. Perhaps one of the most famous Orthodox Churches in the world, a symbol of Moscow and Russia, was built for him: St. Basil's in Red Square. The other famous holy fool, who was also in contact with Ivan the Terrible, was St. Nicolas of Pskov, who might have been the direct inspiration for Pushkin's Nikolka.

Interestingly, it is the travel account of a 16th century Englishman, Giles Fletcher, which provides a contemporary report on the rebellious encounters of these fools with Ivan (see also Saward 22–23 on Fletcher, Ivan and Basil). Of Basil (or Vasily in Russian) Fletcher says he would "reprove the old emperor for all his cruelty and oppressions done towards his people" (219). More dramatically, Nicolas of Pskov sent Ivan a piece of raw meat during Lent, at which time the Orthodox fast from meat. Upon the tsar's confusion over this gift, the fool explained: "doth Ivashka [...] think [...] that it is unlawful to eat a piece of beast's flesh in Lent and not to eat up so much man's flesh as he hath done already?" (220; Ivashka is a familiar, diminutive form of Ivan; its use reinforces the sense of the fool's license to speak his mind. He is essentially verbally indicating his equality with, or even his superiority to, the tsar.) Indeed, it was this interaction that was thought to have precluded Ivan's attack on Pskov for the city's insubordination.[4] Allegedly Tsar Ivan the Terrible was a pallbearer at the funeral of Basil the Blessed (Thompson *Understanding* xiii). Ivan also identified with the *yurodivye*, signing some of his writings as "Parfeni the holy fool," part of his monastic alter-ego (Thompson 1973, 3). Clearly, the holy fool was allowed to be quite direct with the ruler and fear no reprisals, even though anyone else who dared to speak in this manner would certainly have faced arrest, prison, torture and perhaps death. As Ewa Thompson puts it: "neither Ivan nor Boris Godunov, dared to touch a iurodiviyi [yurodivy], so deep was the reverence of the people for the spiritual qualities of these homeless wanderers" (1973, 250). Lear's Fool similarly confronts Lear with his faults and chastises him, and although he is occasionally threatened, he is never punished.

In all of these cases, the fool functions as the "conscience of the king," pointing out to him his weaknesses, evil deeds and stupidity. In this sense he is a political, or perhaps super-political, figure, one in a position very much like the artist or intellectual. The fool's artistry lies in his use of a variety of distancing maneuvers, maneuvers that can be analogized with other artistic forms that "cover" the truth while still revealing it. The fools use humor and jest, singing and dancing, and feigned (although sometimes real) madness to carry their messages. The irony of sending meat as a gift during Lent is an example of such maneuvers: first, it breaks the rules of religious decorum, and as such points out that the tsar is breaking the moral code. Additionally the meat is certainly a quirky gift, which points to the fool's bold madness. The flesh serves as a graphic metaphor or symbol for the Tsar's violence, hence showing a rudimentary poetic sensibility as well as gallows humor. The outrageousness of the gesture and the perception of the fool's compromised mental state are also protective: his behavior could be dismissed or emptied of meaning, and thereby defused. Lear's Fool uses jesting, laughter, oblique language such as riddles, and song to provide a screen of amusement and cleverness in front of his chastisements. Kozintsev makes a particular effort to show his Fool's use of music, although he employs a full range of other tactics, such as linguistic acrobatics and humor. The parallels to the situation of the Soviet artist are striking: the artist is allowed to push the limits of what a subject can do and say, because, although he is dangerous to those in power, he is also loved by the people; indeed, he is needed by the people. Hence, he is needed by those in power as well, who can only take their tyranny and censorship just so far; at a certain point, the people must have their voice. Sometimes even despots have to face facts. Shostakovich's survival through the toughest times of the Soviet period attests to the tyrant's difficulty in ridding himself of the voice of the people: their truths revealed in art.

As in *Hamlet*, humor and irony, as well as feigned madness, are used as techniques of subversion. Laughter is very important in Kozintsev's *Lear* and most prominent with the Fool. Thompson cites edicts from the 16th and 17th centuries discouraging merriment in the Muscovite Kingdom; therefore the fools and minstrels "helped to develop an unusual kind of association between merriment and disobedience. In the Muscovite Kingdom, laughter and jest were associated with breaking the law" (22). Mockery of pre–Revolutionary figures and practices was encouraged by the Soviets, yet humor, satire and irony directed against the State were decidedly not (Thompson 1987, 23). Official displeasure over Akimov's farcical depiction of rulership in his *Hamlet* and the depiction of the police in Shostakovich's *Lady Macbeth* attest to the Party's inability to laugh at itself or to allow anyone else to do so. Kallistos Ware discusses the hagiography of the monk St. Symeon the Fool in Christ (circa the 6th century) and mentions its frequent use of the words "game" and "play": "here, in the playfulness of the fool in Christ, in his purifying laughter, we have perhaps a genuine christianization of irony, the basis for a theology of jokes" (164). St. Symeon's use of humor and his feigned madness, as well as his predilection for befriending undesirables such as actors and prostitutes, enhanced his outsider status since he subverted the seriousness and piety of the supposedly pious, respectable and powerful of his community. Ware writes: "but, if the fool plays, he is also serious: his laughter is close to tears, for he is sensitive to the tragedy in this world as well as to the comedy. He embodies both the sorrow of life and the joy of life" (170). Indeed, this is an area in which clear distinctions can be made among Brook, Kott and Kozintsev.

In Kott and Brook, their sense of absurdity and irony takes on a certain seriousness that verges upon nihilistic despair. Brook's film in particular ends up in a very hopeless place. Kozintsev keeps the reality of things in sharp focus, yet also brings in humor, hope and love. Brook kills his Fool, Kozintsev does not.

Edgar, Christ, the Hovel, and "Unaccommodated Man"

Edgar is an extremely important figure in the play and in Kozintsev's film, however his role in the film has not been examined as closely as it deserves. Edgar is not as prominent as Edmund in the Gloucester subplot, yet he emerges the hero and only survivor of those who populate his family. Edgar is another type of the Russian holy fool; in fact, his characterization is even closer to this Russian figure than Lear's Fool. Edgar combines characteristics of the holy fool, the *yurodivy*, and the wanderer, or *strannik*, as well as those fool-saints who are referred to as "blessed" or *blazhennyi*. Prompted by his brother's perfidy, and out of fear for his father's wrath, Edgar takes on his new role, becoming "a person who, totally lacking vainglory, consciously decides to feign madness in order to produce religious or moral reflection in others" (Thompson 1973, 246). In addition to his *yurodivy* "insanity" he takes on the homelessness and poverty of the *strannik*. As such "he shares with the iurodivyi [yurodivy] the lack of vainglory pushed to extremes, as well as living in perpetual insecurity and homelessness yet living with people and not as an anchorite" (Thompson 1973, 246). In the cases in which *yurodivy* and *strannik* converge, there is a clearly pedantic motivation: "the strannik takes up stranichestvo just as the iurodivyi takes up iurodstvo, for moral and spiritual reasons" (Thompson 1973, 246). As in much of the New Testament inversions of worldly folly and Godly wisdom, Kozintsev finds a similar kinship between folly and redemption: "without anyone noticing, the ridiculous casts off the fool's cap, and somehow appears in the crown of thorns" (*KLST* 172). Edgar's initial motivation to play the Poor Tom role is to evade discovery, but in the process he ends up guiding Lear and Gloucester through their moral and spiritual journeys.

Edgar is allied with the *narod* more directly than the Fool, as is seen in the hovel scene in which he participates in their suffering willingly, deliberately and directly. In the Orthodox Christian tradition, this is precisely the purpose of the Incarnation of Christ. The hovel further calls to mind the stable or cave in which Christ was born. Edgar's Christ-like

Edgar (Leonhard Merzin) leading his blinded father, Gloucester (Karlis Sebris) in the film *King Lear* (1970) directed by Grigory Kozintsev.

appearance and actions serve to ally him with the religious holy fool more so than Lear's Fool, who seems to be more a figure from secular (or even pagan or shamanistic) folk culture. At the end of the film, Edgar and the Fool are brought together in the *mise-en-scène* as emblems of the future currents of Soviet dissidence. The Fool represents artists and intellectuals, while Edgar represents the more general forces of courage, conscience, freedom and truth, as well as the renewal of faith and religious life. The people, to whom Kozintsev refers to as the "chorus" (*KLST* 198), are a sort of character and motif unto themselves in Kozintsev's film and he describes them in ways similar to his descriptions of Edgar, who joins them, and then Lear, who later becomes indistinguishable from them (these three, the people, Edgar and Lear, are linked in *KLST* 198–204). Kozintsev speculates that it was difficult for Cordelia's men to locate Lear not because he was hiding or out of the way, but because he came to be identical to the rest of the people (195). In this way Lear too becomes human in a manner similar to the Incarnation: he descends from his god-like position as ruler and becomes one of the suffering masses. Lear's position relative to the chorus is a key motif for Kozintsev. We see "Lear's face among the multitude of faces, among the people's grief, the destruction which has befallen the country" (*KLST* 202). Later on in the action, it is important to Kozintsev that Edgar not suddenly appear as a beautiful, heroic knight; rather, he must look like an ordinary soldier: "he has taken a dead soldier's tunic and picked up a sword and shield on the field of battle" (203). The emphasis on the *narod* is a constant theme in the film, and all the most positive characters are in some way allied with them visually or thematically.

Edgar's simple folk songs are another theme connecting him to the people. Kozintsev opens the film with the sound of one voice singing and then the image of the people in movement across the screen: the *narod* is the subject of his film, they frame the action and simple melodies are their score. At the end of the film, the people are rebuilding from the rubble as the Fool's pipe plays: "but his voice, the voice of the home-made pipe, begins and ends this story; the sad, human voice of art" (*KLST* 238). Nine crowd scenes were created for the film, each with a specific fragment of Shostakovich's musical "Lament": as with many of his other compositions, the people's suffering is expressed by the composer's voice. "In its ancient meaning the chorus was part of the action and took its rightful place in the tragedy. It was a tribal community raising its voice in lamentation for the dead. And so here in the film, in the very place where the powers of hatred and madness, the demonic element of tragedy had broken free and raged, this voice grew strong; grief brought people together, united them, the community grew and now it was enveloping mankind" (*KLST* 251). Edgar, the Fool and the people are aligned in sadness and its expression is found in music. Kozintsev includes bits of letters from Shostakovich in his chapter on the composer and the music for the film. In them, Shostakovich repeats the words "sad" and "sadness" in discussing his music for these two characters. Lear and Cordelia are brought into the association in Kozintsev's decision to replace the musicians who play for Lear when he wakes from his delirium in the play with just the Fool and his pipe (243, 244).

The positive inclusion of Edgar as a holy fool type, especially one so clearly Christian, is in itself a defiance of the Soviet state, which sought to destroy all faith practices. Yet the people of Russia and the lands of the USSR continued their faith practices and continued to value the holy fool despite efforts to the contrary. Again, the needs and beliefs of the narod supersede the dictates of the State: "and what of the Soviet Union? According to an émigré from the 1970s, holy fools were still at that time to be found in Russia: 'They keep hidden and others hide them'— if discovered, they were interned in psychiatric asylums. Modern tyrannies have reason to be afraid of the fool's freedom" (Ware 159). The influence of Pasternak's translation and the broader movement in the 60s and 70s of a resurgence of interest in and practice of Christianity are evident in Kozintsev's film and his *Lear* book.

The elements of spirituality, faith and Christian imagery in *Doctor Zhivago* stand firmly against Revolutionary and Soviet Socialist rhetoric and ideology. Pasternak was censored and punished — one might even say martyred — by the state as a result. Anna France, in her study of Pasternak's Shakespeare translations, notes Pasternak's use of Christian themes in his later works and suggests that this influence is especially palpable in his *King Lear* translation (79–80). Although in his *Translating Shakespeare*, Pasternak identifies *Lear* as "written in the language of the Old Testament prophets and situated in a legendary epoch of pre–Christian barbarism" (147), France notes that his translation of 1949 "may be linked closely with the profoundly Christian strain in Pasternak's own late work" (79). Despite the fact that Pasternak portrays much of the "brute violence and evil" of the play in his translation, he also "found more scope in this play than in any other for the almost irrepressible expression of compassion. [...] And evidence of selfless concern for others is sustained, often strengthened in Pasternak's handling of the text" (France 80). These facets of the translation appear to have influenced Kozintsev's interpretation of the play on the screen and in his book. The territory between the very farthest poles of love and hope, suffering and evil is traversed in the film, and Kozintsev's writings constantly reassert the power of the best of humanity to will out against its worst, especially through the medium of art, however abused and "tongue-tied" it may have seemed to be.

Kozintsev embraced Christian themes and imagery in his film. The play itself is often identified as taking place in pagan, pre–Christian times, but Kozintsev indicated that Christianity existed in Lear's time, even though Lear and his kingdom's population are mostly pagans. Lear calls upon "the gods" and "Apollo," Gloucester believes in astrology, Edmund in "nature." Yet the film suggests that Christianity exists within the realm and outside the realm, and allies the two most positive characters in the play, Cordelia and Edgar with this faith. Before Cordelia departs with France, we see them kneeling before a large cross by the seashore, being married by a figure in a friar's robe who intones in Latin. They slowly and deliberately cross themselves in Western fashion and kiss the cross on the cleric's rosary. For Soviet believers, especially the Orthodox, this brief scene had to have been loaded with significance. The Church was for centuries almost synonymous with Russia itself and the Liturgical year was the focus of personal and community orientation. The Bolsheviks, inspired by Marx and Lenin, took square aim at Orthodoxy and all religions, persecuting clerics and believers, destroying Churches, outlawing practices and taking control of the hierarchy of what remained of the Church. Cordelia's association with Roman Catholicism, which was considered heresy and apostasy by the Orthodox Church, would strike a chord of both longing and fear in the audience: longing for religious freedom, which only existed elsewhere, and fear that the decline of the Russian Orthodox Church might give over supremacy to the Roman Church as the pre-eminent international symbol of the Faith.[5] Later on in the film, when Gloucester dies, Edgar fashions a cross out of sticks and fabric to mark his place of burial, pausing to pray over his grave. This scene indicates that Christianity is not merely a foreign phenomenon in Lear's world, but that it also exists within the kingdom, even though it is clearly not practiced or endorsed by the King. Again, the resonance with the audience is immediately apparent: the pagan kingdom parallels the atheist Soviet state, and Edgar's private act of devotion and ritual evokes the private, secretive practices of faith that continued among believers throughout the Soviet era. Instead of Shakespeare's pre–Christian England, we find a post–Christian Russia.

Edgar's nearly naked frame strikes Lear upon their meeting and precipitates his realizations about who and what he is. In the play, Lear even tries to remove his own clothes in order to become closer to Edgar and the people. Nakedness figures prominently in the hagiography of Russian holy fools: Basil the Blessed was also known as Basil the Naked (see Volkov 2004, 33, Thompson 1987 xiii, Heller & Volkova 155). These images are reminiscent of Christ's Incarnation and Crucifixion: he was naked at birth and on the cross. Thompson mentions nakedness and other markers of the holy fools, such as wearing iron things, bells, peasant clothes in disrepair (very like both Edgar and the Fool). Giles Fletcher's accounts in *Of the Russe Commonwealth* provide an outsider's chronicle of the holy fools. He specifically mentions their nakedness, the people's reverence for them, their difficulties with the Church and monastics (he refers to the holy fools as "eremites" implying their existence outside of the community of Church or monastery), and most pointedly, their ability to speak out against the government and the tsar without punishment. Rather amusingly, Fletcher observes: "of this kinde there are not many, because it is a very harde and colde profesion, to goe naked in Russia, specially in Winter" (Fletcher *Facsimile Edition* 90). Edgar's nakedness, although uncomfortable, is also a sort of freedom: a freedom from cultural, personal and institutional strictures that attracts Lear. "Tramps, beggars, newly released convicts — the many faces of Poor Tom; in their midst Edgar and later Lear are homeless among the homeless, on the 'rock bottom' of the kingdom" (*KLST* 39). Lear becomes similarly freed from his possessions, position, family, etc., which initially causes him to feel angry and afraid, but after his enlightening conversion encounter with Poor Tom in the storm, he embraces this freedom as the "unaccommodated man."

Kozintsev's storm and hovel sequences are central to the film and crucial in his understanding of the play and its relevance for his audience (*KLST* 191–197): "the space of the tragedy is a penal wash-house" (*KLST* 197). Quoting from Dostoevsky's *House of the Dead*, Kozintsev connects the hovel with the hut of a prison camp — one that could be German or Soviet. As in Dante's famous trilogy, Lear must pass through this Hell in order to attain his Purgatory, "the meeting with Cordelia" (*KLST* 193), and then, presumably, to join her in Paradise after their deaths. Dostoevsky's description of the prison camp in Siberia "concludes, 'if we all end up in Hell one day, it will be very like this place'" (quoted in *KLST* 193). Certainly, Kozintsev has chosen his quotes and analogies purposefully: he does not describe a German camp, but a Russian one. He explains the fate of his own country, not that of any other: "the penal settlement washhouse is a model of life itself. It is the fate of those whom life has banished from its systems, and has forcibly driven together; has herded them into a confined space from which there is no exit, has mangled them with injustice and twisted them with want" (*KLST* 193). The hovel sequence and the effect that it has on Lear, as elucidated in his "unaccommodated man" speech are the heart of Kozintsev's concept of *Lear*. It is similar to the way that Hamlet's "pipe" speech formed the fulcrum upon which the action turned in that film. "In Hamlet the words about not being a pipe on which the king's men can play whenever they like seemed to be more significant [...] than the famous 'To be or not to be!' The most important part of the storm scene seems to me to be the speech about 'unaccommodated' man rather than the rhetorical 'Blow, winds'" (*KLST* 50). The hovel scene is the turning point for Lear, and Edgar's presence is the catalyst effecting his transformation from delusion to illumination.

Lear himself then enters into the life of the wanderer, and in turn he educates Gloucester in the manner of a holy fool. The *strannik*, like Edgar, "abandons his stable and secure social situation and chooses the unsafe life of wandering. He does it in order to discover authentic life" (Thompson 1973, 261). Lear's "resurrection" is brought about by his dislocation from

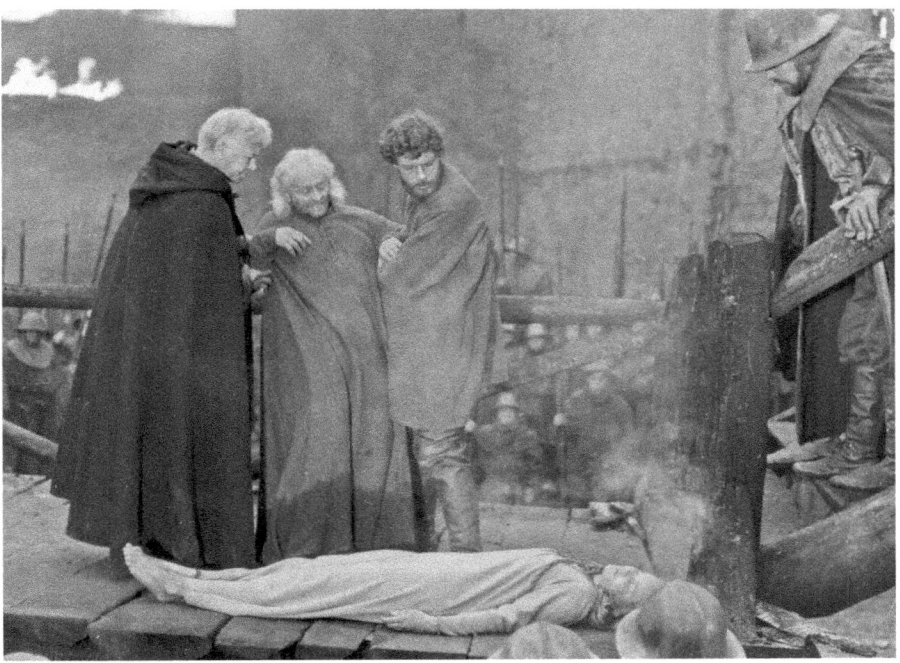

Albany (Donatas Banionis), Kent (Vladimir Yemelyanov) and Edgar (Leonhard Merzin) assist Lear (Yuri Yarvet) over Cordelia's (Valentina Shendrikova) corpse as Edmund's soldiers look on in the film *King Lear* (1970) directed by Grigory Kozintsev.

his place of power and stability and the end of his isolation from others. All of these things must change for him to truly learn. It is as if he goes from a falsely eremitical life into the life of the prophet, and in the process discovers identity with humankind and a deeper experience of love. Importantly, the Fool and Edgar, as well as Kent and Cordelia, continue to act out of love for others and seek to help them. Their outsider status does not preclude their solidarity and care for the people, or cause them to abandon or neglect their relationships with others. Lear's transformation is similar. In the hovel he feels kinship with the "dregs" of society, and later goes on to pass on his knowledge to Gloucester and to reconcile with his estranged daughter.

Of the Pasternak translation France writes, "in this play, however monstrous the actions of some, and despite the tendency towards division, dissention and estrangement, there is always someone to bear witness to suffering, engaged in the effort to overcome it, and Pasternak excels in expressing this" (91). Following from this, Kozintsev's direction brings out "the contrast between suffering borne in isolation, and that which is shared" (France 89). The blinded Gloucester is accompanied by a peasant and then by his estranged son — unlike Edmund, Gloucester does not die alone. Albany, Kent and Edgar are shown standing together throughout most of the final sequence of the film, witnessing Lear's loss and death together. When Lear dies, he is not even in the shot, rather we see the cluster of people surrounding and supporting him as he mourns Cordelia's death. There are many more examples of Kozintsev's *mise-en-scène* depicting people in pairs, trios — often showing people touching each other — and groups both large and small, that stand in contrast to the smaller number of shots and scenes in which a figure appears alone or figures appear together, but with spaces between them, without making physical contact. On the heath the suffering Lear is joined by the Fool, who literally attaches himself to Lear's back, gripping him tightly, then they are joined by Kent, and then Edgar, who himself has already joined ranks with the ever-wandering peasants, themselves always moving in groups across the landscapes of the film. There are very few moments in the film in which anyone is truly alone. Only the villains, such as Edmund, are depicted in isolation from other characters. Anyone who suffers or dies in the film is never alone, except, again, Edmund, who dies abandoned by all, even the slimy soldiers who carried out his evil orders.

King Lear's Ending: Armageddon and Resurrection

The closing sequences of the film serve to summarize Kozintsev's ideological vision for the play, illustrating his hope for the future and transmitting his mandate to his audience to carry on their fight against the entropy of Soviet life. For Kozintsev "the problem is to ensure that the inner action, the intense exploration of life, should not explode at the end of the film but should continue on in the spiritual world of the audience. One should not demonstrate, but provoke" (*KLST* 1). Ware cites Solzhenitsyn's *The First Circle* on the ironic freedom granted to Soviet citizens who feel they have nothing left to lose. In the novel Bobynin rebuts Stalin's Minister of State Security saying, "you only have power over people so long as you don't take everything away from them. But when you've robbed a man of everything, he's no longer in your power — he's free again" (quoted on 156). The Fool and Edgar, even Cordelia and Kent, are free to "speak what they feel and not what they ought to say" because they have

Five. *King Lear* Revisited in the Brezhnev Era

Cordelia (Valentina Shendrikova) and Lear (Yuri Yarvet) being taken prisoner by Edmund's men in the film *King Lear* (1970) directed by Grigory Kozintsev.

nothing left to lose. The holy fool, the wanderer, the eremite, Christ himself, have nothing to lose and therefore speak freely. At the end of the play, Lear goes off to prison happily with Cordelia. In the film, his happiness is complete in his reconciliation with her even as they walk in the midst of Edmund's soldiers, two small, soft figures engulfed by armed, armored men. Lear has been purified and has reconciled with the person he unjustly sinned against, who herself is an emblem of faith and love unconstrained by worldly concerns. The prisoners are victorious in their love. Edmund and his soldiers, as well as the wicked sisters and Cornwall, are the losers, and are ultimately vanquished, adding to the subtle positivity of Shakespeare's play, which is too often interpreted as irredeemably negative.

The image of Lear and Cordelia being taken to prison, yet surrendering with joy and love, which has a palpable effect upon the soldiers and even Edmund, recalls countless hagiographic accounts of martyrdom for Christ. In many such accounts, beginning, in fact, with the conversions of one of the Roman soldiers at the crucifixion and the thief crucified with Jesus, the saints who are tortured and killed bear themselves with such conviction, bravery, humility and joy, that often the people who witness their persecution are converted as a result. As Cordelia and Lear are led to prison by the soldiers, Kozintsev pays special attention to Edmund's reactions in several shots. Edmund is clearly both astonished and angered by his prisoners' love for each other, which seems to render them oblivious to the threat they face. Moreover, it is clear from the faces of the soldiers surrounding them, that they are impressed and moved by the love and compassion emanating from their captives. "The two powerless prisoners become the conquerors" (Kozintsev *KLST* 224). Edmund quickly jumps up on top of a wagon and shouts part of his speech about how "men must be as the times are," not "soft hearted," and then seeks out a man who will carry out his orders to kill Lear and Cordelia.

It is obvious from Kozintsev's choices here that Edmund is threatened by the example that Lear and Cordelia are setting, just as the leaders who sent so many martyr-saints to their deaths must have been dismayed at the conversions that resulted from their attempts to eradicate believers. "The prisoners, with bound hands, walk past the ranks of men armed to the teeth, wicked men — like conquerors. This is the beginning of Edmund's defeat" (Kozintsev *Proceedings* 1972, 199). It appears that even Edmund ends up converted, or at least repentant, since his final act before he dies is to rescind his orders against Lear and Cordelia. Kozintsev shoots the dying Edmund from above; for a few moments it appears that Edmund has a vision from the heavens that motivates his final act of repentance, as if he could see that he would be doomed unless he performed some final redemptive act of compassion. Earlier in the film, Edmund throws a rock up to the sky, as if in defiance of the god(s) he claimed moments before not to believe in. In his final breaths, he looks up to the sky again and accepts his dormant faith.

Kozintsev writes that Edmund's rise to power is basically invisible in the play, so in the film he takes time to show the war, the destruction and his rise to power in order to emphasize his ultimate defeat (*KLST* 209). The final battle between Edmund and Edgar is very important in the film, since it determines which of the new generation's ideologies will prevail. The implications for Kozintsev's audience are the same: will the newer generations succumb passively to the repressions of the Brezhnev era, relinquishing any hope for justice and freedom, or will they continue the quest for a renewal of hope and the assertion of the individual's rights, even under the threat of annihilation? In his writings, Kozintsev raises the stakes here to Apocalyptic proportions: he indicates that a decisive moment has come, one which is every bit a matter of life or death.

Edgar arrives at the moment when it seems that Edmund and his like have won, imprisoning Lear and Cordelia, burning villages and homes, and murdering anyone who resists. Edmund, Goneril, Regan and Cornwall "are all heading towards madness and eternal damnation," and therefore, so is the whole nation (*KLST* 209). Yet Edgar's power is no less potent: "Edmund has behind him the might of the army, the powers of destruction; Edgar — a ruined country, the grief of mankind" (*KLST* 253). Amidst the smoke and chaos of battle, a circle of soldiers forms in which this Armageddon plays out. Importantly, Edgar is wearing a helmet that completely obscures his identity. In this moment, he is not fighting for himself; his personal gripe with his brother pales in comparison to the larger goal, which is to win back the soul of the kingdom on behalf of all the people. Because Edgar embodies the entire will of the people against evil, and Edmund only his self-interest, "Edmund is defeated even before the fight begins" (*KLST* 253). After witnessing many acts of heroic goodness, his armor had already begun to crack, and his faith in himself and his mission had already begun to fade: "why were Lear and Cordelia so fearless? Why did the weak Duke of Albany come out from under his wife's heel and destroy her plans? Where did this faceless man come from who was deflecting his blows? Why was he so assured? How many more were there like him? And what linked them together?" (*KLST* 253) Edmund is not defeated merely by force; rather he is defeated because he has buried within him a conscience, a sense of his own and others' human worth and dignity. He realizes that his project would necessarily lead to his own destruction because no one could survive in the world he sought to create, not even the one who created it. "Edgar finally struck him, or Edmund purposefully impaled himself on Edgar's sword. It is all shrouded in a leaden grey mist, smoke and soot. The hour of judgment" (*KLST* 236). Edmund's death is punctuated by a very short musical composition by Shostakovich titled "The Call of Death." Edmund's final lines are replaced by an overhead shot of his dying and by this music: "at this moment — in the last close-up — the total, the ruin of the inhuman idea, the Shakespearean dialectic of the struggle for power should be played out" (*KLST* 249). Fortunately, for this moment at least, the victor is Edgar, one of the "good guys."

Cordelia and Lear's deaths are followed by images of water and flying birds. Of this positive imagery Kozintsev writes, "the heroes of tragedy do not die, they come to life again with each new generation and again accompany them along the same path, repeating the same words, the answer to the new Edmund. The rebuff of darkness. The repulse of the plague" (*KLST* 224). In the Soviet context, Kozintsev's insistence on a redemptive, even resurrectional, interpretation of the deaths of the play's heroes is clearly intended to encourage the audience to continue to rise above circumstances and to persevere against oppression. The accumulated death-toll up to this point in Soviet history is truly staggering: from the Bolshevik Revolution, through the Stalin era, World War II and into the 1960s, tens of millions of citizens lost their lives, mainly due to the policies and practices of their own government. Indeed, Lear and Cordelia also die in their own homeland, as prisoners of war and victims of tyranny, in no small part due to Lear's errors as a leader and Cordelia's resistance to his irrationality.

Edgar's final line "speak what we feel, not what we ought to say" is a mandate to the Soviet audience, and a difficult one. Despite the clear drawbacks of freely speaking one's mind as citizen, servant or kin of the powerful, Edgar tells the audience that this is exactly what they must do. Perhaps if Lear had not been flattered or cajoled he would not have turned into a tyrant both despotic and childish and perhaps, in a trickle-down fashion, the rest of the links in the chain would have been spared breaking apart. Kozintsev's ending replaces the utterance of this line with a powerful, almost chilling, visual equivalent. Breaking the "fourth wall," Edgar simply stares out at the audience after the bier carrying Lear and Cordelia passes, while fires smolder in the background, peasants begin cleaning and rebuilding and the Fool, perhaps the only constant truth-teller, plays his pipe mournfully after being roughly kicked aside by soldiers bearing the corpses. Kozintsev writes, "the Fool who amused the King at the beginning — the boy in the dog's coat, put on inside out — turned out to be both the last man to stay by him and the only one to mourn him" (238). These visual juxtapositions reinforce the complexity of the seemingly simple aphorism "speak what we feel"; it will always be a world in which challenging speech, especially that which clashes with the dominant narratives of power, will be dangerous. *Lear* drives home the costs of silence; war, and all of its horrors are made visible here; it shakes down even into individual families, as the Gloucester subplot makes manifest. Edgar's final stare into the camera is a call-to-arms. Depending upon the version or edition of the play one consults, the final speech is delivered by either Edgar or Albany. Clearly, Kozintsev preferred it to be Edgar, most likely because he wanted a representative of the younger generation to be the last man standing, one who had less baggage from the past. There is an emphasis on his aloneness at the finale: Kent goes, then Albany, and Edgar is left ... with the audience. The context of the film's era resonates here, since the Soviet regime has moved through the cooling of the Khrushchev "Thaw" into the more repressive Brezhnev years. Kozintsev's somewhat circular view of history in *The Space of Tragedy* suggests his awareness of the continuing and newer dangers facing Soviet Russia. If people are cowed, even with good reason, there will be no end to the despotism of the regime. "I recognized Shakespeare's thought in his eyes. Perhaps the audience would also read these lines in the look he directed at them? ..." (Kozintsev *KLST* 238). Words were not needed given the powerful eloquence of the actor and the film's final images.

Kozintsev's ending betrays greater optimism than Kott's treatment of the play or Brooks' film, which is decidedly bleaker and more influenced by Kott's reading of *King Lear*. Kozintsev appeals to his country's leadership and its people. Kozintsev sees history and human nature as often tragically repetitive; he visits this theme constantly in his Shakespearean writings. Given the era during which this film was created, it seems reasonable to assume that Kozintsev feared a return to the sort of despotism and horror that he and his country had already passed through — the tightening of intellectual and creative controls under Brezhnev and the specter of nuclear war perhaps presaged for Kozintsev another Stalin era, and possibly yet another, perhaps even more devastating, war. This *King Lear* is guardedly hopeful, both a statement about overcoming the past and warning about the future likelihood of repeating it. The end of the film reiterates these fears and heightens the sense that this is Kozintsev's cautionary tale. The biers of Cordelia, Lear, Edmund, Goneril and Regan are marched through the corpse-strewn battlefield and burnt-out town as peasants throw water on the fires and clear away debris. This feeling of closure is not unbroken: as the soldiers pass the Fool playing on his pipe, they kick him out of the way, implying the unending cycle of human brutality. Here in the final scenes the existence of another sort of "all" is revealed:

> Shakespearean characters demand an answering call. Lear's call, "O, you are men of stones" is not unanswered. Who does he expect an answering call, a reply from? From everyone. Does that mean from all who enter the stage? No, rather from those who are in the audience. And not literally from those who that same day bought a ticket and came to see the play, but from all those who continue to live; from those who will come in the future; from those who understand; those who are not made of stone [*KLST* 185].

Edgar, left alone to try to carry on after "those who are older" have all gone away, looks directly into the camera. He says nothing, he merely walks forward staring at the audience; it is the only time anything like this happens in the film. The burden of repairing the kingdom is not one person's, it is the burden of the entire audience who must become a part of the effort to reclaim their country.

Epilogue

Korol Lir was Kozintsev's last film. He died in 1973, evidently with plans to make an adaptation of The *Tempest*. The *Tempest,* with its themes of exile, betrayal and misgovernment would have been yet another significantly loaded choice of material for Kozintsev, and one can only mourn that it never came to fruition. The legacy of Kozintsev's productions and writings, like that of Shostakovich and Pasternak, is clearly felt in the cultural and political events of the decades after his death. Most significantly, Shakespeare continued to serve as a mouthpiece for dissent, and many more subversive theatrical productions were produced throughout the USSR. In fact, the correspondences between the Shakespearean plays and the contemporary situations of their audiences became more and more directly stated, a development I am sure Kozintsev would have greeted with no small satisfaction.

One of the most notable productions of the newer generation was Yuri Lyubimov's *Hamlet* at Moscow's controversial Taganka Theater in 1971, which remained in its repertoire through 1980. Hamlet was played by the incredibly popular protest singer and poet Vladimir Vysotsky, casting that signaled the spirit of dissent intended by the production's entire concept. This casting recalls Kozintsev's choice of former soldier and POW Innokenti Smoktunovski as his Hamlet in the 1964 film, or his choice to use Nikolai Cherkasov as his *Don Quixote,* who had been Eisenstein's controversial Ivan. Lyubimov also used Pasternak's "Hamlet" poem as one of two alternate openings for the play, just as Kozintsev had in his 1954 stage production (in which he used the poem at the play's finale), a choice which remained controversial since *Doctor Zhivago* was still banned through the 1970s. The production was noteworthy for a large curtain that moved ominously back and forth over the stage and sometimes the actors — this was a sort of Iron Curtain motif that reminded many viewers of the 1954 Okhlopkov *Hamlet* as well as Kozintsev's use of the imagery of heavy woven cloth in both of his Shakespeare films. The gravediggers occupied the space between the stage and the audience, turning the orchestra pit into a grave. They dug and removed bones throughout the production, serving as a graphic reminder of the countless lives lost due to Soviet brutality. Dawson sums it all up thus: "the images of the theatre, the prison, and the grave all crucial to Hamlet and *Hamlet*, were adroitly woven together in the production" (236).

The always outspoken Lyubimov was exiled in 1984 and even lost his Soviet citizenship — many commentators posit that this *Hamlet* production didn't help his standing in the USSR. Nonetheless, his *Hamlet*'s long run and subversive content made its mark on the cultural scene and evidenced the continuing relevance of Shakespeare for Soviet artists and audiences — in the case of *Hamlet*, a relevance that was going strong after more than two-hundred years. Indeed, the production may very well have continued even longer than its 9-year run had not its star Vysotsky died prematurely in 1980.

King Lear also continued to be performed in the Soviet Union. A Georgian production directed by Robert Sturua for the famous Rustaveili company even traveled to the United States in 1990 — the Brooklyn theater at which it appeared made a cultural exchange of their *Cherry Orchard* for the visiting company's production, a trade typical of the Glasnost era. The set for this Lear evoked an old decaying theater "meant to give the audience something of the sense of looking into a mirror" according to a contemporary review in *Newsday*. This mirroring is a device we have seen in both of Kozintsev's films — Hamlet's "Mousetrap" and Edgar's final stare, for instance. At the end of the play Lear's world literally comes crashing down around him as set pieces fall, giving the sense of a cataclysm reminiscent of Kozintsev's visions of post-nuclear annihilation in his *Lear* film. Sturua himself deliberately referenced apocalypse in his comments upon the play, fitting imagery for the Cold War audiences in the USSR and the USA (Gussow). For Georgians on the brink of independence from the Soviet Union, Lear's division of his kingdom must have provided an interesting parallel to the contemporary situation that showed something of the anxiety surrounding such changes. The question, as ever, was "what's next?"

The 1970s and '80s saw great upheavals in Soviet society as the USSR continued to disintegrate and eventually collapse. Even the repressive policies of the Brezhnev era could not contain the will of the people to end their oppression. Artists, intellectuals and regular citizens throughout Russia and the republics redoubled their efforts, using *samizdat* and *tamizdat* distribution, independent radio broadcasting and voluntary exile through defection to evade Party censorship. The newer generations who had not experienced the worst of the Stalin era nor the trauma of World War II were even more outspoken than Kozintsev's generation. Having not lived through the worst of times, they did not fear reprisals in the same way as their predecessors. The generational divide is here in Edgar's words, the very last of *King Lear*: "The oldest hath borne most; we that are young/ Shall never see so much, nor live so long" (5.3.326–7). The younger generations indeed rose up and finally helped to bring the dark period of Soviet dictatorship to a close.

Chapter Notes

Chapter One

1. I would add that here it seems Pushkin is also quoting Polonius' "to thine own self be true."
2. This translation © John Woodsworth, Ottawa (Canada); http://kanadacha.ca. Used with permission.
3. See Golub (174–75) on the Decembrists, *Hamlet* and the "aristocratic suicide cult."
4. See article by Grigor'jan on Pecorin and the *Hamlet* influence in *A Hero of Our Time*.
5. N. Grigor'jan's article provides an interesting critique of Turgenev's "arbitrary" interpretation of *Hamlet*, which ends up oversimplifying Hamlet (247–249).
6. Diakonova's and Levin's essays date from the 1970s and 80s and give the impression of treating the 19th century as a screen for talking about the continuing problems of the late Soviet era, illustrating that the critical tactic of doing Shakespeare criticism as a way of commenting upon the present is a tenacious Russian tradition.
7. In Russian names the middle name is usually a version of the father's name, which is called a patronymic.
8. The article by Golumb discusses the choices of translations available to Chekhov and speculates as to why he might have chosen to quote the Polevoy. Golumb discusses the problem of some translators of *The Seagull* using Shakespeare's original language instead of translating from the Polevoy, which is markedly different (76). Moreover, Winner suggests that Chekhov probably did not read English (104). There is a similar problem in the subtitles for Kozintsev's Shakespeare films, which quote the English text of the plays instead of translating Pasternak directly.
9. See Gibian "Tolstoj and Shakespeare" (43–44) on Tolstoy's chagrin over Shakespeare's language in *Hamlet*.
10. See Knight on Tolstoy's ideas about Hamlet's lack of character and Shakespeare's versus Tolstoy's vision of characterization (15–19).

Chapter Two

1. Communist Party members loved to use this word as a slight upon anything spiritual or religious.

2. As with "mystical" and "feudal," "humanism," "humanist," etc., were more Party-line buzzwords indicating a people-centered social organization: a proto-Communist ethos.

3. See Golub's chapter on the theater in this period, "The Silver Age, 1905–1917" (278–301) in *A History of Russian Theatre*.

4. Kozintsev himself had been co-director of FEKS in the 1920s, which was an experimental theater company. He and his longtime artistic partner Leonid Trauberg made many highly experimental theatrical pieces and films together.

5. See Law for more descriptions of the stylized sets, costumes and makeup, which look like they could be from an F. W. Murnau film, so dramatic is the use of expressionist style.

6. The post-war situation is compellingly dramatized in Pasternak's *Doctor Zhivago*, and treated in the brutal historical drama of Solzhenitsyn's *The Gulag Archipelago: 1918–1956* (1956 being the date of Khrushchev's "secret speech" that effectively ended the Stalin cult).

7. See *STC* (212–225) for samples of letters between the two; (221) for their debate on the ending of the play.

8. France notes that the verb used here, *rastroit*, can mean to unsettle and to untune, much like the double meaning of "fret" in English, meaning to worry or irritate and to play an instrument with one's fingers.

Chapter Three

1. Mayakovsky was a famous Revolutionary poet who committed suicide in 1930 (at the age of 36) as a result of his despair over the Stalinist state.

2. A radio broadcast in 1961, quoted *Hamlet* in English and compared Ivinskaya to Gertrude: "frailty thy name is woman!" (Conquest 184)

3. This translation is © John Woodsworth, Ottawa (Canada); http://kanadacha.ca. Used with permission. For more on the Christian implications of the poem see Sergay.

4. France's chapter on Pasternak's translation expands upon its Christian themes and imagery.

5. This is similar to the depiction of Western Christianity in Kozintsev's *King Lear* film, in which Cordelia and France are married by a Latin friar.

6. The KJV translates the verses thus: "For the preaching of the cross is to them that perish foolishness; but unto us which are saved it is the power of God. For it is written, I will destroy the wisdom of the wise, and will bring to nothing the understanding of the prudent. Where is the wise? where is the scribe? where is the disputer of this world? hath not God made foolish the wisdom of this world? For after that in the wisdom of God the world by wisdom knew not God, it pleased God by the foolishness of preaching to save them that believe [...] Because the foolishness of God is wiser than men [...] But God hath chosen the foolish things of the world to confound the wise" 1 Corinthians 1.18–29.

Chapter Four

1. Pushkin's story "The Postmaster" (or "The Stationmaster") from the *Tales of Belkin* features a somewhat *Lear*-inspired relationship between a widowed father and his daughter, who appears outwardly to be an ungrateful Goneril or Regan character, but turns out to be much more like Cordelia, despite her apparent abandonment of her father (Bethea 87).

2. See Stribrny (36–40), Bethea (82), for comparisons to *Richard III* and *Henry V*; Blustain notes that the play is often called the "Russian Macbeth" (191); other sources cite similarities to *Julius Caesar*, such as O'Neil (37–44).

3. Kozintsev pays homage to this ending in his finale of the 1970 film of *Lear*.

4. Strangely, there are very few critical works devoted to the theme of war in *King Lear*. Gary Taylor's 1980 article is one of few entirely focused on war in both versions of the play, Quarto and Folio. Taylor cites the importance of civil war, invasion and apocalypse as tropes governing many of the relationships within the play, discussing the different emphases in Q and F as well as citing film treatments such as Kozintsev's. Kozintsev's book on *Lear* frequently uses the language of Biblical apocalypse in reference to war.

5. Surprisingly, there is almost no Shakespearean scholarship on *King Lear* and utopia, dystopia or anti-utopia, just as there is very little written that engages the meaning of the domestic and international wars that take place in the play's action: Russo-Soviet scholars have picked up on themes other academics and artists seem to have minimized.

6. Radlov's fate after World War II is discussed in Stribrny (88–89), where it is also mentioned that Radlov put on a production of *Lear* in 1954 in Riga with Shostakovich's music, clearly following his post-war "disappearance" and Stalin's death — it is unclear what happened to Radlov when he returned to the USSR after the war. He was most likely imprisoned, exiled or relocated to some remote region or anonymous post. For more information on Yiddish theater and GOSET see Henry, Veidlinger and Zivanovic.

7. See Kachuck, Prager, and Waldinger for more on *King Lear* and Shakespeare in Yiddish.

8. That any of this might be debatable as historically factual is not important for this study. This is, rather, the consensus of the majority of Marxist and Soviet critics. To alter it factually would entail misunderstanding contemporary Russo-Soviet interpretations and adaptations of Shakespeare.

9. For more on Stalin's anti-Semitism, especially in his later days, see Conquest, *Stalin* (290–291); (304–311).

10. Stalin's wife committed suicide in 1932, see Service (195).

11. The essay is reprinted in *STC* (49–102).

Chapter Five

1. Kozintsev's presentation at the screenings of his films in Canada for the 1971 World Shakespeare Conference was published in its Proceedings in 1972. It reiterates many of the ideas about *Lear* found in the 1973 book.

2. More Soviet critical buzzword here: "cosmopolitan," "formalist" and "decadent" were used to describe works, especially musical ones, that were unduly influenced by the West or that were too difficult to understand.

3. Volkov's work is controversial, but several other works corroborate his assertions and the sentiments he attributes to Shostakovich. For example, Elizabeth Wilson's *Shostakovich: A Life Remembered,* and *Shostakovich Reconsidered* by Ho and Feofanov.

4. There seems to be some confusion among sources about this story: Saward asserts that it was St. Basil who appeared, after his death, to Ivan in a dream with the meat and blood, others say this was the act of Nikolka, who was living in Pskov.

5. The writings of Fyodor Dostoyevsky illustrate the deep hostility to Roman Catholicism in Russian culture. See especially the "Grand Inquisitor" section of *The Brothers Karamazov.*

Bibliography

Andrei Rublev. Dir. Andrei Tarkovsky. 1966.
Andrews, Nigel. "King Lear." *Sight and Sound,* Summer 1972: 171–172.
Baer, Brian James. "Literary Translation and the Construction of a Soviet Intelligentsia." *The Massachusetts Review* 47.3 (2006): 537–560.
Barrie, Robert. "Telmahs: Carnival Laughter in Hamlet." *New Essays on Hamlet.* Mark T. Burnett and John Manning, eds. New York: AMS Press, 1994: 82–100.
Bazin, Andre, Alain Piette, Bert Cardullo. "The Myth of Stalin in the Soviet Cinema." *New Orleans Review* 15.3 (1988): 5–17.
Benedetti, Joan. "Stanislavsky and the Moscow Art Theatre, 1898–1938." *A History of Russian Theatre.* Cambridge: Cambridge University Press, 1999: 254–277.
Bethea, David. "Pushkin: From Byron to Shakespeare." *Routledge Companion to Russian Literature.* London: Routledge, 2001: 74–88.
Billington, Sandra. *A Social History of the Fool.* Brighton: Harvester Press, 1984.
Blok, Alexander. "Shakespeare's King Lear." *Shakespeare in the Soviet Union.* Moscow: Progress Publishers, 1966: 17–24.
Borovsky, Victor. "The Organization of the Russian Theatre 1645–1763." *A History of Russian Theatre.* Cambridge: Cambridge University Press, 1999: 41–56.
Bourdeaux, Michael. *Risen Indeed: Lessons in Faith from the USSR.* Crestwood, NY: St. Vladimir's Seminary Press, 1983.
Braun, Joachim. "The Double Meaning of Jewish Elements in Dmitri Shostakovich's Music." *The Musical Quarterly* 71.1 (1985): 68–80.
_____. "Jews in Soviet Music." *Jews in Soviet Culture.* Ed. Jack Miller. New Brunswick, NJ: Transaction Books, 1984: 65–106.
Brode, Douglas. "Monologue without Words." *Shakespeare in the Movies.* Oxford: Oxford University Press, 2000: 210–214.
Brown, Royal. "Hamlet." *Cineaste,* Winter 31.1 (2005): 69–71.
_____. "Not to Be." *Shakespeare in the Movies.* Oxford: Oxford University Press, 2000: 127–129.
Burnett, Mark Thornton. "The 'Heart of My Mystery': Hamlet and Secrets." *New Essays on Hamlet.* Mark T. Burnett and John Manning, eds. New York: AMS Press, 1994: 21–46.
Byrns, Richard. "Aleksandr Blok and 'Hamlet.'" *Canadian Slavonic Papers* 18 (1976): 58–65.
Carmelli, Audrey. "Allegory and Metaphor: Soviet Productions of Shakespeare in the Post-Stalin Era." Dissertation. University of Illinois at Urbana-Champaign, ProQuest: Ann Arbor, 2002.

Carnovsky, Morris, and Paul Berry. "On Kozintsev's King Lear." *The Literary Review* 22 (1979): 408–15.
Chamberlin, William H. "Russians Against Stalin." *Russian Review* 11.1 (1952): 16–23.
Chekhov, Anton. *Anton Chekhov's Selected Plays*. Trans. Ed. Laurence Senelick. New York: Norton Critical Edition, 2005.
Clayton, J. Douglas. "The Hamlets of Turgenev and Pasternak: On the Role of Poetic Myth in Literature." *Germano-slavica* Ontario 2 (1978): 455–461.
Clowes, Edith W., ed. *Doctor Zhivago: A Critical Companion*. Evanston, IL: Northwestern University Press, 1995.
Cohen, Brent M. "'What is it you would see?': Hamlet and the Conscience of the Theatre." *ELH* 44 (2), 1977: 222–247.
Collick, John. *Shakespeare, Cinema, and Society*. New York: St. Martin's, 1989.
Conquest, Robert. *The Pasternak Affair: Courage of Genius*. Philadelphia: J.P. Lippincott, 1962.
_____. *Stalin: Breaker of Nations*. New York: Penguin, 1991.
Cooperman, Stanley. "Shakespeare's Anti-Hero: Hamlet and the Underground Man." *Shakespeare Studies* 1 (1965): 37–63.
Dawson, Anthony. "International Shakespeare." *Cambridge Companion to Shakespeare on Stage*. Stanley Wells and Sarah Stanton, eds. Cambridge: Cambridge University Press, 2002: 174–193.
_____. *Shakespeare in Performance: Hamlet*. Manchester: Manchester University Press, 1995.
Davidson, Clifford. *Fools and Folly*. Kalamazoo: Medieval Institute Publications, Western Michigan University, 1996.
Derdzinski, Mark. "Richard II: Shakespeare's Referents and the Problem of Deposition." *The Upstart Crow* 23 (2003): 17–30.
Diakonova, Nina. "Three Shakespearean Stories in Nineteenth-Century Russia." *Russian Essays on Shakespeare and His Contemporaries*. A.T. Parfenov and Joseph G. Price, eds. Newark: University of Delaware Press, 1998: 97–112.
Diamond, Wilhelm. "Wilhelm Meister's Interpretation of Hamlet." *Modern Philology* 23.1 (1925): 89–101.
Don Quixote. Dir. Grigory Kozintsev. 1957.
Donskov, Andrew. "Tolstoi and Drama." *Canadian Slavonic Papers* 18 (1976): 125–140.
Dostoyevsky, Fyodor. *The Brothers Karamazov*. 1881.
_____. *The House of the Dead*. 1862.
Dunning, Chester. "The Tragic Fate of Pushkin's Comedy." *The Uncensored Boris Godunov: The Case for Pushkin's Original Comedy with Annotated Text and Translation*. Chester L. Dunning, et al., eds. Madison: University of Wisconsin Press, 2006: 94–135.
Dye, Ellis. "Wilhelm Meister and Hamlet, Identity and Difference." *Goethe Yearbook* 6 (1992): 67–85.
Egorova, Tat, B. A. Ganf, and N. A. Egunova. *Soviet Film Music: An Historical Survey*. Contemporary Music Studies, v. 13. Australia: Harwood Academic Pub., 1997.
Eisenstein, Sergei. *Film: Russian Essays and a Lecture*. Ed. Jay Leyda. Princeton: Princeton University Press, 1982.
El-Gabalawy, Saad. "Christian Communism in Utopia, King Lear and Comus." *University of Toronto Quarterly* 47.3 (1978): 228–238.
Emerson, Caryl. "Back to the Future: Shostakovich's Revision of Leskov's 'Lady Macbeth of Mtsensk District.'" *Cambridge Opera Journal* 1.1, 1989: 59–78.
_____. "Introduction." *Boris Godunov*. Trans. James Falen. Oxford: Oxford University Press, 2007: vii–xxxii.
Ettinger, Shmuel. "The Position of Jews in Soviet Culture: A Historical Survey." *Jews*

in Soviet Culture. Ed. Jack Miller. New Brunswick, NJ: Transaction Books, 1984: 1–21.
Fairclough, Pauline. "Facts, Fantasies and Fictions: Recent Shostakovich Studies." *Music & Letters*. Oxford: Oxford University Press 83.3 (2005): 452–460.
Fay, Laurel. *Shostakovich: A Life*. Oxford: Oxford University Press, 2000.
Ferenc, Anna. "Music in the Socialist State." *Russian Cultural Studies*. Catriona Kelly and David Shepherd, eds. Oxford: Oxford University Press, 1998: 109–119.
Fleishman, Lazar. *Boris Pasternak: The Poet and His Politics*. Cambridge: Harvard University Press, 1990.
Fletcher, Giles. *Of the Russe Commonwealth*. Cambridge: Harvard University Press, 1966.
Fomichev, Sergei. "The World of Laughter in Pushkin's Comedy." *The Uncensored Boris Godunov: The Case for Pushkin's Original Comedy with Annotated Text and Translation*. Chester L. Dunning, et al., eds. Madison: University of Wisconsin Press, 2006: 136–156.
France, Anna K. *Boris Pasternak's Translations of Shakespeare*. Berkeley: University of California Press, 1978.
Friedberg, Maurice. *Literary Translation in Russia: A Cultural History*. University Park: Penn State University Press, 1997.
Frye, Roland Mushat. "Hitler, Stalin and Shakespeare's Macbeth: Modern Totalitarianism, Cinema, and Ancient Tyranny." *Proceedings of the American Philosophical Society*. 142.1 (1998): 81–109.
Gerlach, Henry. "Wilhelm Meister's Observations about Hamlet." *The University of Dayton Review* 7.3 (1971): 25–33.
Gerstel, Jennifer. "Irony, Deception, and Political Culture in the Works of Dmitri Shostakovich." *Mosaic* 32.4 (1999): 35–51.
Gibian, George. "Shakespeare in Soviet Russia." *Russian Review* 11.1 (1952): 24–34.
_____. "Tolstoj and Hamlet." *Tolstoj and Shakespeare*. The Hague: Mouton, 1957: 40–44.
Gillespie, David. "Adapting Foreign Classics: Kozintsev's Shakespeare." *Russian and Soviet Adaptations of Literature, 1900–2001*. Stephen Hutchings and Anat Vernitski, eds. London: Routledge Curzon, 2005: 75–88.
_____. *Early Soviet Cinema: Innovation, Ideology and Propaganda*. London: Wallflower, 2005.
Glazov-Corrigan, Elena. "A Reappraisal of Shakespeare's Hamlet: in Defense of Pasternak's Doctor Zhivago." *Forum for Modern Language Studies* 30: 3 (1994): 219–238.
Golomb, Haral. "Hamlet in Chekhov's Major Plays." *Coventry* 2 (1986): 69–88.
Golub, Spencer. *The Recurrence of Fate: Theatre and Memory in Twentieth Century Russia*. Iowa City: University of Iowa Press, 1994.
_____. "The Silver Age, 1905–1917." *A History of Russian Theatre*. Cambridge: Cambridge University Press, 1999: 278–301.
Graves, Michael. "Hamlet as Fool." *Hamlet Studies* 4.1–2 (1982): 73–88.
Greenberg, Robert. "Great Masters: Shostakovich — His Life and Music." The Great Courses: Fine Arts and Music. The Teaching Company. Chantilly, VA, 2002. (CDs and booklet of academic lecture.)
Griffin, Alice V. "Shakespeare through the Camera's Eye: IV." *Shakespeare Quarterly* 17: 4 (1966): 383–387.
Griggs, Yvonne. "On the Road: Reclaiming King Lear." *Lit/Film Q*, Spring (2009): 97–108.
Grigor'jan, N. "Pecorin and Hamlet as Fool." *Hamlet Studies* 4.1–2 (1982): 73–88.
_____. "Pecorin and Hamlet: Towards a Typology of Character." Trans. Carolyn Roberts. *Canadian Review of Comparative Literature*, Fall (1974): 235–252.
Gross, John, ed. *After Shakespeare: Writing Inspired by the World's Greatest Author*. Oxford: Oxford University Press, 2002.

Gussow, Mel. "Soviet Georgians' Essential Lear: Review." *New York Times* 4 April 1990: C.17.
Hamlet. (Gamlet). Dir. Grigory Kozintsev. 1964.
Heller, Dana, and Volkova, Elena. "The Holy Fool in Russian and American Culture: A Dialogue." *American Studies International* 41.1&2 (2003): 152–178.
Henry, Barbara. "Jewish Plays on the Russian Stage." *Yiddish Theatre: New Approaches*. Ed. Joel Berkowitz. Oxford: Littman Library, 2003: 61–75.
Ho, Allan B., and Dmitry Feofanov. *Shostakovich Reconsidered*. London: Toccata Press, 1998.
Hodgdon, Barbara. "Kozintsev's King Lear: Filming a Tragic Poem." *Lit/Film Q* 5.4 (1977): 291–8.
_____. "Two King Lears: Uncovering the Film Text." *Lit/Film Q* 11.3 (1983): 143–151.
Holland, Peter. "'More Russian than a Dane': The Usefulness of Hamlet in Russia." In *Translating Life: Studies in Transpositional Aesthetics*. Shirley Chew and Alistair Stead, eds. Liverpool: Liverpool University Press, 1999: 315–338.
Hortmann, Wilhelm. "Shakespeare on the Political Stage in the Twentieth Century." *Cambridge Companion to Shakespeare on Stage*. Stanley Wells and Sarah Stanton, eds. Cambridge: Cambridge University Press, 2002: 212–229.
Hosking, Geoffrey. *Russia and the Russians*. Cambridge: Harvard University Press Belknap, 2001.
Hutchings, William. "Structure and Design in a Soviet Dystopia: H. G. Wells, Constructivism, and Yevgeny Zamyatin's We." *Journal of Modern Literature* 9.1 (1981–82): 81–102.
Ivan the Terrible (Ivan Grozny), Parts 1 (1944) and 2 (1946). Dir. Sergei Eisenstein. 1944, 1946.
Johnson, Emily. "Nikita Khrushchev, Andrei Voznesensky, and the Cold Spring of 1963." *World Literature Today* 75.1 (2001): 31–39.
Jorgens, Jack. "Image and Meaning in the Kozintsev Hamlet." *Lit/Film Q* 1 (1973): 307–15.
_____. *Shakespeare on Film*. Bloomington: Indiana University Press, 1977.
Kachuck, Rhoda Silver. "The First Two Yiddish Lears." *The Globalization of Shakespeare in the Nineteenth Century*. Krystyna Courtney and John M. Mercer, eds. Lewiston: Edwin Mellen Press, 2003: 55–67.
Katerina Izmailova. Dir. Mikhail Shapiro. 1966.
Kelly, Catriona, and David Shepherd, eds. *Russian Cultural Studies*. Oxford: Oxford University Press, 1998.
Kenez, Peter. "Soviet Cinema in the Age of Stalin." *Stalinism and Soviet Cinema*. Richard Taylor and Derek Spring, eds. London: Routledge, 1993: 54–89.
Kernan, Alvin B. "Politics and Theatre in Hamlet." *Hamlet Studies* 1(1), 1979: 1–12.
Khlevniuk, Oleg. *The History of the Gulag: From Collectivization to the Great Terror*. New Haven, CT: Yale University Press, 2004.
King Lear (*Korol Lir*). Dir. Grigory Kozintsev. 1970.
Knight, George W. *Shakespeare and Tolstoy*. London: The English Association, 1934.
Kott, Jan. *Shakespeare Our Contemporary*. Trans. Boleslaw Taborski. New York: W. W. Norton, 1974. (Polish 1st edition 1964.)
_____, and Mark Minsky. "On Kozintsev's Hamlet." *The Literary Review* 22 (1979): 383–390.
Kozintsev, Grigory. "Hamlet and King Lear: Stage and Film." *Shakespeare 1971*.
_____. *King Lear: The Space of Tragedy*. Berkeley: University of California Press, 1977.
_____. *Shakespeare: Time and Conscience*. Trans. Joyce Vining. New York: Hill and Wang, 1966.
Kozlov, Leonid. "The Artist and the Shadow of Ivan." *Stalinism and Soviet Cinema*. Richard Taylor and Derek Spring, eds. London: Routledge, 1993: 109–130.

Law, Anna. "Chekhov's Russian 'Hamlet.' (1924)." *The Drama Review* 27.3 (1983): 34–45.
Leach, Robert. "Revolutionary Theatre, 1917–1930." *A History of Russian Theatre*. Cambridge: Cambridge University Press, 1999: 302–324.
Leskov, Nikolai. *Lady Macbeth of Mtsensk*. Trans. Robert Chandler. London: Hesperus, 2003.
Levin, Yuri. "Shakespeare and Russian Literature: Nineteenth-Century Attitudes." *Russian Essays on Shakespeare and His Contemporaries*. A.T. Parfenov and Joseph G. Price, eds. Newark: University of Delaware Press, 1998: 78–96.
_____. "Tolstoy, Shakespeare, and Russian Writers of the 1860s." *Oxford Slavonic Papers*. New Series Volume I. Oxford, Clarendon, 1968: 85–104.
Leyda, Jay. *Kino: A History of the Russian and Soviet Film*. Princeton, NJ: Princeton University Press, 1983.
Liebman, Stuart. "Que Viva Eisenstein? A Life for the Revolution." *Cineaste* 26.4 (2001): 6–12.
Liehm, Mira, and Antonin. *The Most Important Art: Eastern European Film After 1945*. Berkeley: University of California Press, 1977.
Loseff, Lev. *On the Beneficence of Censorship: Aesopian Language in Modern Russian Literature*. Munchen: Sagner, 1984.
Lunacharsky, Anatoli. "Bacon and the Characters of Shakespeare's Plays." *Shakespeare in the Soviet Union*. Moscow: Progress Publishers, 1966: 25–50.
MacDonald, Ian. *The New Shostakovich*. Boston: Northeastern University Press, 1990.
Magarshack, David. *Chekhov the Dramatist*. New York: Hill and Wang, 1960.
Makaryk, Irena. "Wartime Hamlet." *Shakespeare in the Worlds of Communism and Socialism*. Irena Makaryk and Joseph Price, eds. Toronto: University of Toronto Press, 2006: 119–135.
Manvell, Roger. *Shakespeare and the Film*. New York: Praeger, 1971.
The Maxim Trilogy: *The Youth of Maxim* (1935); *The Return of Maxim* (1937); *The Vyborg Side* (1939). Dir. Grigory Kozintsev with Leonid Trauberg.
McBurney, Gerard. "Soviet Music after the Death of Stalin: The Legacy of Shostakovich." *Russian Cultural Studies*. Catriona Kelly and David Shepherd, eds. Oxford: Oxford University Press, 1998: 120–137.
McNeir, Waldo. "Grigory Kozintsev's King Lear." *College Literature* (January 1978): 239–48.
Medzhibovskaya, Inessa. "Hamlet's Jokes: Pushkin on Vulgar Eloquence." *The Slavic and East European Journal* 41.4 (1997): 554–579.
Mendel, Arthur. "Hamlet and Soviet Humanism." *Slavic Review* 30.4 (1971): 733–747.
Morozov, Mikhail. "On the Dynamism of Shakespeare's Characters." *Shakespeare in the Soviet Union*. Moscow: Progress Publishers, 1966: 84–112.
_____. *Shakespeare on the Soviet Stage*. Trans. David Magarshack. London: Soviet News, 1947.
Moss, Kevin. "A Russian Munchausen: Aesopian Translation." *Inside Soviet Film Satire: Laughter with a Lash*. Ed. Andrew Horton. Cambridge University Press, 1993: 20–35.
O'Dell, Margaret. "Yuri Olesha's Play Spisok Blagodeyaniya (A List of Blessings): Hamlet and the Artist in Soviet Society. Proceedings Pacific Northwest Council of Foreign Languages 29.1 (1978): 136–139.
O'Neil, Catherine. *With Shakespeare's Eyes: Pushkin's Creative Appropriation of Shakespeare*. Newark: University of Delaware Press, 2003.
Orwell, George. "Lear, Tolstoy and the Fool." *The Collected Essays, Journalism and Letters of George Orwell: In Front of Your Nose, 1945–1950*, Volume IV. New York: Harcourt, Brace & World, 1968: 287–302.

Ostrovsky, Arkady. "Imperial and Private Theatres, 1882–1905." *A History of Russian Theatre*. Cambridge: Cambridge University Press, 1999: 218–253.

_____. "Shakespeare as Founding Father of Socialist Realism: The Soviet Affair with Shakespeare." *Shakespeare in the Worlds of Communism and Socialism*. Irena Makaryk and Joseph Price, eds. Toronto: University of Toronto Press, 2006: 56–83.

Othello. Dir. Sergei Yutkevich. 1955.

Otto, Bernice K. *Fools are Everywhere*. Chicago: University of Chicago Press, 2001.

Pasternak, Boris. *Doctor Zhivago*. Trans. Max Hayward and Manya Harari. New York: Pantheon, 1958 (reprint 1991).

_____. "Translating Shakespeare." In *I Remember*. Trans. Max Hayward and Manya Harari. New York: Pantheon, 1958 (reprint 1991).

_____. *The Uncensored Boris Godunov: The Case for Pushkin's Original Comedy with Annotated Text and Translation*. Chester L. Dunning, et al., eds. Madison: University of Wisconsin Press, 2006: 136–156.

Porter, Robert. "Hamlet and The Seagull." *Journal of Russian Studies* 41 (1981): 23–32.

Prager, Leonard. "Shakespeare in Yiddish." *Shakespeare Quarterly* 19.2 (1968): 149–158.

Prochazka, Martin, and Zdenek Stribrny. "A Vision of Soviet Russia: H. G. Wells's Russia in the Shadows as an Alternative in the Development of His Utopian Social Thought." *Philologica Pragensia* 30.4 (1987): 183–193.

Pushkin, Alexander. *Boris Godunov*. Trans. James Falen. New York: Oxford University Press, 2007.

_____. *Boris Godunov*. Trans. Philip Barbour. New York: Columbia University Press, 1953.

_____. "The Postmaster." (Also known as "The Stationmaster.") *The Captain's Daughter and Other Stories*. Trans. T. Keane. New York: Vintage Books, 1936: 187–201.

Radcliff-Umstead, Douglas. "Order and Disorder in Kozintsev's King Lear." *Lit/Film Q* 11.4 (1983): 143–51.

Riley, John. *Dmitri Shostakovich: A Life in Film*. London: I.B. Tauris, 2005.

Rogers, Philip. "Tolstoy's Hamlet." *Tolstoy Studies Journal* 5 (1992): 55–65.

Rogers, Thomas. *Superfluous Men and the Post-Stalin Thaw*. The Hague: Mouton, 1972.

Rothwell, Kenneth S. *A History of Shakespeare on Screen*. Cambridge: Cambridge University Press, 1999.

_____. "How the Twentieth Century Saw the Shakespeare Film: 'Is it Shakespeare?'" *Lit/Film Q* 29.2, 2001: 82–95.

_____. "Representing King Lear on Screen: From Meta-Theatre to 'Meta-Cinema.'" *Shakespeare and the Moving Image*. Anthony Davies and Stanley Wells, eds. Cambridge: Cambridge University Press, 1994: 211–231.

_____. *Shakespeare on Screen: an International Filmography and Videography*. New York: Neal-Schuman, 1990.

Rowe, Eleanor. *Hamlet: A Window on Russia*. New York: New York University Press, 1976.

Rowe, Kenneth. "Values for the War in Hamlet, Othello, King Lear and The Tempest." *College English* 5.4 (1944): 207–213.

"The Rustaveli Theater Company: They're No Fools: Finding the Magic of King Lear." *Newsday* 2 April 1990.

Rzepka, Charles. "Chekhov's The Three Sisters, Lear's Daughters, and the Weird Sisters: The Arcana of Archetypal Influence." *MLS* 14.4 (1984): 18–27.

Sandler, Stephanie. "Baratynskii, Pushkin and Hamlet: On Mourning and Poetry." *Russian Review* 42.1 (1983): 73–90.

Saward, John. *Perfect Fools: Folly for Christ's Sake in Catholic and Orthodox Spirituality*. Oxford: Oxford University Press, 1980.

Seligsohn, Leo. "A Bold, Innovative and Musical King Lear." *Newsday* 4 April 1990.
Senelick, Laurence. "Chekhov's Letters." *Anton Chekhov's Selected Plays*. Trans. Ed. Senelick. New York: W. W. Norton, 2005: 379–459.
_____. "'Thus conscience doth make cowards of us all': New Documentation on the Okhlopkov Hamlet." *Shakespeare in the Worlds of Communism and Socialism*. Irena R. Makaryk and Joseph G. Price, eds. Toronto: University of Toronto Press, 2006: 136–156.
Sergay, Timothy. "'Blizhe k suti, k miru Bloka': The Mise-en-Scene of Boris Pasternak's 'Hamlet' and Pasternak's Blokian-Christological Ideal." *The Russian Review* 64 (2005): 401–421.
Service, Robert. *A History of Twentieth-Century Russia*. Cambridge: Harvard University Press, 1997.
Shakh-Azizova, Tatiana. "A Russian Hamlet ("Ivanov" and His Age)." *Soviet Literature* 1 (1980): 157–163.
Shaw, Nonna D. "The Only Soviet Literary Peasant Utopia." *The Slavic and East European Journal* 7.3 (1963): 279–283.
Shklovsky, Viktor. "On Eisenstein." Trans. Benjamin Sher. Public Domain, 1991. http://www.websher.net/srl/shk-eis.html (1/16/2003).
Shurbanov, Alexander. "Politicized with a Vengeance: East European Uses of Shakespeare's Literature." *Proceedings International Shakespeare Association* 1 (1980): 157–163.
Siberian Lady Macbeth. Dir. Andrzej Wajda. 1961.
Simmons, Ernest. "Catherine the Great and Shakespeare." *PMLA* 47.3 (1932): 790–806.
_____. "Catherine the Great Tragedies." *Shakespeare and the Twentieth Century*. Newark: University of Delaware Press, 1996: 137–147.
Simple People. Dir. Grigory Kozintsev with Leonid Trauberg. 1945. (Suppressed, re-released in 1956.)
Smirnov, A. A., "Shakespeare, the Renaissance and the Age of Barroco." *Shakespeare in the Soviet Union*. Moscow: Progress Publishers, 1966: 58–112.
Sokolva, Boika. "Between Religion and Ideology: Some Russian Hamlets of the Twentieth Century." *Shakespeare Survey* 54 (2001): 140–151.
Sokolyansky, Mark. "'Giant-like Rebellions' and Recent Russian Experience: Shakespearean Irony as an Approach to Modern History." Michael Hattaway, Boika Sokolova and Derek Roper, eds. *Shakespeare in the New Europe*. Sheffield: Sheffield Academic Press, 1994: 221–228.
_____. "Grigory Kozintsev's Hamlet and King Lear." *The Cambridge Companion to Shakespeare on Film*. Russell Jackson, ed. Cambridge: Cambridge University Press, 2000: 199–211.
Solzhenitsyn, Aleksandr. *The Gulag Archipelago: 1918–1956*. Trans. Thomas P. Whitney and H.T. Willetts. Edward E. Ericson, ed. New York: Harper Collins Perennial Classics (abridged edition), 2002 (previous full editions Harper & Row, 1985).
Stribrny, Zdenek. *Shakespeare and Eastern Europe*. New York: Oxford University Press, 2000.
Stroud, T. A. "Hamlet and The Seagull." *Shakespeare Quarterly* 9.3 (1958): 367–372.
Szabo, Emma P. "Shakespeare's Hamlet and Pasternak's Poem." *Shakespeare and His Contemporaries: Eastern and Central European Studies*. Jerzy Limon and Jay L. Halio, eds. Newark: University of Delaware Press, 1993: 169–174.
Taylor, Gary. "The War in King Lear." *Shakespeare Survey* 33 (1980): 27–34.
Teachout, Terry. "The Composer and the Commissars." *Commentary* (October 1999): 53–56.
Thompson, Ewa. "The Archetype of the Fool in Russian Literature." *Canadian Slavonic Papers* 15 (1973): 245–73.

_____. *Understanding Russia: The Holy Fool in Russian Culture*. Lanham, MD: University Press of America, 1987.
Tolstoy, Leo. "Shakespeare and the Drama." *Recollections and Essays*. Trans. Aylmer Maude. London: Oxford University Press, 1952: 307–383.
_____. "Shakespeare and the Drama." *Recollections and Essays*. Trans. Antonia Bouis. New York: Alfred Knopf, 2004.
Turgenev, Ivan. "King Lear of the Steppes." *First Love and Other Stories*. New York: Oxford University Press, 1989: 203–273.
Twelfth Night. Dir. Jan Frid. 1955.
Veidlinger, Jeffrey. "Let's Perform a Miracle: The Soviet Yiddish State Theater in the 1920s." *Slavic Review* 57.2 (1998): 372–397.
_____. *The Moscow State Yiddish Theater*. Bloomington: Indiana University Press, 2000.
Volkov, Solomon. *Shostakovich and Stalin*. Trans. Antonia Bouis. New York: Alfred A. Knopf, 2004.
_____, ed. *Testimony: The Memoirs of Dmitri Shostakovich*. Trans. Antonia Bouis. New York: Harper & Row, 1979.
Von Geldern, James. "The Thaw." Soviethistory.org. Web. N.d. March 31, 2012.
Walsh, Martin. "The King His Own Fool: Robert of Cicyle." *Fools and Folly*. Clifford Davidson, ed. Kalamazoo: Medieval Institute Publications, 1996: 34–46.
Ware, Kallistos. "The Fool in Christ as Prophet and Apostle." *The Inner Kingdom: Collected Works* Vol. 1. Crestwood, NY: St. Vladimir's Seminary Press, 2000.
Weimann, Robert. "Shakespeare on the Modern Stage: Past Significance and Present Meaning." *Shakespeare Survey* 20 (1967): 113–120.
Welsford, Enid. *The Fool: His Social & Literary History*. London: Faber and Faber, 1968 (paperback reprint, orig. 1935).
Welsh, James. "To See It Feelingly: King Lear Through Russian Eyes." *Lit/Film Q* 4 (1976): 153–8.
White, R. S. "Marx and Shakespeare." *Shakespeare Quarterly* 45 (1992): 89–100.
Willson, Robert. "Lear and Dispossession: The Peopled Space of Kozintsev's King Lear." *Shakespeare Survey* 20 (1967): 113–120.
_____. "On the Closing of Gloucester's Door in the Kozintsev Lear." *Shakespeare on Film Newsletter* 2.1 (1977): 3, 5.
Wilson, Arthur. "The Influence of Hamlet upon Chekhov's The Sea Gull." *Susquehana University Studies* 4 (1952): 309–316.
Wilson, Elizabeth. *Shostakovich: A Life Remembered*. Princton: Princeton University Press, 1994.
Winner, Thomas. "Chekhov's Seagull and Shakespeare's Hamlet: A Study of a Dramatic Device." *American Slavic and East European Review* 15.1 (1956): 103–111.
Womak, Kenneth. "Assessing the Rhetoric of Performance in Three Variant Soviet Texts of King Lear." *Yearbook of Comparative Literature* 1993 (41): 149–59.
Wood, Antony, trans. "From Pindemonte." Untitled collection of Pushkin's lyric verse. London, Angel Classics, Forthcoming.
Yarrow, Andrew. "U.S. Cherry Orchard for a Soviet Lear." *New York Times* 13 July 1988: C15.
Zamyatin, Yevgeny. *A Soviet Heretic: Essays by Yevgeny Zamyatin*. Ed. and trans. Mirra Ginsburg. Chicago: University of Chicago Press, 1970.
_____. *We*. Russian original circa 1921.
Zivanovic, Judith. "GOSET: Little-known Theatre of Widely Known Influence." *Educational Theatre Journal* 27.2 (1975): 236–244.

Index

Aesopian language 5–6, 10–11, 24
Akimov's *Hamlet* production 58–59
Alexander I 32, 110–11
allegory 5–7, 59, 63, 148, 185
Anikst, A. 59, 141

Belinsky, V. 30, 37–41, 43, 135
Blok, A. 117–19, 121, 124, 129, 185
Bolshevik Revolution 4, 6, 21, 26, 30, 52–53, 55, 57, 59, 61, 63, 65, 67, 71, 80, 83, 85, 88, 117, 121–22, 127, 137, 154, 176
Bolsheviks 51, 55–56, 65, 70, 116–20, 122, 127, 131, 146, 169
Boris Godunov (opera) 19, 23, 28, 31, 110, 151–52, 163, 186–87, 190
Brezhnev, L. 22, 82–84, 105–6, 137, 152, 154, 177
Brook, P. 139–40, 142, 164–65, 177
Brook's *Lear* film 140, 165

censorship 6–8, 20, 26, 28, 34, 55–56, 59, 61, 66, 75, 94, 96, 104, 111, 128–29
Chekhov, Anton 26, 40, 43, 113, 186, 191; letters 44, 46–47, 191; production 55
Christ 11, 17, 35, 77, 103, 164–65, 173, 192
Christianity 77, 101–3, 137, 168–69
Church 17, 77, 110, 123, 127, 159–60, 168–69
Civil War 21, 52, 56–57, 64, 107, 118, 120, 124, 127–28, 130, 134, 154, 184

Doctor Zhivago 17, 19, 76, 87–89, 168, 179, 186, 190
Dostoevsky, F. 42–43, 113
Druzhinin, A. 108, 116, 123

FEKS 82, 92, 136, 140–41, 161–62, 183
folk music 152–53

"Hamlet" (poem, Pasternak) 17, 87, 89–90, 179
"Hamlet and the Seagull" 190–91
Hamlet in Russia 7, 25, 27, 29, 31, 33, 35, 37, 39, 41, 43, 45, 47, 49, 51
Hamletism 19, 21, 26, 29–30, 38–39, 41, 43–44, 46, 48, 52, 54, 67, 89–90
Hitler-Stalin pact 22, 64
holy fools 19, 23, 110, 151, 162–63, 165, 167, 169–70, 173
humanism 65, 70, 101, 104, 131, 139, 157, 183

Ivan (film, Eisenstien) 81, 135
Ivan the Terrible 4, 80–81, 135, 151, 162–63, 184, 188, 192

Jewish music 153–54
Jews 10, 35, 125, 127–28, 152–55, 157, 186

Karamzin, N. 107–9
Khrushchev, N. 20, 26, 62, 74–77, 82–84, 87–88, 99, 101, 103, 105–6, 137, 152, 154, 176, 183
Kott, J. 4, 13–14, 109, 142, 164–65, 177, 188
Kozintsev, Grigori 1, 11, 15, 69, 184

Lady Macbeth of Mtsensk (opera) 145–46
Lear's Fool 7, 17, 23, 110, 113–15, 121, 125, 140, 151–52, 154–55, 159–67, 171–72, 176, 192

Marxism 14, 54, 65, 84, 86, 121, 127, 132, 142

MAT2 Hamlets 54, 57
Mikhoels, S. 127, 152, 155–56
Mochalov, P. 38–39, 45

narod 51, 91–92, 111, 140, 152, 159, 165, 167
Nicholas I 31, 33, 35–36, 106, 109–12, 151
Nikolka (fool in *Boris Godunov*) 18, 110, 184

Okhlopkov, N. 62–65, 67–68; *Hamlet* 180, 191
Orthodox Church 17, 102–3, 127, 162, 169

Pasternak, Boris 10, 16, 18–19, 117, 187, 191; affair 88; death 89, 141; *Hamlet* 17, 90; translation 17, 21, 55, 62, 66, 72, 85–86, 141, 143, 168, 183
Paul I 19, 28, 111
Polevoy, B. 36, 38, 182; *Hamlet* 35, 47
progressives 5, 19, 26, 34, 37–38, 116–17, 127
Prokofiev, S. 59–61
Pushkin, Alexander 26, 30–31, 108–9; comedy 186–87; death 33, 35, 110

Radlov, S. 60–61, 184
religion 17, 55, 77, 88, 101, 103, 124–25, 127, 169, 191
Renaissance 97, 123, 125, 131, 191
Revolutionary Hamlet 19, 43, 54, 83
Russian holy fools 152, 165, 169
Russian Theatre 183, 185, 187, 189

Shakespeare in Yiddish 184, 190
Shostakovich, D. 2, 4, 16–19, 21, 23, 57, 58, 60–61, 75, 86, 128, 134, 143–54, 160–61, 167, 187, 190, 192; music 143, 150–51, 184; opera 145–46; testimony 17–18, 143, 150–51, 157, 192

Socialist realism 11, 37, 55, 59–60, 79–80, 100, 106, 116, 122, 129, 131–32, 137–38, 142, 144, 162
Soviet artists 9, 12, 15, 17, 20–21, 45, 94, 149, 164, 180
Soviet critics 3, 14–15, 57–59, 72, 108, 119, 121, 124–25
Soviet film music 186
Soviet Jews 126–27, 154–55
Soviet Marxist Shakespeare criticism 83
Soviet Shakespeare criticism 15, 70
Stalin, Joseph 10, 13, 20, 35, 61, 65, 68, 96, 105, 122–23, 127–29, 151, 176–77, 181; death 1–2, 18–20, 22, 27, 37, 52–53, 55, 57–59, 61–65, 67, 71–74, 77, 80–81, 135, 137–38
Stalinism 49, 70, 99, 101, 107, 134, 153
State Jewish Theatre 125–26
strannik 165, 170

Terror era 16, 21–22, 60–61, 126, 146, 149
Thaw era 20, 22, 26, 62, 68, 74–77, 79, 81–83, 85, 87, 89, 91, 93, 95, 97
Tolstoy, L. 49–51, 113–16, 182, 188–89, 192
translating Shakespeare 7, 36, 90, 107, 121, 159, 168, 190
Trauberg, L. 17, 82–83
Turgenev, I. 21, 41–43, 77, 79, 111–13, 182, 192

Western critics 15, 140
World War II 21–22, 57, 71, 77, 86, 88, 106–7, 121, 125–26, 128–30, 133, 137, 153, 154, 158, 176

Yiddish 125–27, 155, 184
yurodivy 18, 23, 110, 150–52, 160, 163, 165

www.ingramcontent.com/pod-product-compliance
Ingram Content Group UK Ltd.
Pitfield, Milton Keynes, MK11 3LW, UK
UKHW042010140426
5217IPUK00015B/1080